"This amazing personal accou
siderable historical knowledge
the present. Kennedy presents his subject in an innovative spiritual light that changed my view of what it meant to grow up in the fertile religious environment of Southern California."

—JARRELL C. JACKMAN,
Santa Barbara Trust for Historic Preservation, Retired CEO

"Narrated with the salty wisdom of a storytelling sailor and the seasoned eye of a historian, *Winds of Santa Ana* offers an abundance of riches for the reader. With a revitalizing, evangelical consciousness—distinctively Californian and dynamically erudite—Kennedy's journey as a sailor-scholar aboard his beloved boat, Boethius, is a hopeful consolation for our generation, and a good reminder of our theological roots. This book is both timely and delightful."

—KAREN AN-HWEI LEE,
Wheaton College

"There is no better guide to the California Bight, its natural beauty, human history, and spiritual potential than Rick Kennedy, a pilgrim who has sailed its shores for decades. Read this book and see its wonders through the eyes of Rick's heart. You will never be the same."

—DOUGLAS SWEENEY,
Beeson Divinity School

"Kennedy is not only a gifted academic historian, he is also a pilgrim-sailor with the head of a philosopher, the heart of a Christian mystic, and the soul of a poet. These traits are wonderfully on display in this imaginative and enchanting book. . . . Winds of Santa Ana nurtures the spiritual imagination. It is a book for those longing for a thicker description of nature, the past, and life than the reductive methodologies of the modern academy offer."

—DONALD A. YERXA,
former Editor, *Historically Speaking*

"This book will be appealing to readers on several scores: those interested in the environmental, maritime history of the San Diego area and those interested in how a noted Christian historian weaves the religious history of the region into a unique connection to the sea and the vocation of sailing."
—RONALD A. WELLS,
Calvin University, emeritus

"To sail into the waters of Rick Kennedy's memoir, *Winds of Santa Ana*, is to voyage with a most affable, engaging captain. Part philosopher, part sage, part poet, Kennedy approaches his audience as a friend in his invitation to apprehend rich interior and exterior seas and landscapes."
—KAY HARKINS,
author of *Queen of the Leaves: A Memoir of Lost and Found*

"Nobody tells the story of Southern California like Rick Kennedy. Winds of Santa Ana expounds his own experience of the place—in his case, the bight, seen from his nautical, sojourning, historian's eyes looking at the coast of Southern California from the water. . . . Seen through his vessel Boethius and accompanied by the personified Philosophia for the journey, this book is a true love letter to the Southern California coast."
—JASON S. SEXTON,
UCLA Institute of the Environment and Sustainability

"Kennedy's ruminations on the California Bight present a Christian spiritual topography of the Los Angeles Basin and its environs. . . . This sailor-pilgrim reflects on his vocation, the evangelical cause, and the interplay of place and faith in the Bight. This fine memoir uses Kennedy's life journey and evocations of the Mediterranean to describe the islands and coastlines, winds and waves as the means and fruits of Christian yearning for God's presence in the world."
—GLENN SANDERS,
King University

Winds of Santa Ana

Other Books by Rick Kennedy

Aristotelian and Cartesian Logic at Harvard: Morton's "System of Logick" and Brattle's "Compendium of Logick" (1995).

Faith at State: A Handbook for Christians at Secular Universities (1995, reprint 2002).

Student Notebooks at Colonial Harvard: Manuscripts and Educational Practice, 1650–1740. Co-written with Thomas Knoles and Lucia Zaucha Knoles (2003).

A History of Reasonableness: Testimony and Authority in the Art of Thinking (2004).

Jesus, History, and Mount Darwin: An Academic Excursion, (2008)

The First American Evangelical: A Short Life of Cotton Mather (2015).

John and Acts, vol. 8 of *Cotton Mather's* Biblia Americana, 10 vols. Reiner Smolinski and Jan Stievermann, general editors. Co-edited with Harry Clark Maddux and Rebecca Stephens Falcasantos (2023).

Winds of Santa Ana

Pilgrim Stories of the California Bight

Rick Kennedy

WIPF & STOCK · Eugene, Oregon

WINDS OF SANTA ANA
Pilgrim Stories of the California Bight

Copyright © 2022 Rick Kennedy. All rights reserved. Except for brief quotations in critical publications or reviews, no part of this book may be reproduced in any manner without prior written permission from the publisher. Write: Permissions, Wipf and Stock Publishers, 199 W. 8th Ave., Suite 3, Eugene, OR 97401.

Wipf & Stock
An Imprint of Wipf and Stock Publishers
199 W. 8th Ave., Suite 3
Eugene, OR 97401

www.wipfandstock.com

PAPERBACK ISBN: 978-1-6667-3613-7
HARDCOVER ISBN: 978-1-6667-9402-1
EBOOK ISBN: 978-1-6667-9403-8

APRIL 18, 2022 9:11 AM

Scriptures taken from the Holy Bible, New International Version®, NIV®. Copyright © 1973, 1978, 1984, 2011 by Biblica, Inc.™ Used by permission of Zondervan. All rights reserved worldwide. www.zondervan.com The "NIV" and "New International Version" are trademarks registered in the United States Patent and Trademark Office by Biblica, Inc.™

Scripture quotations taken from the (NASB®) New American Standard Bible®, Copyright © 1960, 1971, 1977, 1995, 2020 by The Lockman Foundation. Used by permission. All rights reserved. www.lockman.org

Dedicated to
Harold Kirker, Jeffrey Burton Russell, and Harold Drake
Professors of History at UC Santa Barbara

You who go down to the sea,
you creatures in the sea,
you islands, and all who live among them,
sing a new song to the Lord.

ISAIAH 42: 10

He makes the clouds his chariot;
He walks upon the wings of the wind;
He makes the winds his messengers.

PSALM 104: 3–4

Ask the beasts, and let them teach you;
And the birds of the heavens, and let them tell you.
Or speak to the earth, and let it teach you;
And let the fish of the sea declare to you.
Who among all these does not know
That the hand of the Lord has done this,
In whose hand is the life of every living thing,
And the breath of all mankind?

JOB 12: 7–10

Ask the beauty of the earth,
Ask the beauty of the sea,
Ask the beauty of the air amply spread around everywhere.
Ask the beauty of the sky,
Ask the serried ranks of the stars,
Ask the sun making the day glorious with its bright beams,
Ask the moon tempering the darkness of the following night
    with its shining rays,
Ask the animals that move in the waters, that amble about on dry land,
    and fly in the air.
Their souls are hidden.
Their bodies evident.
They all answer, 'Here we are! Look! We're beautiful!'

ST. AUGUSTINE, EASTER SERMON, 241

Contents

Ventura's Advice: Investigate with Wonder,
Speculate with Devotion | 1

Those In San Diego Who Go Down to the Sea | 19

The Snake Path in La Jolla | 31

As Refreshing as a Great Rock: Dana Point | 40

Streams of God, Full of Water, in the Los Angeles Basin | 56

Mission Bay Baroque | 77

The Rivers Santa Margarita and San Luis Rey | 92

The Point of Immaculate Conception
and the Wedding Banquet in Santa Barbara | 111

The Alexandrian Waters of San Pedro and Santa Catalina | 130

Prisoners and Pelicans on Santa Cruz Island | 150

Santa Barbara Island | 166

The Santa Ana Condition | 172

Acknowledgements | 183

Bibliography | 185

Index | 191

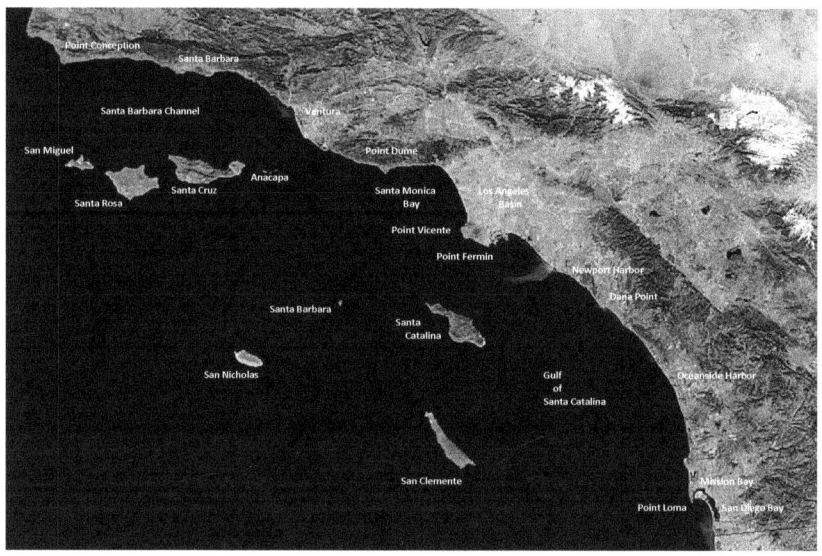

The California Bight (NASA with labels added by the author)

Ventura's Advice
Investigate with Wonder, Speculate with Devotion

BEGINNING sharply in the north at Point Conception and curving down to the estuary of the Tijuana River is the Bight of California. By definition, a bight is a geographical feature too wide and open to be a bay, but still a distinctive cut into a coast. California's bight is more than just geographically distinct. The cartography and collective histories of this coast and the islands it embraces point to a unifying character, a cultural identity, an underlying ecology. The waters of the Bight, the Santa Barbara Channel, Santa Monica Bay, San Pedro Channel, and the Gulf of Santa Catalina, are more benign than waters to the north or south. Winds in the region often cycle like an eddy on the edge of a curving river rather than blow full force like a trade wind coming off the world's largest ocean. It is hard to be an atheist here. Notions of purposelessness have to struggle to survive in a place so beautiful. The California Bight is distinctly revelatory, sacramental, and hopeful.

The Winds of Santa Ana

Those who sail the Bight's waters, ride its winds, and seek its harbors are offered a spiritual experience. When a sailor unrolls a large nautical chart of the California Bight on a cabin table, spreads weights out to the corners to hold it down, leans over it, and reads it carefully, the chart itself teaches that these waters are an ecosystem of faith. Navigating the Bight is like wandering inside a cathedral where the floorplan, statues, and chapel alcoves are dense with the names of saints, memorials of prayer, and messages of salvation. Santa Monica's son, St. Augustine, writes that all creation is on pilgrimage. The California Bight's cartography, ecology, and history tell of its pilgrimage.

For many years I have been a pilgrim on this pilgrim coast. I think of myself as created, in part, by the California Bight. I have long taught the history of this place at one of its little colleges. I am nearing retirement and need to assess what this place has made of me and gather together what I think this place says about itself. I follow the advice of Job in the Old Testament:

> Ask the animals, and they will teach you;
> or the Birds of the air, and they will tell you;
> or Speak to the earth, and it will teach you;
> or let the fish of the sea inform you.[1]

Pilgrims, as I understand the role, are not explorers. Pilgrims are not cynics. Pilgrims go where others before them have gone and believe what others before them have believed. They do not begin with doubt; instead, they willingly believe more than most. They do not stand, obstinately, in one place; rather, they ponder as they travel, expecting to find more to ponder when they round the next bend. Pondering is an accumulative method of thinking. In the New Testament, Mary ponders by storing things in her heart. A Christian and classical image for pondering is the honeybee wandering among flowers, gathering pollen, then, like Mary, storing them, waiting for the honey that will come. Another classical and Christian model of scholar-pondering, the remnants of which are still evident in modern universities, is flower-picking and flower-arranging. The scholar wanders in literary fields, picking flowers, arranging them upon return for an accumulated purpose. Prior to our modern times, a scholar's published flower-arrangement would be called, in Latin, a *florilegia*. In our times,

---

1. Job 12:7–8.

these flower arrangements are still called at universities by their Greek name, *anthology*.

This book is a pilgrim-sailor's hive, his *florilegia,* his *anthology.* The pilgrimages here are bee-like in that they do not go far, always return, and are intent upon the possibility that honey might result from accumulation. They are a flower arrangement intent upon the possibility that an assemblage of flowers can communicate more fully when arranged together than when dispersed in the wild. The hope is not to produce a proof or even an argument; rather, the goal is an anthology of signs, the sum of which is greater than its parts. This book is an account of bee-like wanderings, asking questions and listening for answers, in the hope of honey.

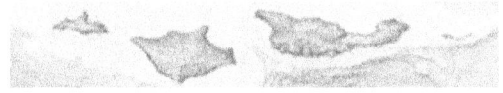

IN THE SPRING of 1979, while a student at the University of California, Santa Barbara, I partnered with a couple of roommates to buy and refurbish a small plywood sloop with a cuddy cabin. When at the end of the year I got married, the boat came with me as a package deal. I named the boat "Pilgrim." Around the same time, I read *Life of St. Francis* and *The Soul's Journey into God* by the patron saint of the nearby coastal city of Ventura. I embraced these two books as a pilgrim manual for life in general and sailing in particular. Both methodically teach a reader to think like St. Francis, especially a way of wide-angle living that takes the Bible straight-up. All creation is a family, a household, an ecosystem. The sun is my brother and the wind my sister. All creation is wild with life and communication. Answers do blow in the winds. If humans don't praise God, the rocks will. For Francis, if the Bible says God has concern for birds, then Francis preaches to birds—and if he is going to preach to birds, he might as well preach to fish too. While reading these books and sailing in the Santa Barbara Channel, I found myself becoming a type of Protestant-evangelical-Franciscan-pilgrim-sailor-ecologist.

Author and wife on left, summer of 1980, east campus of UC Santa Barbara. (Author's photo.)

In *The Soul's Journey into God* Bonaventure advises pilgrims who wish to live and think like St. Francis to first cultivate desire. Only with prayerfully cultivated desire can the journey begin in earnest. Only with a sense of joy will an observer fully see creation. An investigator must investigate with a sense of wonder. Speculation needs to be fired with devotion. Work needs to be accompanied with piety. Understanding cannot be attained without humility and love. Prayer is essential. Scripture is essential. Having cultivated desire and proper modes of inquiry, the pilgrim must "Open your eyes, alert the ears of your spirit, open your lips, and apply your heart, so that in all creatures you may see, hear, praise, love, and worship, glorify, and honor your God."[2] Bonaventure, in good pedagogical style, mixes his prose with poetry:

> We gather that all the creatures of the sense world
> lead the mind
> of the contemplative and wise person
> to the eternal God.
> For these creatures are
> shadows, echoes, and pictures,
> vestiges, representations, spectacles
> proposed to us

---

2. Bonaventure, *Soul's Journey*, 67–68.

Ventura's Advice

> and signs divinely given
> so that we can see God....
>
> For every creature is by its nature
> a kind of effigy and likeness of the eternal Wisdom,
> but especially one
> which in the book of Scripture
> has been elevated through the spirit of Prophecy
> and more especially, those creatures
> in whose likeness God wished to appear
> through the ministry of angels;
> and most especially, a creature which God willed to institute
> as a symbol
> and which has the character
> not only of a sign in the general sense
> but also of a sacrament.[3]

Signs, symbols, even sacraments: "Every creature is by its nature a kind of effigy and likeness of the eternal wisdom." Bonaventure codified, for me, the essential thinking method of a pilgrim-sailor. Boats became spiritual companions. Actions such as raising sail, tacking, and anchoring became liturgies of investigation mixed with wonder, speculation mixed with devotion. The wind, the birds, and the islands, I came to accept, are angels.

LIVING ON THE CALIFORNIA BIGHT encourages belief in patron saints. Maps and nautical charts of this place promote belief. To live thoughtfully in Santa Barbara, Ventura, Los Angeles, Santa Monica, San Pedro, Santa Ana, or San Diego is to be confronted, regularly, with the notion that life does not end in death and there are some who after death are charged with watching over us. To deny the existence of saints is to dismiss the prayers of people whose prayers should not be treated lightly. This book shares the faith of Apolinaria Lorenzana who, after arriving in California as an orphan, became the gentle and pious manager of the *monjerio*, the women's quarters, at Mission San Diego. She is remembered as a wise woman, devoted to

---

3. Bonaventure, *Soul's Journey*, 76–77.

the health and welfare of women at the mission. Her duties included teaching girls to read and pray. When the mission disbanded she was given two ranchos not far up the Sweetwater River from San Diego Bay. In her old age she told an interviewer that "Whenever I acquired land, I had it blessed and named it in honor of a saint. I have always had faith in the power of saints, and above all, faith in the one who surpasses them all—God himself."[4] This kind of thinking, this kind of faith, is behind the names that fill our maps and charts.

I have no systematic theology of saints. The California Bight does not demand one. I embrace the existence of saints with a mind open to the quandary of what people are doing after death while waiting for the second coming of Christ. Christianity offers many ways to think of life as having three stages. First, there is *life before death*, then a *life after death* before a final *life after life after death* when the true church will be gathered to Christ after the second coming and final judgement. The Bible indicates a mysterious second life when it tells of Moses and Elijah meeting with Jesus in the Transfiguration, graves being opened in Jerusalem at the time of the crucifixion, and the bodily appearances of Jesus after his resurrection but before his ascension. Purgatory is a possibility between the first and third stages of life. Many Christians have long believed some people in the *life after death* are commissioned by God as guardians, patrons, and prayer-partners to people in the *life before death*. I do not press the issue. I only note that life on the California Bight encourages belief in patron saints.

Saint names on the Bight are almost always tied to prayers. The Franciscan missionaries coming up the coast with the first Spanish colonizers recorded Indian names for villages and did not try to stop the use of these names. On the other hand, they had been ordered by José de Gálvez, the man in charge of the Spanish colonization of Alta California, to request of God the patronage of Franciscan saints on significant sites. For example, Gálvez specifically commanded that San Buenaventura, the saint and author of the *Life of St. Francis* and *Soul's Journey into God*, be prayed down as patron of a mission to be built somewhere on the Santa Barbara Channel. When in August 1769 the Spanish first arrived at *Shisholop*, the Franciscan friars in the exploration party first prayed down onto the site the name *La Asunción de Nuestra Señora*. The date on the calendar of saint's days guided them to pray for the patronage of Mary for the site. Fr. Juan Crespí, one of the friars, wrote in his diary: "I hope that through the intercession of this great lady, such a

---

4. Beebe and Senkewicz, *Testimonios*, 184.

fine site, which lacks nothing, will become a good mission."[5] The great lady did intercede. A Franciscan mission to the Indians was eventually established there. Because of Galvez's order, God was requested to appoint St. Bonaventure as patron of the mission. Eventually, because the mission dominated the area, the names *Shisholop* and *La Asunción de Nuestra Señora* fell into disuse. After the United States took over California, the town's name was shortened to "Ventura." Mere conquest and the shortening of a name, however, does not dismiss a saint from patronage duties. St. Bonaventure, we can assume, still watches over the region as does Mary.

The most prominent patron saint of the Bight is Mary although her name is sometimes hidden. Rufugio State Beach is under the patronage of Mary as *Refugium Peccatorum,* Refuge of Sinners. The river, city, and port of Los Angeles are under the patronage of Mary as *Nuestra Señora la Reina de los Ángeles de Porciúncula.* The Point of the Immaculate Conception calls upon the patronage of Mary and her parents Santa Ana and San Joaquín. This name was prayed down in 1602 by a Spanish sailing expedition. The doctrine of the Immaculate Conception of Mary in the womb of Anne was not yet an official teaching of the church, but it was a popular belief promoted by Franciscan missionaries.

Santa Ana has become the saint most popularly associated with the California Bight. Her name is spread wide as much more than just a prayer-marker. The long river at the southern border of the Los Angeles Basin is named Santa Ana. Much of what is now Orange County is in the *Vallejo de Santa Ana*. The town of Costa Mesa sits on the old Santa Ana ranch that was managed by Indians under the jurisdiction of mission San Juan Capistrano. The line of mountains behind Dana Point and Camp Pendleton is the Santa Ana Range—lying parallel to, but much larger than, her husband, the San Joaquín Hills. The name Santa Ana River was contracted to "Santana" on a Mexican map drawn in 1823, and that shorter name is today attached to burrito stands, public parks, a high school, and even a production line of sailboats built by W. D. Schock, one of Southern California's most prolific boat builders. Most famously in Southern California, the name Santa Ana is given to a distinctive wind and meteorological condition. The wind seems to have been named after the saint in the late nineteenth century because it concentrates most forcefully along the route of the Santa Ana River before spewing into the San Pedro Channel toward Santa Catalina Island. The meteorological condition is named for its most famous wind. During autumns

---

5. Palou, *Historical Memoirs of New California*, 2:146.

and winters, the National Oceanographic and Atmospheric Administration (NOAA) announces when Southern California is experiencing "Santa Ana Conditions." Often the announcement comes as a warning. High pressure in the desert will soon be sending hot winds racing down onto the California Bight. Under such conditions, out on the islands and at Point Dume, what are normally safe anchorages turn into dangerous lee shores. In extreme cases, the east facing harbor at Avalon will be pummeled by tall waves. In less extreme cases, the announcement of Santa Ana Conditions is simply a grandmotherly heads-up. Be alert. Keep watch. Things can change.

ALONG WITH THE patronage of saints, one of the principal assumptions of this book is that sailing is a simple yet intricate craft that entangles persons, boat, wind, water, and sky in ways that reveal there are no sharp distinctions between the physical and spiritual, the visible and invisible. Every excursion away from the dock, the smaller the boat the better, powered by unstable winds, held aloft by undulating water, covered over by an expansive sky, is a journey into creation's fullness. All the energy in it is a gift. Sailing is necessarily passive, and best understood as an art of gratitude. Walking is the world's most popular mode of pilgrimage, but walking is not necessarily an art of gratitude. The walker tends to believe oneself self-powered and self-willed. Sailing is a more true-to-life mode of pilgrimage. Sailor-pilgrims must necessarily be more obedient than walkers. Walkers can fool themselves into thinking themselves independent. They often cling to puffed-up notions of freedom and their ability to stride to the beat of their own drum. No sailor, becalmed on a glassy sea, stands up and declares to the cosmos "I'm free!"

I like to walk, but sailing teaches me more. A walker can walk through a slight puff of wind without noticing. To a sailor every slight puff is accompanied by a dance. The windward gunwale rises then dips back. The hanging lines swing to leeward then back. The tiller tugs as the bow tries to nudge itself toward the puff. Winds, the Bible says, are messengers. Sailboats are amplifiers. A walker simply can speed up. A sailor petitions the wind for more speed by trimming a sheet or adjusting the rigging. A walker can simply turn around and head home. To come about on a sailboat

Ventura's Advice

requires genuflection. Lines must be prepared. Wind direction, sea state, and boat speed correlated. "Ready about?" yells the person at the helm. (I do so even when alone.) "Ready!" yells the existent or non-existent crew. "Helm's a lee!" is then yelled as the tiller is pushed leeward. The sails begin to luff as the bow swings up into the wind. The boat gives up any leverage it had, yielding itself to water, wind and sky. Stalled at the top of a swell, the sails flogging, the bow dips in obeisance to the source of all power in the universe. Rising up with the next swell, the wind catches the backside of the jib, its sheet still wrapped around what was the leeward, but now becoming, the windward winch. The back-winded jib pushes the bow toward its homeward-pointing direction as the boat revives out of its momentary stall. The jib sheet, awkwardly now holding the jib back from its proper new position, is let loose. The jib then flaps across the forward deck, gathers itself to leeward, fills, then stiffens as its sheet is tightened. The genuflection is complete. The boat is now headed in a new direction. What began as a petition to wind, water, and sky ends in gratitude.

Jesus was a sailor. A keyword search of the gospels has Jesus getting into a boat nineteen times, going into a house six times, and never going into a classroom. A simple application of "What Would Jesus Do?" indicates that Jesus would have us all sailing often. Jesus knows what he is talking about when he says "The wind blows wherever it pleases. You hear its sound, but you cannot tell where it comes from or where it is going. So it is with everything born of the spirit."

At any given moment, a sailor thinks in terms of multiple wind speeds and directions. First, there is the regional wind speed and direction offered by weather reports. These are generalizations. Second, there is what is called "true wind." This is awkwardly named because true wind is not the actual wind experienced by a moving sailboat. True wind is an intellectual model for what a theoretically stationary object would experience. The third type of wind, "apparent wind," is the actual wind with which a moving sailboat must negotiate. Apparent wind is the wind that matters. Trouble is: At any given moment a boat experiences several different apparent winds. The apparent wind experienced at the top of the mainsail as a sloop rolls through the seas is not the same as the apparent wind experienced lower or up front on the jib.

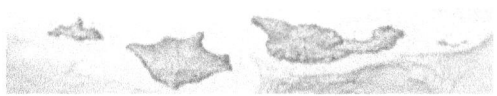

The Winds of Santa Ana

ONE LAST SUBJECT of introductory importance: The "we" in this book means me and my boat. It is both traditional and appropriate for boats to be thought of as having personal identities. We—my boat and I—make pilgrimages together like the scholar and his horse in the prologue of *Canterbury Tales*. My boat is my Rocinante, the horse of Don Quixote and the pick-up truck of John Steinbeck. We depend on each other and share in each other's weaknesses and strengths. More than this, a sailboat can serve as a showstone, a physical communication-help, a physical object that enhances the listening side of prayer. The most famous of these communication-helps appear in the Old Testament as Urim and Thummim, apparently stones or jewels woven into the clothing of the High Priest. Samuel's Ebenezer was a showstone, and like an Ebenezer, my boat never lets me forget my reliance on powers beyond my control. I do not say that any distinctively higher sanctity is infused into my boat. I only note that a common grace is manifest in, with, and through sailboats in general. Sailboats are amplifiers. If creation sings, as it does, then creation sings more loudly through a sailboat.

Since the mid-1960s, I have sailed a variety of boats on the California Bight, but my pilgrim-companion for this book is a twenty-four foot Yankee Dolphin built in Santa Ana during the fall and winter of 1969–70. At that time the coastal cities surrounding the mouth of the Santa Ana River were the center of an American boat-building boom. Fiberglass had been developed. World War II had brought a lot of techno-aeronautical inventive types to Southern California who, after the war, turned their energies to watercraft. With the Pacific Ocean being usually pacific in the confines of the Bight, the ocean called for post-war families to come and play. Fiberglass made boat-building cheaper and boat maintenance less burdensome. Recreational marinas were dug into the coastline. The growing middle class of Southern California had motive, means, and opportunity to go boating.

My boat, *Boethius,* was initially designed in New England by Bill Shaw and revised into the Dolphin-class by the Sparkman & Stephens Company. In the 1950s and 1960s, Sparkman & Stephens set the standard for the look, feel, and performance of well-balanced, beautiful, sailboats. In 1962, John Shumaker brought the design to the California Bight and built the first Yankee Dolphin in Marina del Rey. He began production of a series of Yankee Dolphins in Inglewood, then, in 1969, moved production to Santa Ana. The Yankee Dolphin sold well. It is perfectly designed to take a young family over to Catalina Island and back. But competition was tough.

Ventura's Advice

Newer, lighter, cheaper, less substantial boats were also being produced in and around Santa Ana. Yankee Yachts went out of business in 1974.

Boethius the author's 24' Yankee Dolphin, moored with downtown San Diego in the distance (author's photo).

Boethius in San Diego Bay with Point Loma in the background (author's photo).

The Winds of Santa Ana

I found *Boethius* in 2001, well-used and much-loved at the mouth of the San Gabriel River in Alamitos Marina. I paid $5,000 for her. Our first trip together was a run south, coasting in a pleasant northwesterly wind past Huntington Beach, Newport Beach, Laguna Beach, then docking for the night at Dana Point. The next morning, we were joined by my architect-friend, Kevin deFreitas. We motored till the wind filled in, then sailed further south past La Jolla Point. In the late afternoon off Point Loma, another friend, my diving instructor Robin Jacoway, the person who introduced me to Dolphin sailboats and advised me to buy this one, sailed out to greet us in his Dolphin. It was a good first pilgrimage on some of the most pleasant sailing waters in the world. The winds were gentle and consistent. The sky cloudless. The water blue. The friends good. The coast clear and distinct.

Much happiness has come with this boat. She is designed well, stronger than she needs to be, and pleasing to the eye. Her name, *Boethius*, is derived from a Greek word meaning helper. The person, Boethius, who is the namesake of the boat, was a Christian scholar and politician who lived during the last gasps of the Roman Empire. He wrote a beautiful little book called *The Consolation of Philosophy*, a copy of which I keep in the boat's cabin. On passages along the coast or between the islands when the boat is steering itself, I sometimes go below and retrieve *The Consolation of Philosophy*. I read favorite chapters, especially the poem at the end of Book Two where he waxes lyrical about the cosmos being held together by love. In the book, Boethius uses a surprising amount of ocean, wind, and wave imagery—all together making me think he must have, himself, made some long coastal passages. He wrote the book in Northern Italy while awaiting execution for a crime he did not commit. He was a high government official whose king turned paranoid. In the book, Boethius is frustrated. Why do bad things happen to good people? The book can be understood as an extended application of the opening lines of the New Testament's Book of James: "If any of you lacks wisdom, he should ask God, who gives generously to all."[6] In *The Consolation of Philosophy*, God gives generously to Boethius when a woman, *Philosophia*, appears in his cell, angel-like, ancient, and tall. She rebukes him for whining about his situation. "If you spread your sails for the wind," she tells him, "you must go where the wind takes you, not where you wish to go."[7] Don't worry, she consoles him. Be happy. Even as "the winds howl and stir up the waves of the sea," creation is a ship

---

6. James 1:5.
7. Boethius, *Consolation of Philosophy*, 2. prose 1, 179.

Ventura's Advice

on a journey—a pilgrimage—and God is rightly believed, she says, to be holding the tiller.[8]

Philosophia, at times, visits *Boethius* and me as we are sailing. The California Bight is blessed with guardian angels and saints that exist bodily in a liminal social stratum, sometimes visible, often invisible. *Philosophia* is a type of book-angel, a pondering-partner, a teacher, a mentor. When she appears, she is tall and thin, usually stretched out on the opposite side of the cockpit, sometimes she sits next to me. She is Ethiopian, her skin a deep black. She is usually barefoot, wearing long skinny blue jeans and a red fleece pullover. Her hair is cropped short. She is beautiful. She could be forty or four thousand years old. Renaissance artists tended to depict her as Nordic. Boethius, a thousand years earlier, would not have been surprised by her actual color. In the Mediterranean's antiquity, the most vigorous winds of knowledge and wisdom blew Sirocco not Mistral, from the south not the north. Herodotus, the Greek historian who sailed the Nile, described the men of Ethiopia as "the tallest in the world, the best looking, and the longest lived."[9] The people of the Nile, both from the lower and upper river, he said, were the most learned of any nation he had experienced. They were also "the healthiest people in the world."[10] The California Bight is often described as Mediterranean, but we forget that we are best associated with the African side of the Mediterranean. Santa Monica, San Pedro, and Santa Catalina were Africans. So is Boethius' *Philosophia*.

Boethius is a camp-out boat. She is what is called a weekender. She is seaworthy in a coastal sort-of way, having a long keel and four thousand, two hundred and fifty pounds of displacement. I can stand anywhere on her, and she does not tip to my weight. On the other hand, I cannot stand inside her. She is not designed to cross oceans, ride out hurricanes, or promote the kind of yachting in which people wear white and enjoy drinks with little umbrellas. She is a coastal vessel, perfect for island hopping and ranging between Santa Barbara and San Diego. Inside, *Boethius* expects you to hunker low and watch your head. For a stove, she has a one-burner propane contraption that is very efficient. For light, I most often wear a headlamp. For non-drinking fresh water, I have a sink with a pump connected to a two-gallon collapsible container. Next to the sink is a top-loading insulated icebox. My outboard motor, when it is running, is supposed to re-charge

---

8. Boethius, *Consolation of Philosophy*, 1.poem 2, 137.
9. Herodotus, *Histories*, 3.114.
10. Herodotus, *Histories*, 2.77.

the battery. I also carry a portable solar panel that can connect directly to the battery. I have a mounted VHF radio, and in 2017 I purchased a combination VHF and AIS that can tell me if large ships are nearby. My GPS is handheld, as is a second VHF radio. I have trailed behind on the communication curve, but eventually bought my own cellphone. I have family responsibilities and need to be connected. In the bow compartment, I have my scuba gear along with a six-foot inflatable raft. As for the needs of nature, I have a bucket with a plastic lid. This means I try to submit to the needs of nature only when I am beyond three miles out to sea where the bucket can be dumped overboard. Otherwise, I have to store the bucket in a well-ventilated space, usually in the cockpit when I am below and below when I am in the cockpit.

Head of quarter berth and galley in *Boethius* (author's photo).

Boethius teaches me, with every outing, the ancient discipline of household management. The boat teaches me to be aware of how things fit together, to think in terms of particulars rather than abstractions, and to rely on durable traditions. *Boethius* wants me to know how to splice an eye into various types of rope, tie certain knots, and coil lines properly so as to not tangle when next needed. The boat talks to me. She tells me directions she prefers and sail positions that are better. I am chastised when I don't take into account the angle of the wind, the depth of the water, and signs of a gust. *Boethius* likes me. She wants us to be happy together. Life on land lulls me into patterns of thought that are national, professional, and supposedly

Ventura's Advice

progressive. *Boethius* insists that I be local, work with my hands, and trust traditions. *Boethius* teaches an intensive, waterborne, home economics. I don't want to disparage life on land as necessarily problematic. Wendell Berry has learned similar lessons from his farm on the Kentucky River, Henry Beston from his Outermost House on Cape Cod, Kathleen Norris in a monastery in Minnesota, Edwin Way Teale on his nature preserve in Connecticut, and Annie Dillard at Tinker Creek in Virginia. I simply want to say that, untied from the dock with sails up, *Boethius* encourages ways of thinking that tend to be less encouraged on land.

What *Boethius* teaches best is slowness. Her hull shape and length are such that the laws of creation have set a limit to her hull speed at about the speed of your average neighborhood jogger. Even when using our outboard motor, our fastest speed is slow. Slow is good for pilgrims. Slow is the appropriate speed for investigation, contemplation, and belief. Slow encourages pondering. If *Boethius* and I want to go on long pilgrimages up through the islands of the California Bight, the cosmos says "Fine. Just be happy doing it slowly."

Slow, however, is not unexciting. Up along the southern side of the Santa Barbara Channel there is a current of big winds that first concentrate by swinging around Point Conception from the west and then concentrate again along the north side of the islands. The boaters of Santa Barbara call this current "Windy Lane," as if it were a pleasant neighborhood street lined with eucalyptus trees and cute bungalows. Truth is: this so-called "lane" often channels the roughest winds and waters on the whole California Bight.

Being alone with *Boethius* in those waters tends to heighten our sense of excitement. One trip I remember well. *Boethius* and I needed to cross from Santa Barbara over to Anacapa Island. All started out quite Presbyterian, but two thirds of the way into the channel, all went Pentecostal.

We left Santa Barbara mid-morning in a pleasant wind coming at us a little aft of a broad reach. By mid-afternoon, high winds were blowing the tops off increasingly tall swells. At the tops of these swells, gravity would loose its hold on us. Time would stop. Then powers deep in the swell would rise up and sometimes fling us forward. Sledding down the face of a swell, *Boethius* would stretch out as she surpassed the physical limits of her mathematical hull speed. Sometimes a swell would, after lifting us by the stern, drop us backward, letting us fall with our bow pointing into the sky. Steering through the swells became harder and harder as the boat would lift the bow into a gust of wind at the same time a wave top blew into spray and threatened to throw us sideways.

I needed to get rid of more sail. Earlier I had reefed the mainsail, making it smaller. After dropping backwards into a trough, I pushed the tiller away from me and let loose the sheets. With the sails wildling flogging about, the boat languished. Properly harnessed, I crawled up to the base of the mast, loosed the jib halyard, then crawled forward to the bow in order to gather in the sail. Big rollers, over and over again, lifted the bow high into the air then splashed us down. Having temporarily secured the jib with the short line kept by the anchor for this purpose, I crawled back to the cockpit and pulled in the mainsheet. *Boethius* immediately perked up, stopped rolling wildly, and surged forward. Regaining our course, she was much happier. We were still flying Pentecostal, but with only a half-sized triangle of mainsail full of wind, we did not worry about being rolled over.

Eventually, having passed by Cavern Point on the northeast corner of Santa Cruz Island, we were lifted by a last burst of Pentecostalism that squirted us out of Windy Lane into the relatively flat water of the passage between islands. It was now late afternoon. We were gloriously sledding between tall island cathedrals. Anacapa Island is high gothic. Santa Cruz Island is broad shouldered and Romanesque. White water froths at the foundations of each. We were enchurched. Both of us were being lifted into high praise. *Boethius* was stretched out in yearning with almost no sail flying. Back to the wind, I clung to the boat with my right hand while steering the tiller with my left.

After wearing the boat eastward, gybing the reefed mainsail to bring the wind across our stern over to our port side, we ran underneath Anacapa Island. After about half an hour, we anchored in thirty feet of water next to a high protective cliff. There are no protected anchorages on Anacapa, just tall cliffs. Our anchorage, a little alcove in the island's south-facing wall, is called East Fish Camp. We spun bow eastward into the wind and snuggled close in to the island. Anacapa lighthouse rose high behind us, and to the south, a hundred yards away, high winds were still blowing the tops off short swells. No person was in sight. But we were not alone in the cathedral. Birds were everywhere. As I stood on the bow, waiting for full confidence in our anchor, I felt exhilarated, joyful, amazed.

Anacapa Island is famous among ornithologists as a haven for birds. The scraggy cliffs offer temporary homes for flocks of transient birds along with being the West Coast's largest breeding colony of the California brown

Ventura's Advice

pelican. *Boethius* and I had anchored in a Pentecostal aviary. Thousands of birds, small and large, were swirling and diving while others were squawking and singing from perches on the cliffs. We were in Bird-church. I closed my eyes, and listened to the bird-ecstasy. The patron of Ventura tells of St. Francis asking a flock of birds to be quiet while he preached—the birds immediately complying. *Boethius* and I were in an opposite situation. Our job was to listen while the birds preached.

Jesus commands us in the Sermon on the Mount to be bird watchers. Birds, like winds, can be embodiments either of the Holy Spirit or lesser angels. They watch us. It is always appropriate to ask a bird if it is an emissary with a purpose or just hanging around. One morning when *Boethius* and I were motoring north up the outer side of Point Loma, two osprey flew out to play with us. They swooped and swerved before one settled in on top of the swaying mast while the other continued to inspect the rigging. Were these osprey angels? Am I so cocky as to think that these two osprey might have flown out from the coast for the purpose of giving *Boethius* and me a blessing, a little affirmation, a little wisdom? I think the cocky people are those who insist that birds are just birds. As a pilgrim, I am willing to risk the cockiness of thinking that God, the Creator and sustainer of all, smiled and sent two osprey out to wish us well.

Two Osprey visit *Boethius* (Author's photo.)

I have friends I trust, who say they have actually heard God speak audibly to them. I myself have never heard a human-like voice from God.

The Winds of Santa Ana

On the other hand, sailing from Santa Barbara, through Windy Lane, to an evening anchorage at East Fish Camp, *Boethius* and I heard creation singing about its creator. We watched the sunset inside a Pentecostal bird-church. I did not hear words, but *Boethius* and I were singing with angels.

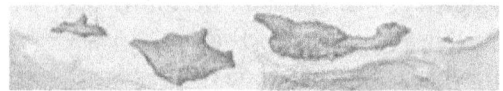

THE CALIFORNIA BIGHT is a wilderness only superficially civilized. The whole of sailing, if one is willing to accept it, is a wild conversation with creation, and through creation with the Creator. I like sailing alone, but as a pilgrim-sailor on *Boethius,* I never feel alone when sailing. I am a college professor, educated and educating on the California Bight, a card-carrying product and employee of the Knowledge Industry. I have learned well the rules of separating matter and spirit, physics from metaphysics. I know how to dissect an argument, color within the lines, and get tenure. However, when *Boethius* and I leave our mooring, industrialized rationalism loses its grip on us. Insistent analysis gives way to abundant possibilities. Mysteries cease to be merely that which we have not yet figured out and become the facts of life that are beyond our capability of knowing. When *Boethius* and I leave our mooring the whole of the California Bight embraces us in pilgrim-fellowship. *Boethius* and I do not pretend to hear everything we are told or learn everything we should. We do, however, come back to our mooring having heard things, seen things, and experienced things that cumulatively give me confidence that this world is enchanted.

Point Loma and San Diego Bay (NASA.)

Those In San Diego Who Go Down to the Sea

*B*OETHIUS moors under the local patronage of Santa Isabel, a saint-queen from Portugal. Isabel came late to what Spanish sailors had long called *La Punta de la Loma* (roughly: the Point of the Hill), the peninsula that creates San Diego Bay. Santa Isabel came with the Portuguese whaling and fishing families from the Azores who established themselves at the core of Point Loma's culture in the early twentieth century. She, herself, was born a Spanish princess in the thirteenth century. When she was thirteen, she was given to the Portuguese as a political wife. Isabel could have been despondent, but instead she chose to adopt her new country and people. Throughout her life she tried to do better by her people than her husband, who was greedy and mean. Depictions of her usually show her with a bundle of flowers. This is because once, when she was sneaking food out of the palace to feed the poor, her husband, who had forbidden such kindness, confronted her. He demanded to see what was hidden under her cloak. When she spread her arms, flowers poured out onto the floor, not the food she had actually concealed.

Point Loma has a *festa* every year in honor of Santa Isabel. A parade begins and ends at a tiny fishermen's chapel built in 1922 as a facsimile of chapels remembered from the island of Terceira in the Azores. Inside is a statue of Santa Isabel and, in front of it, engraved into the sidewalk, is a depiction of her. Sometimes when I walk down to the harbor, I turn down the short side-street called Avenida de Portugal and stop in front of the chapel. I don't know if she is supposed to watch over Presbyterian sailors like me, but I hope so. I usually say a quick prayer asking for protection for me and the rest of us going to sea that day.

Going to sea encourages piety. It is customary for Roman Catholic fishing boats to carry, up by the helm, little statues of Mary or baseball-card sized images of patron saints. Beginning in the 1920s, when tuna fishing became a big industry in San Diego and huge tuna boats lined the waterfront, the boats often had chapels built inside them. These chapels were often elaborate floor-to-ceiling cabinets where sailors could place a picture-card of their particular patron saint, light a candle (in good weather), and say a prayer before venturing on deck for a day's work. The Maritime Museum of San Diego has an exhibit of one of these tuna-boat chapel-cabinets. The cabinet has three arched enclosures, and the exhibit displays a random collection of picture-card saints along with a mid-century snapshot of a scruffy teenage sailor, kneeling before a similar chapel-cabinet, with hands clasped in prayer. I suppose there are some who visit the museum and smile at what they think to be evidence of superstition among immigrant sailors. I smile, but out of appreciation. Those who go down to the sea in ships, and do business on great waters, they see the works and wonders of the Lord. The oceans of the earth love us, but we are right to fear them. They cleanse the atmosphere and coastlands as they churn in cycles, rise and fall as tides, and are agitated into tumultuous seas. It is smart to say a prayer before venturing out to sea and again daily before going on deck.

Waterfront neighborhoods are surprisingly pious. They are superstitious in the best sense of the term. *Boethius* and I have found the water-folk around us to be quick to discuss mysteries and spiritual matters. Water-folk tend to be acutely aware of the spirit in nature. On the dinghy dock or out in the mooring field, we boaters tell each other tales of uplifting sights, miraculous escapes, fickle winds, rogue waves, and insistent pelicans. We don't talk the ins and outs of theology, but conversation easily slips from boastful escapades to reverence and appreciation. Boat people have seen the works of the Lord and the wonders of the deep.

Those In San Diego Who Go Down to the Sea

Richard Henry Dana Jr., who published the classic *Two Years Before the Mast* in 1840, lived here on Point Loma for six months of his two years. In the book, he describes a tough old sailor wanting to borrow a Bible from a pious young one. The young one fears that the other wants to make sport of it. "No," says the man, "I don't make sport of God Almighty." Dana adds: "This is a feeling general among sailors." Dana describes a household of faith on boats and in ports. He advocates the free distribution of Bibles. He admits that many a sailor leaves the Bible at the bottom of his sea chest for the whole length of a voyage, but "he never treats it with positive disrespect." He continues, "I never knew a sailor but one who doubted its being the inspired word of God."[1] Dana is adamant that to be a good ship captain is to be a religious captain. A ship should keep the Sabbath in some way at sea, and as much as possible, the captain should look out for the souls of the crew. Dana writes also of the important influence of Bethels, the port chapels that appear often in sailing literature.

Boethius and I are members of a maritime fellowship that thrives here the lee of Point Loma. Portuguese Catholicism is strong, and so too is evangelical Protestantism. We moor, parking-lot style, tied to bow and stern to buoys, in the middle of a cove next to Shelter Island. A surprising number of individuals, couples, and families live around us. Rent is cheap. A public toilet is on shore next to the dinghy dock. A grocery store, chandlery, and bookshop are all within easy walking distance. The live-aboard boats rarely move off their moorings. They have solar panels and TV satellite dishes hanging awkwardly off makeshift brackets. Plastic awnings are often stretched over cockpits. Extra gear is usually stacked on deck. Many boats have flower pots hanging off various spars or over their sterns. There is a retired mechanic named Joe who lives a couple of boat rows down from *Boethius*. He is happy to give advice and is inexpensive to hire. Chris, down the row from me, plans on getting his boat in working order for a long cruise, but is happy now being friendly to all the boaters around him. Daniel is another who seems to know everyone in the neighborhood. I see him often standing in his dinghy at the side of boats chatting with their owners. There are several former students from my college who live here in the mooring field. Two of them just had a baby and ferry the child back and forth to shore every day in a dinghy. There is a retired psychologist on a beautiful ocean-going yacht further down. He flies a large Christian flag, and, for a long time, had a banner tied to his boat stanchions declaring "Jesus Saves."

---

1. Dana Jr., *Two Years Before the Mast*, 406.

The Winds of Santa Ana

When *Boethius* and I, after many years at a channel mooring, were moved into this inner mooring field, we were welcomed by our neighbors. Michael off our bow and John off our starboard, both lived aboard their boats. Each helped me figure out how best to set lines and offered good advice to keep the boat safe through the seasonal weather changes. They were patient with me, and we often had many nice chats as I rigged or de-rigged *Boethius*. Neither of them sailed their boats. Like nautical hermits, they each lived alone on their boats while participating by dinghy in fellowship with other live-aboards. Michael told me he was living on his boat because this is where he ended up after too many years taking bad drugs. He readily volunteered he had cleaned up his life with the help of a Higher Power. Now he lived on the bay. His son had helped him attach large solar panels to his mast. John, on the boat to our starboard, had been for many years a deckhand on fishing and sport-fishing boats that sailed in and out of Newport Harbor. He would lean out over the edge of his cockpit, sticking his head out from underneath the tarp that protected him from the sun. He talked pretty much non-stop to me about anything that happened to be crossing his mind. One day he was complaining about the taste of canned refried beans and said he had learned to cook refried beans the right way when he was in a Mexican prison. I paused while rigging *Boethius* for a trip out to sea, "Mexican prison! When was that?" He said it was after being a deckhand and before moving onto this boat. He did not say what he had done. After several years in prison, he came north to live on the streets of San Diego. His sister bought for him his beat-up twenty-seven foot sloop. "This boat cost her about $7,000," he said. "I've been living on it for seventeen years."

About a year after I moved into the neighborhood, John died. He had been having health problems. On a bad night John called the Coast Guard on his VHF radio. Apparently, he had suffered a stroke. The Coast Guard lifted him off his boat and put him ashore into an ambulance that took him to a local hospital. The next day I rowed out and saw his boat in disarray. Michael told me about the night's events. He said he did not think John would ever be back. About a month later, Michael sent me a text saying John had died.

Those In San Diego Who Go Down to the Sea

John at the stern of Michael's boat in the mooring field of America's Cup Harbor, San Diego (author's photo).

We all liked John. As I was rowing by one day he called for me to come alongside his boat. When I got over to him, he gave me a pointy thing to glue onto the top of my mast. "I got this for you," he said. "It will fix your bird-crap problem. No bird will want to stand on this up there."

On another day, as we were talking boat to boat while I was getting ready to head out to sea, he said, "You're a Christian, right?" I said yes. He said he was one too. He described himself back in 1970 being saved while working on the waterfront in Newport Harbor. He said he went to Chuck Smith's Calvary Chapel on the border between Costa Mesa and Santa Ana. As a historian, I know Chuck Smith to have been one of the most influential evangelical pastors in the world—not as one of those pastors on TV, but rather as one that changed way church services are set up, the way congregations sing, and expectations of what it means to be seeker-friendly. In the late 1960s, Pastor Smith and his family welcomed wayward beach-people and boat-bums like John into church services even if they showed up covered with sand, shirttails out, jeans cut-off, long hair straggling, and feet bare. Smith encouraged a local soft-rock band called "Love Song" to lead the singing in church. Eventually, Smith and his church set up a record company called *Maranatha! Music* to promote what is now called "worship music." Calvary Chapel became a type of waterfront Bethel like the one depicted in Melville's *Moby Dick*. Young Ishmaels, arriving at the coast, homeless from the hinterland, would find themselves in church listening to a powerful message. Chuck Smith wrote in his autobiography: "The ocean has a lesson to impart every time a person comes near, so long as they have ears to hear. 'The voice of the Lord is upon the waters,' no less today than when the psalmist heard Him speak centuries ago."[2] My boat-neighbor John was much moved by Chuck Smith's sermons. After being in prison and coming to live in San Diego, he bought at a garage sale a cardboard box full of cassette tapes of Smith's sermons. Still today, he told me, he listens every morning to a sermon by Chuck Smith.

I find it pleasant to picture John, old and cramped in the bow of his little boat, waking up every morning to the noise of squawking birds following sport-fishing boats heading out to sea. I see him, reaching over to his cardboard box of tapes, punching one into an outdated portable cassette player, lying back, and listening to a sermon by Chuck Smith. Such are the ways Christianity thrives on the waterfronts of Southern California.

For my generation of young middle-class sailors, we lived vicariously through another young seeker who lived in Newport Beach: Robin Lee Graham. In 1965, sixteen years old, Graham sailed out of Newport Harbor on a boat no bigger than *Boethius* wanting to live deliberately. For the next five years he sailed around the world. I am nine years younger than Graham. I followed his voyage in *National Geographic* magazine, later read *Dove*, his popular account of the adventure, then years later, read his second book, *Home is the Sailor*. In this follow-up book, Graham is still seeking meaning for his life after sailing around the world. He, his wife, and a new baby are living on their sailboat in Long Beach. One evening, sitting on a chair at the end of the dock, gun in hand, Graham is going to end it all. His wife, however, sees what is happening. She walks up behind him, slides an arm over his shoulder and with the other grabs the gun and throws it into the water. He writes that his wife knelt down beside him and "I leaned my head against her breast and sobbed."[3]

Graham tells readers he and his wife then decided to go to church. It was February 1971 and a "hot, dusty, Santa Ana was blowing." Nearby Calvary Chapel set the example of beach-friendly churches for a Jesus Movement thriving along the coast of the California Bight. The Grahams found a coastal church filled with what looked like two thousand young people. "You could sense the love in the place," his wife, Patti, wrote in her diary.

2. Smith, *Memoir of Grace*, 16.
3. Graham, *Home is the Sailor*, 22-23.

But they remained guarded. They did not want to be simply swept up in the excitement. They did, though, go back on Wednesday night. Graham says: "I had a strange and almost nautical feeling that we were being swept along by some sort of current—a current so strong that we might not be able to fight it."[4]

Many of us on this coast know the feeling.

Within a few blocks of where *Boethius* and I moor is one of the most dynamic megachurches in Southern California. It has a black pastor, Miles McPherson, who wears loose Hawaiian shirts while leading a church of more than twenty thousand members of all sorts of skin colors and economic situations. McPherson is a Bible-thumping evangelical of the sort that came out of the Jesus Movement. He gives his people the Bible's what-for. The music is great. The congregation sings loudly with raised hands waving. The church is called The Rock. It follows in the Chuck Smith tradition, a tradition born on the Santa Ana/Costa Mesa border, the tradition of a coastal Bethel.

My wife and I went to The Rock one Saturday to hear Francis Chan preach. Chan is another of the Bight's famous and powerful preachers. The church he long pastored is over the hill from Malibu on the north side of Santa Monica Bay. The portrait of him on the program shows him on a Southern California cliff with the coastline stretching behind him. On the morning Sue and I listened to him, over two thousand people of all ages and colors were gathered in an African-American pastor's church, listening to a Chinese-American preach. Francis Chan, to add to the mix, was named by his parents to honor his birthplace in San Francisco, a city named in honor of Italian missionary-preacher whose organization sent to the Bight its first preachers. Chan spoke in the morning of a day-long event called "Awaken Southern California." After singing songs in the tradition of Chuck Smith's *Maranatha! Music,* Francis Chan preached like the pastor in Herman Melville's *Moby Dick*, full of intensity and deep piety. He preached with an open Bible in his hands on Jesus' prayer in John 17 that all of us here in Southern California should be unified in Christ. He preached of Catholics and Protestants, charismatics and traditionalists, tongues-speaking Pentecostals and miracle-working healers all finding unity in Jesus and the work of spreading the gospel to the larger world. Chan, himself, would soon be leaving California to plant churches in Southeast Asia.

---

4. Graham, *Home is the Sailor,* 37-39

The Winds of Santa Ana

Melville declared in *Moby Dick*: "The pulpit leads the world.... Yes, the world's a ship on its passage out, and not a voyage complete; and the pulpit is its prow."[5] There is deep truth in this. Creation is a ship on pilgrimage. The Creator is at the helm steering. As Melville describes them, Smith, McPherson, Chan, and many other pastors on this coast, are leaning out over the prow, leading the earth to a voyage complete.

When I go down to the sea here in San Diego to go sailing for a short afternoon pilgrimage, I perform rituals required by the craft of sailing. There are liturgies to the craft. Tugging the outboard motor to life raises anticipation, but the most meaningful of all the liturgies is the raising and lowering of sails. Once clear of other boats and obstructions, the tiller is pushed to port, and the bow swings to starboard until *Boethius* is head-on into the wind. With her motor puttering forward with just enough weigh to keep us headed into the wind, I climb onto the cabin roof and pull down on halyards while the main and jib rise, both flogging back and forth in the wind. After cleating the halyards and returning to the cockpit, I pull the tiller over to starboard. The bow swings to port. Sheets are pulled in and secured as the sails cease their flogging and cup the wind. A wave develops at the bow and a wake forms behind the stern. Grace abounds. The motor is turned off and *Boethius* and I surge through the channel so as to exit the bay. The liturgy is reversed when we return. The motor is tugged on. Sails are lowered, flaked, and tied down. Halyards and sheets are coiled. There is usually a late afternoon shimmer to the waters of the mooring field. Often, watching us slowly putter in or out of the harbor, is a pelican perched on the rail of a fishing trawler or hunkered on the top of a dock pylon.

Along with physical liturgies, pilgrim-sailing requires liturgies of the mind. There are mental crafts within the physical craft. There are processes of thought that need to be learned and applied just as there are processes of raising and lowering sails that need to be learned and applied. Take, for example, seeing a pelican. We see them often. When out at the entrance to the bay, they elegantly swoop low, wings spread wide. They swerve in so close I can look them in the eye. They often seem to be looking back at

---

5. Melville, *Moby Dick*, 836.

Those In San Diego Who Go Down to the Sea

Boethius and me. At such moments, it is appropriate to practice a thought-liturgy long taught in Christian tradition called *physiologia, a thought-craft of seeking, seeing, and hearing nature speak great Biblical truths. Physiologia* assumes that creation teaches about the Creator. In my office I have a copy of a textbook on the subject used in medieval European schools titled, in Latin, *Physiologus*. Among the examples given in the book is a liturgy of the mind one should perform when one sees a pelican.

The first step of the method is for the observer of a pelican to go to the Bible and see if the Bible has anything to say about pelicans. *Physiologus* points out that "David says in Psalm 101 [our 102:7], 'I am like the pelican in loneliness.'"[6] As an aside, I note the word for the bird in the original Hebrew Scriptures does not have to signify, exactly, a pelican (the word could indicate a cormorant or something similar), but the Latin translation of the Bible used by *Physiologus* has David clearly compare himself to a lonely pelican: "*Similis factus sum pellicano solitudinis*." The next step in the method is to apply what is called biblical typology. This is the reading craft that recognizes that rocks, in the Bible, can signify God, winds can signify the Holy Spirit, trees can signify the cross, and King David can signify Jesus. Typology recognizes that God uses an expansive grammar of figures, signs, and types when communicating. A sailor-pilgrim, having seen a pelican, then remembering the Bible's evocative identification between King David and a lonely pelican, should then ask a pelican what it has to teach about Jesus.

Having established this link, physiologic method encourages the observant and thoughtful sailor-pilgrim to go further. The third step in the textbook recommends the observer turn again to the Bible, asking "Where does Jesus say something similar to David about being a lonely pelican?" The answer is when Jesus quotes Psalm 22 while dying on the cross: "My God! My God! Why have you forsaken me?" Therefore, using physiologic method, the thoughtful and observant sailor is encouraged, when seeing a pelican, to ponder the lonely Jesus, suffering alone on the cross in order to redeem a fallen and sinful creation.

There is now a fourth step that is, I think, a big stretch. But it can be good and useful. In this step, the observer is encouraged to create a parable, create a story. The example given in *Physiologus* merges rumor and fancy into this: A pelican loves its young exceedingly, but the young ones, as they grow, strike their parents in the face; the parents both strike back and kill

---

6. Curley, *Physiologus*, 9–10.

their little ones; immediately they lament the deaths and weep over the chicks for three days; on the third day, the mother pelican strikes her own side, then spills her own blood over the dead bodies. This blood awakens the chicks from death. The fifth and final step in Alexandrian physiological method is to go back to the Bible for support for the story in step four. In this case, *Physiologus* quotes from Isaiah, Romans, and the four gospels about the work of Jesus, especially how Jesus was stabbed in the side.[7]

Protestants tend to worry about the practice of *physiologia*. It is thought to be too wild and dangerous. Protestant theologians have tended to worry that people can too easily be led away from the Bible into fanciful parables. They are right to be worried, especially about steps four and five; however, *Boethius* and I don't want to throw the baby out with the bathwater. *Boethius* and I believe our home waters encourage us to keep *physiologia* in our toolbox of thinking methods. We who go down to the sea in ships, who do business on great waters, need to practice liturgies, both physical and mental, in order to best see the works of the Lord and the wonders of the deep. Reality here is abundant and calls for abundant thinking.

Boethius and I are most often day-sail pilgrims. Our most common sail is a late-afternoon tack out to the Point Loma lighthouse and back before dinner. Even though these are short sails, they can be abundant if we use philologic method. When a lone pelican swoops low and crosses our bow, we take it as a sign. We say like John the Baptist when he watches Jesus pass by, "Behold, the lamb of God who takes away the sin of the world." Are we in danger of worshiping a pelican? No. Our danger is ignoring what God wants to show us. The philosopher C. Stephen Evans warns us about ignoring signs in his excellent book *Natural Signs and Knowledge of God*. As for *Boethius* and me, we play it safe. When we sail in our home waters we try to be sign-searchers. When we see interesting sea-life, we watch. When the wind and the water are playful, we perk our senses. If a cloud is particularly prominent, we listen. The Bible teaches us to do this. If we see, feel, or hear something that appears to be a sign, symbol, or type, we concentrate harder and even push our speculations. Christians have often said there are two books of revelation: Nature and the Bible. The two are not mutually exclusive.

Annie Dillard in her well-known *Pilgrim on Tinker Creek* uses physiologic method in her chapter called "Fecundity," a chapter about the abundance of death required here on earth for the abundance of life we see here.

---

7. Curley, *Physiologus*, 10.

Those In San Diego Who Go Down to the Sea

Dillard writes: "This world has signed a pact with the devil; it had to . . . . The terms are clear: if you want to live, you have to die."[8] In that chapter, Dillard says she is not promoting despair, only an abundant realism about this fallen world. Similar to the way *Physiologus* observed pelicans, she observed thistles and goldfinches. "The thistle," she writes, "is part of Adam's curse." When in a painting we see the baby Jesus clutching a goldfinch, we are to remember that goldfinch are found among thistles, that Christ became incarnate in "the thorny beauty of the real."[9]

As a pilgrim-sailor, I mourn for those unwilling to think in the ways taught by St. Bonaventure, *Physiologus*, Chuck Smith, and Annie Dillard. William Cronon, a highly-respected historian of environmentalist ways of thinking, visited our coast and dismissed all methods of listening for the Creator to speak though creation. Living in Irvine near Newport Harbor for a semester, a place that proudly calls itself "the largest planned community in the nation," he and a group of scholars gathered to write a book subtitled: *Rethinking the Human Place in Nature*. In the book, Cronon insists the natural world does not communicate with us; rather, we humans project ourselves onto nature. Nature, he writes, is mute. There are no signs in nature. Listeners to creation are merely listening to themselves. Cronon is a sensitive and deep thinker, but he embraces the modern belief in human isolation. He writes of walking into the highly manicured park at the center of the UC Irvine campus, musing, but not actually seeking a muse. He wandered toward the center of the park where the campus map names "Rock Outcrop 1" and "Rock Outcrop 2."

> I sat down on Rock Outcrop 1 and stayed there about half an hour. The air was cool and the sky hazy, and as a bird called quietly from one of the pines, I found my mind moving back and forth between the thoughts in my own head and the landscape around me. Because the problem I was trying to solve had something to do with wilderness, I ran my hand over the outcrop and meditated, as the [park] planners no doubt intended I should do, about the meaning of stone and my relationship to it. No epiphany occurred, and I certainly did not experience a mystical flash of enlightenment. Still it was a beautiful moment in a lovely place, and I left with a much clearer sense of where I was going and what I wanted to say.[10]

---

8. Dillard, *Pilgrim at Tinker Creek*, 181.
9. Dillard, *Pilgrim at Tinker Creek*, 215.
10. Cronon, *Rethinking the Human Place in Nature*, 54–55.

William Cronon is a great lover of nature, even a great listener. I am saddened that he walked out of the park that day not allowing for the possibility that the birds, pines, and rocks were speaking to him; or that the Creator spoke to him through them.

San Diego Bay to La Jolla Shores (NASA image with labels added by author).

The Snake Path in La Jolla

GIVEN only one day, dawn-to-dusk, *Boethius* and I go on a "there and-back-again" pilgrimage to La Jolla Shores. This bit of coast promotes spiritually dense forms of science, architecture, and sculpture. We sail with ears to hear and eyes to see. We will allow experiences and information to accumulate, collage-like, into messages. We follow the advice of the patron saint of Ventura who recommends pilgrims to be investigators, contemplators, and believers.

I first felt the spiritual density of the architecture on the La Jolla ridge, not while sailing with *Boethius,* but while pondering the *Snake Path* leading up to the base of the main library at the University of California, San Diego. In the 1960s, William Pereira, one of the Bight's most famous mid-century modernists, designed the library to look like two hands, joined at the wrist, fingers splayed out, lifting knowledge upward. Some two decades later, Alexis Smith, a member of the art community of Venice and Santa Monica, transformed the iconic message of the library from joined hands into a tree—the Tree of Knowledge of Good and Evil in the Garden of Eden. She did this by designing the *Snake Path* that leads up the hill to the base of the library. Walking on a snake below a tree-like library calls for contemplation. As I walked up and down the length of the snake, I did what we professors tell students to do: "Let the art speak." As I walked, I listened to the sculpture and its surroundings. I let geography and proximity interact with design. I allowed the place to speak as a whole.

UC San Diego's Geisel Library designed by William Pereira and the Stuart Collection's *Snake Path* designed by Alexis Smith (author's photos).

Alexis Smith is an artist of "collage" or "assemblage." Her art assumes that when diverse things are juxtaposed, a fuller or even different message emerges. Place a glass of red wine on a table and an observer might simply remember the biblical line "wine gladdens the heart." Place a Christian cross and a loaf of bread next to the glass of red wine and the spiritual density of the assemblage thickens with sacramental associations and a higher message emerges. 1 + 1 + 1 no longer equals only 3. Smith's snake not only accumulates meaning with the library, but also in association with the massive cross—in biblical terms the Tree of Life—in the distance on top of Mount Soledad. This huge modern-style cross, designed in 1954 by Donald Campbell rises above the highest point along the San Diego coast and can be seen from within the library. The snake and two trees join also with the Structural Systems Laboratory at the tail of the snake. In 1988, before Smith designed the *Snake Path*, Bruce Nauman wrapped the top of this lab

The Snake Path in La Jolla

building with seven-foot tall neon letters that spell out Roman Catholicism's seven vices and seven virtues. When the *Snake Path* was constructed four years later it linked artwork at the snake's tail about humanity's ethical choices to the ultimate choice at the Tree of the Knowledge of Good and Evil at the snake's head.

There is more to this assemblage. Halfway up the *Snake Path*, Smith has the snake's body encircle a granite statue of an enlarged copy of John Milton's Christian classic *Paradise Lost* in which Milton juxtaposed in Eden the Tree of Life and the Tree of Knowledge of Good and Evil. Smith even offers a bench to contemplate a quote inscribed onto the granite cover of the book: "Then Wilt Thou Not Be Loth To Leave This Paradise, But Shall Possess A Paradise Within Thee, Happier Far."[1] This quote comes at the culmination of Milton's epic when the archangel Michael—San Miguel who is patron of the island in the northwest of the Bight—tells Adam about the future coming of Christ and the eventual salvation of creation. San Miguel tells Adam and Eve, even as they are venturing into the newly fallen cosmos, there will be, later, a future redemption. The earth shall again be a paradise! The "Paradise Within thee, Happier Far," inscribed on the book is not a reference to scholarly self-satisfaction or some form of individualistic euphoria. It is a reference to human flourishing accomplished in the cross—the Tree of Life depicted on Mount Soledad. It is a reference to the hope we have for all creation. This become clear in the final lines of the book when Eve responds to San Miguel after learning that a future daughter of hers will give birth to creation's savior:

> This further consolation yet secure
> I carry hence; though all by me is lost,
> Such favor I unworthy am vouchsaf'd,
> By mee the Promis'd Seed shall all restore.[2]

At this point in the book, San Miguel holds hands with both Adam and Eve as they walk out of the garden and enter our present, fallen, world. Creation is cursed, but the curse will be reversed. On the ridge above La Jolla, the *Snake Path* two tree-shapes, a laboratory, and a statue of a book, assembled in reference to each other, declare nature's hope in a Creator who restores Paradise. Inscribed into the southeastern corner of the California

---

1. Milton, *Paradise Lost*, 12.586-87.
2. Milton, *Paradise Lost*, 12.620-24.

Bight is St. Paul's promise in Romans 8:21: "All creation will be liberated from its bondage to decay."

Did Alexis Smith in 1992 plan to use the *Snake Path* to create a collage that tells Christianity's overarching and central story? Maybe. Probably. Why else would there be a statue of Milton's book with that particular quote? But whatever her personal motive, what is important is that the juxtaposition is there, on the ridge, walkable and visible to any and all who care to investigate. The assemblage of buildings, *Snake Path,* and cross come together as a geoglyph written into the top of La Jolla Ridge. Robert Irwin, the teacher of Alexis Smith when she was at UC Irvine and creator of another artwork on the UC San Diego campus, wrote in 1985 that an artist, before starting a work, must go to the site. Then while "sitting, watching, walking," the artist must listen for what is "conditioned/determined" by the place.[3] It makes sense to me to think that Alexis Smith heard the ridge speak. The ridge, itself, conditioned/determined her work. The ridge above La Jolla Shores, like the wind, is an angel with a message. The whole of the California Bight seems to be a geoglyph telling a story. As pilgrims on the Bight, *Boethius* and I keep watch for more of the story written into the coast.

Down at sea level on our day-long pilgrimage, *Boethius* and I listen for more of such messages. We expect this coast to speak. We expect birds, plants, and fish to speak. We expect geography and human history to speak. We expect architecture and sculpture to speak. Our research method is first to wander then ponder our experiences and book-learned knowledge. We believe that in the assemblage of such things, pilgrims can get a glimpse of the role of the California Bight in what Santa Monica's son called the pilgrimage of all creation.

At noon after leaving San Diego Bay early in the morning, *Boethius* and I round the outside of La Jolla Point's kelp forest. We have been motoring, but now, after seeing some ruffling on the surface of the water, we raise sails. Soon a moderate wind steadies itself from the northwest. Raising sails changes everything. *Boethius,* pushed by its little outboard, is a boat,

---

3. Irwin, *Primaries and Secondaries,* 180.

The Snake Path in La Jolla

a good boat, a functional boat, even a pleasant boat. But when we raise sails and turn off the motor, *Boethius* becomes something more, something wholly integrated into the cosmos, something meant to be in ways that motor boats can't. The sound of wind in the rigging and splashing of water are amplified, not drowned out. *Boethius* leans over and surges forward. She is happy. The boat's designer accommodated the motor with a lazaret opened from the stern deck with a square hole at the waterline; but the boat has no commitment to its motor. Raise sails in a steady wind and the whole purpose of *Boethius's* existence is enabled. Her tiller comes alive. She becomes lighter, more buoyant. She smiles. She laughs. She flourishes.

I pull the tiller windward and the bow swings to the northeast. I loose the sheets to let the sails swell. We steer toward the tall cliffs at the upper end of Torrey Pines State Park. After a while, we fall further off the wind, letting the boom go wide and the sails bulge. The boat ceases to lean as the bow hunkers down and points toward the cliffs south of the park. Along the top of the cliffs are a string of modern bio-tech firms.

Soft swells lifting us by our stern quarter come in from the northwest. Pelicans fly by, low in a long line. Terns flit about erratically. Sea lions breech for air then watch us pass. We are awash in sunshine, and all is beautiful. I lean back on a cushion, let the boat steer itself, and contemplate the grandeur of this little bight within the California Bight. Southward, the cliffs give way to the flat land of La Jolla Shores. From this angle, Mount Soledad with its cross rises above La Jolla Shores. Sloping down to the right of Mt. Soledad is downtown La Jolla. I can see the iconic blue-domed tower of The Bishop's School. The tower is marked on my nautical chart and beautiful to see from a distance offshore. The architecture of The Bishop's School softens the harshness of the La Jolla's skyline. The school's tower signals the town's aspiration. It points heavenward with a combination of Spanish, Craftsman, and Modernist dignity. It initiates conversation with the cosmos. It signals the pursuit of truth.

Boethius and I continue to sail toward the cliffs above Black's Beach. We gybe the mainsail over to port. My knee pushes the tiller as I reach up to pull the boom over my head. Now headed southward, parallel to the coast, I reset the jib and lean back to contemplate the bio-tech buildings lining on the top of the cliff. Eventually we are straight off the coast from Louis Kahn's Salk Institute of Biological Studies built in 1962–63. We are sailing below what is probably the most architecturally famous building on the whole California Bight. Standard textbooks of art history talk of it as a modernist temple. The *New York Review of Books* of June 2017 featured a picture of the building on its cover with the title "Mystic Monumentality." The article notes that Kahn, in 1944, defined "architectural monumentality" as finding "a spiritual quality inherent in a structure which conveys the feeling of its eternity."[4] The book being reviewed in the article is *You Say to Brick: The Life of Louis Kahn*. The title comes from Kahn's belief that an architect must discuss with construction materials what should be designed. Kahn would give students an example of such a conversation: "You say to a brick, 'What do you want, brick?' Brick says to you, 'I like an arch.'"

Sailing south into the La Jolla Bight I can see the original Scripps Institution building, built in 1909–10. It stands unobtrusively at the shore end of Scripps Pier. The building looks like two attached cubes. Its architect, Irving Gill believed "There is something very restful and satisfying" about a cube, there is "bare honesty" in it, a "childlike frankness and chaste simplicity."[5]

Today, there are many who think artists talk gibberish when they tell their students to expect a brick or a cube to communicate. There are an increasing number in the sciences, the humanities, the arts, and even the environmental movement who insist the cosmos cannot communicate honesty, frankness, or chastity. Statements to this effect are merely tricks played on a silent cosmos. They deny the possibility, and therefore refuse the opportunity, to hear a site, a brick, or a building speak. Parsimonious, not abundant, thinking has become standard in modern industrialized education. *Boethius* and I, as we circle clockwise along the La Jolla coast, contemplate the awkwardness of people living here who appreciate the assemblage created by the *Snake Path,* the aspiration to truth declared by the tower of the Bishop's School, the mystic monumentality of the Salk building, and the ethics taught by the Scripps Building but deny the mysticisms of the designers of these artworks. Many of the educated elite along this coast want to deny the widespread existence of souls. They believe in a stark separation between inanimate and animate, then seem to want to think parsimoniously about even their own animation.

The historic Boethius in *The Consolation of Philosophy*, in his despair, fell into thinking narrowly about the existence of souls. *Philosophia*, rebuked him. Flames, he reports her telling him, fly upward out of desire to fulfill their created purpose. A rock, she says, is solid because of its desire to

4. Filler, "Mystic Monumentality," 14.
5. Gill, "Home of the Future," 12.

cling tenaciously to itself within itself. She affirms the classical and Christian tradition that there are many kinds of souls that animate all creation: souls with desires, souls with a sense of purpose, souls with inklings of ultimate love, joy, and beauty in them. *Philosophia* describes the Creator as the whole fullness of boundless life, the one who offers all fulfillment to all creation's desires. In *The Consolation of Philosophy* she heartily affirms that the earth, our human bodies, and life itself are machine-like, but she does not allow Boethius to think the earth, humans, and life are merely machines. Mechanical and mathematical relationships, she says to Boethius, are everywhere but do not hold the center and are not the end. Beware this notion: "inanimate." What holds both creation's center and end is the Creator's boundless fullness of life.[6] *Philosophia* taught this to Boethius. Life is the great reality. Nothing is actually inanimate. All creation sings.

It is an old idea from deep in history: Nature is music. As *Boethius* and I sail pleasantly in a Presbyterian breeze, I start to sing lines from a great old hymn:

> This is my Father's world,
> And to my listening ears
> All nature sings and round me rings
> The music of the spheres.
>
> This is my Father's world:
> I rest me in the thought
> Of rocks and trees, of skies and seas;
> His hand the wonders wrought.
>
> This is my Father's world,
> The birds their carols raise,
> The morning light, the lily white,
> Declare their maker's praise.
>
> This is my Father's world,
> He shines in all that's fair;
> In the rustling grass I hear him pass;
> He speaks to me everywhere.[7]

I am sure the founders of Scripps Institution of Oceanography sang this popular hymn. William and Mary Ritter were church goers. They

---

6. Boethius, *Consolation of Philosophy*, 3.prose 11, 289–95.
7. Babcock, "Father's World."

believed in nature as creation in the way most Christian naturalists thought about such things at the beginning of the twentieth century. Even those who were uninterested in whether nature was their Father's world still thought of biology as a spiritual wonder. Andrea Wulf in *The Invention of Nature* writes of the biological mysticism of the amazingly influential Alexander von Humboldt. He believed the world "pulsated with life." Nature, for Humboldt, is "a never-ending activity of animated forces." Nature is "a living whole" in which organisms are bound together in a "net-like intricate fabric." Humboldt, probably the most revered natural historian of the nineteenth century, believed nature to be enchanted. Wulf notes that, without mentioning God, Humboldt's book *Cosmos* asserts that nature is animated: "one breath—from pole to pole, one life is poured on rocks, plants, animals, and even into the swelling breast of man."[8] Wulf notes that Charles Darwin, who took Humboldt's volumes with him around the world on the *Beagle*, derives his famous metaphor of "entangled" nature from Humboldt. She then points to Humboldt's direct influence on the biologists Ernst Haeckel who invented the term "ecology."[9]

William and Mary Ritter were Christian Humboldtians, the scientific founders of the Scripps Institution of Oceanography. They lived on the top floor of Gill's Scripps Building at the end of the pier I see in the distance. They were one of the important intellectual power-couples in California history. Both were intensely interested in what Mary called "The Problem of Human Wholeness." Mary was a physician. She had been the first female faculty member at UC Berkeley. She taught women's health and served as dean of women. She became a national leader in women's health organizations such as the Young Women's Christian Association (YWCA). William Ritter's most important book, published in 1919, was *The Unity of the Organism: Or the Organismal Conception of Life*. Biology, for Ritter, should have a commitment to understanding that the way life is greater than its elements, that wholes can be greater than the sum of their parts. Biology, he wrote, should not ignore the "indubitable psychic life of organisms."[10] Ellen Scripps and her little brother Edward, the high-thinking patrons of La Jolla, were drawn to the Ritters' plan to create an oceanographic institution. We are told by Ellen's biographer, Molly McClain, that the Ritters and Scripps

---

8. Wulf, *Invention of Nature*, 245–46.

9. Wulf, *Invention of Nature*, 307.

10. William Ritter, *Unity of the Organism*, 23. See also Mary Bennett Ritter, *More Than Gold in California*.

The Snake Path in La Jolla

together believed "the study of the ocean promised to mediate the truths found in both science and religion."[11]

Needing to go home, I haul in the sheets as we swerve westward into a broad reach. We need to put the Salk and Scripps buildings behind us and shape a course with the Bishop's School's tower to port so as to pass on the northern side of the kelp off La Jolla Point. All nature is singing as we gurgle through the water. Everything round us rings with the music of the spheres.

To be a sailor is to be a student of how creation is organismal, how it works together, how it speaks, how it loves. *Philosophia* in Boethius's *Consolation*, writes of love as the highest of the natural laws. She sings, "O happy human race, if the love that rules the stars may also rule your hearts."[12]

A wave of sadness hits *Boethius* and me broadside. Maybe you, dear reader, are worried that we are believing too much. Maybe you are one of the multitude of the STEM-trained who insist on the wisdom of Ockham's Razor, a thinking tool that favors parsimony over abundance. Allow me to remind you that William of Ockham, the great medieval philosopher with whose razor our schools increasingly insist we shave our minds, believed, like *Boethius* and me, in prayer, patron saints, assemblage, the harmony of the spheres, and the love that rules the stars. Throughout his life he believed in miracles and the crucial importance of Santa Cruz. Properly understood, Ockham's "Razor" never proposes that creation should be thought of as anything but abundant. Ockham was a Franciscan, a follower of St. Francis of Assisi. Like Bonaventure, he believed creation speaks of its Creator.

In the middle of the afternoon, *Boethius* and I round the outer edge of the kelp off La Jolla Point. We sail wide then ease our sheets to shape a course for the entry buoy to the San Diego Channel. We have miles to go and hours to sail before we will be moored in San Diego Bay. With *Boethius* rushing through the water and the sun on my back, I imagine Francis, Bonaventure, Ockham, and *Philosophia* crammed into the cockpit with me. We talk of the *Snake Path* as an assemblage preaching the gospel of hope for all creation. We talk of the mystical in architecture. We talk of the Ritters and their organismal biology. We talk the importance of wholes over parts, assemblage over dissection, and abundance over parsimony. We laugh together, and at one point we all break into singing Francis's hymn to Brother Sun, Sister Moon, Brother Wind, and Sister Water.

---

11. McClain, *Ellen Browning Scripps*, 72.
12. Boethius, *Consolation of Philosophy*, 2.poem 8, 227.

Richard Henry Dana Jr. by John Terken, 1972, Dana Point Harbor. (Author's photo.)

As Refreshing as a Great Rock
Dana Point

LATE in the afternoon, I hear a whale breathe. The wind is noisy and blowing hard. I am concentrating on sailing wing-and-wing in rough conditions, but I clearly hear the whoosh of a whale exhaling close behind me. I turn immediately and see its back underneath a dissipating spout. Then, close by, a second whale's back hunches up into view, spouts, and lumbers back underwater. The backs of neither whale looked familiar. I had seen the backs of grey and humpback whales. These two whales I had just seen had broad backs that barely washed above the surface before sinking below. I was moving fast, the wind and the waves were rough, I did not see much. I yelled to them: "Hey! Come back!"

Boethius and I are sailing in charismatic conditions, wing-and-wing, heading southeast in the middle of San Pedro Channel between Santa

As Refreshing as a Great Rock

Catalina Island and Dana Point. Wing-and-wing is a downwind way to configure the rig. It requires concentration to keep one sail filled to port and the other filled to starboard. It is pretty to see a boat sailing this way, but it is precarious. The person at the helm is not relaxed—especially if there is a following sea combined with a wind regularly blowing the tops off the swells before they roll underneath the boat. Stupidly, I make a mistake and break the boom. I lean forward to reach down into the cabin. Suddenly the stern lifts and swings sideways, the port rail rises high into the sky, and the starboard rail dips low into the water. Boethius is now broaching sideways to a white-capped swell. The mainsail is back-winded. I had set a "preventer," a line from the boom to a cleat that will "prevent" the boom from swinging all the way across the boat in the case of an accidental gybe. The preventer is holding the boom so that it won't crash all the way to leeward, but I had used only a short rope and tied a cheater-preventer to the bale in the middle of the boom. *Bang!* The wind pushing against the back side of the sail is too strong. The boom breaks at the bale to which the preventer is tied. The back half of the boom begins to flail wildly as the boat begins to right itself, still broadside to the waves. Lines whip back and forth. I push the tiller deep to leeward trying to point *Boethius* into the wind. The bow, however, keeps being beaten back. The back half of the metal boom continues to flail about. I duck low and tug the outboard motor to life and rev the throttle. When *Boethius* gains some momentum I push the tiller again to leeward. As the bow starts to point into the wind, I pull the mainsheet tight, stabilizing, somewhat, the boom's movements. All is safe now with the bow punching directly into oncoming swells. I attach the autohelm to the tiller. Harness on, I crawl up to the mast and drop the mainsail and jib. I wrap lines around heaps of sail, crawl back to the cockpit, release the autohelm, push the tiller to starboard and swing the boat back onto a course to Dana Point. An hour or so later when the sea calms, I again connect the autohelm and begin to clean up the mess. Eventually all is secure. I am mad at myself. This is my fault. Long into the night, we will motor toward Dana Point. Tomorrow, we will limp back to San Diego. Tonight, we will anchor in the lee of a great rock that refreshed Richard Henry Dana Jr. when he was depressed. I also hope for a little refreshment.

The Winds of Santa Ana

Limping toward San Diego the day after we broke our boom. (Author's photo.)

BACK TO THE whales. They were like no other I had ever seen, and *Boethius* and I have seen our fair share. The population of whales in the California Bight has been increasing during my decades here. The older I get, the more whales I see and seeing them is always a thrill. They lumber along and allow us boaters to come close. I always feel blessed by them. They show us how to live deliberately. They have a slow dignity to which we humans should aspire, but they also like to frolic, a quality to which we humans should also aspire. Seeing them fling themselves into the air is a wonderful sight.

In May of 2006 in the Santa Barbara Channel, when I was teaching California History on a rented fifty-foot yacht, my students and I saw two grey whales propel themselves up into the air. I was teaching about Mexican California on a calm bright morning with no wind. We were all in the cockpit when one of the students saw the first whale break the surface of the water. She called out and pointed to the sea up ahead beyond the bow. Class immediately dismissed itself as students clamored up along the rails and scrambled forward. Soon another whale breached, breaking through the surface of the water, poking its nose high into the sky, and splashing down on its side. Students continued to watch waiting for another show as

As Refreshing as a Great Rock

we continued to motor forward. After a few minutes, one of the students at the bow called out and pointed. She was not, however, pointing out to sea. She was pointing down to the water below her feet. I was steering back in stern. I looked down into the water and saw the back of a whale as big as our boat crossing diagonally under us. Fear and wonder overwhelmed me at the same moment, but the whale just swam on. Those whales were giving us a thrill.

A few years later on a bright sunny day when *Boethius* and I were sailing south several miles off the estuary of the San Dieguito River with La Jolla Point ahead, a small humpback whale swam up close to take a look at us. Whale emotions are hard to read, but I sensed that this one wanted to be social. It surfaced next to us again, then again, then again, keeping the same distance from us at the same speed. I started talking to it. Lines of pelicans flew by as terns and gulls wheeled about in the distance. We swam together for about thirty minutes, Boethius smiling with sails wide and full. The whale keeping pace with us. Eventually the whale decided to go its own way. After it disappeared, *Boethius* and I watched for a while, hoping it would join us again.

I confess to talking often with whatever sea or air creatures are nearby. I talk often to *Boethius*. At home, my whole family regularly talks to our cats. St. Francis talked with animals and birds. Moses talked with a bush. Jesus talked to a tree. In the Book of Isaiah, cypress and cedar trees speak. The Bible encourages readers to be in conversation with rocks, plants, and animals. One of the most fun stories in the Bible is about a stubborn and obtuse prophet and his talking donkey. An angel tells the donkey and the prophet, Balaam, riding him to stop. Balaam does not see or hear the angel and starts whipping the donkey that is trying to help him obey the angel. God then miraculously gives the donkey the power of human speech: "Why are you beating me?" the donkey asks.

Balaam responds, "You have made a fool of me! If only I had a sword in my hand, I would kill you right now."

The loyal animal answers, "Am I not your own donkey, which you have always ridden, to this day? Have I been in the habit of doing this to you?"

Balaam replies, "No," apparently realizing that the donkey is, in fact, loyal and should be listened to.

At that moment, the Lord allows Balaam to see the angel blocking the road. The angel is angry with Balaam for beating the animal. "I would have killed you by now," says the angry angel, but for the good donkey.[1]

The miracle in the story is not communication with an animal; rather, it is the donkey talking in human language. We should not expect human language from all the beings around us. We should simply be alert to the possibility that beings with souls are communicating with us. I am pretty confident that a whale once offered me some consolation when I needed it. It happened very early on a spring morning back in 1987. I was walking alone, westward, along the beach below UC Santa Barbara and Isla Vista. Waves were washing up to my bare feet. Santa Cruz Island was crisp in the distance. All was beautiful. But the beauty made me sad. I had accepted a job that would take my wife and me away from the California coast. I knew the whole world is full of different kinds of beauty, but I loved my life on the Santa Barbara Channel. As I walked, I saw in the surf to my left, the whole length of a grey whale. I walked faster and matched its speed. Together we walked/swam next to each other for maybe a quarter of a mile. Neither the whale nor I said anything out-loud to each other. I did sense, however, that it was consoling me. We had a give-and-take, a back-and-forth, between us. The communication was non-verbal, but it was communication nonetheless.

Later in life I began to doubt my memory of the event. It was too perfect, too poetic, too symbolic: a whale commiserating with me about my immanent departure from the Bight. Did an angel higher up in the heavenly bureaucracy assign the whale the duty of swimming over in order to give me an emotional lift? Where, by the way, are whales on the Great Chain of Being? Are they above or below humans? I don't know. If I were writing an academic article on the consciousness of whales, I would not be allowed to cite my memory of a whale visit as evidence of inter-species communication. Happily, family, church, and sailing teach that life is bigger and wilder than what appears in academic articles.

My doubt about the whale encounter left me, when on a sailing version of my California History class. My students and I were headed south on a Bavaria 46 named *Wizard*. We were near the mouth of the Santa Ana River headed for the entrance to the harbor at Newport Beach. The beach was crowded and the sky bright blue when a student called out that there was a whale in the surf. We were motoring at that point, the sails having been

---

1. Numbers 22:21–34.

furled, flaked, and secured for our entrance into the harbor channel. The whale was headed north, opposite to us. I swung the boat around, dropped the engine speed, and we motored parallel to a grey whale swimming at the edge of the surf. People on shore crowded down to the waterline pointing. From the other side of the whale, my students and I were also pointing. Everybody on the beach and the boat was laughing and calling out to each other. A clump of people on the beach began walking northward, keeping pace with the whale. After about five or so minutes, the whale headed out to deeper water and disappeared. The crowd dispersed, and I turned the boat back around toward the breakwater at the entrance to Newport Harbor.

Standing at the helm, I thought back to my whale experience in Santa Barbara. I am pretty sure those two whales, the one in Santa Barbara and this one in Newport Beach, knew, in some way, what they were doing. The one intentionally consoled me, and the other purposefully gave a thrill to the crowd. Am I a fool to think the cosmos is organized in such a way that whales would want to uplift people? Maybe. But so much that is foolish is true. Why shouldn't whales, in their minds, reach out to people? The extent of communication in the cosmos is a great mystery. The Bible assumes rocks can praise, trees can wail, donkeys can talk, and all creation can yearn. Yes, this is poetry. Yes, this is prophesy. Can it not also be factually true?

Back to the whales I heard breathe in the San Pedro Channel. I am pretty sure they were blue whales! I had glimpsed two of the largest animals that have ever lived on earth! I heard them breathe! After the boom broke, after I had cleaned up the mess, when *Boethius* and I were motoring with the setting sun behind us and Dana Point ahead, I went below to retrieve my *Whales and Other Marine Mammals of California and Baja* by Tamara Eder and Ian Sheldon. The book shows a profile sketch-sequence of the rise and dive of every kind of California whale. Sure enough! I had seen two blue whales! More than seen, I had heard them breathe!

There is a Hebrew phrase, *nishmath chajim*, which means "breath of life." Sailing is, at its essence, a constant affirmation of the *nishmath chajim*. *Boethius* and I suspect that whales have an extra portion of *nishmath chajim*. Imagine their giant lungs. Who is not thrilled by hearing one breathe? In the Old and the New Testaments, the Hebrew and Greek words for wind, breath, spirit, and soul are mostly interchangeable. *Boethius* and I are wind-driven, breath-driven, spirit-driven, and soul-driven. To have the boom on *Boethius* broken by a charismatic wind is to be yelled at. Today,

Boethius and I heard two blue whales breathe. What we hear is a command: Be humble. Be grateful. Be amazed!

In 2002, the Maritime Museum in San Diego began renovating the schooner *Californian*. I proposed to the museum director that together we create for the boat a college-level history class based on Richard Henry Dana Jr.'s *Two Years Before the Mast*. We gave the class an initial run from San Diego to Santa Barbara in 2003, but we did not attract enough students. A big boat like that with a paid captain needs to generate significant revenue. We needed around twenty-two students on board to break even. We did the first class at a financial loss to the museum and the next year cancelled the class when not enough students signed up. In the meantime, my college paid the cost for me to get the certification to charter large sailboats and eventually a master's license from the U.S. Coast Guard. By chartering large yachts and sailing them, it became economically viable for me to teach Dana's book within a maritime-oriented California history class every summer over the next fifteen years.

For two weeks every May, my teaching job included gathering some students around me on a sailboat in order for us to investigate, contemplate, and experience California history. In the following years, we sailed many different routes along the coast and through the islands, but often, we spent the first night at anchor in the lee of Dana Point. I would rent a sloop in Long Beach or Newport Harbor between forty and fifty feet long, with three or four cabins and two heads. Then, after loading the boat with food and gear, the students and I would do an easy afternoon sail down the coast to Dana Point. We would spend the day talking about the coastline, its rivers and estuaries, and the way a boat needs to anchor in the lee of big rocks where it can be safe from winds and especially swells. Swells push against the hull and can pull an anchor loose. Before the construction of modern harbors, the Southern California coast had only one really good rock, Point Loma. In its lee, boats could anchor and feel safe all year round. The rest of the Southern California coast had only touch-and-go anchorages that were good only when the wind and waves were moderate and came from the right direction. The best of these touch-and-go anchorages was San Pedro

As Refreshing as a Great Rock

behind Point Fermin. The moderately good ones were behind Point Conception, Santa Barbara Point, Point Dume, and Dana Point.

When my class and I, sailing south, passed Dana Point rock and had the modern breakwater of Dana Point Harbor off to port, I would encourage the students to imagine the scene without houses hanging on the cliff and a modern harbor below. Indians for thousands of years, European explorers, and all sorts of multinational sailors on this coast before recent times yearned for this tall, wart-like, rock that creates, on normal days, a patch of flat water in its lee. Where the cliffs drop down and the land spreads out toward what is now Doheney State Beach is a creek offering fresh water. Eventually Mission San Juan Capistrano was built nearby in order to be close to the patch of flat water behind this rock.

On that first leg of our maritime field trip, I would teach what would become our daily liturgy of dousing sails and preparing the boat for entering an anchorage. This first time at the ritual, we would go slow. I would turn on the engine, ask one of the students take the helm, and have that person round us up then hold us steady into the wind. When the jib and main were about to lose their hold on the wind, a student would loosen the jib sheet while two students winched in the jib's roller-furler line. As the mainsail began to luff, another student would haul in the mainsheet to center the boom. With the jib furled and the boom centered, another student would loose the main halyard. By that time I would be standing at the mast to guide down the mainsail. With the mainsail down, a couple of students would then help me gather the loose sail, flake it over the boom, and tie it down with what are called gaskets. Finally, still pointing into the wind with the engine running barely above idle, with jib furled, lines cleated, and the mainsail tied to the boom, the student at the helm would then swing our stern quarter to the wind, and we would head toward the buoy that marks the entrance to the channel. At the buoy we would swing the bow to port and motor into the lee of the long breakwater that shelters a narrow channel. Inside the breakwater, having dropped engine speed so that we produced no wake, we would slowly pass the statue of Richard Henry Dana Jr. The young man in the statue stands shirtless and strong. His feet are bare, one foot raised on top a dock bollard. He leans onto that raised foot with a book clutched in one hand. He is, I would tell the students, an excellent example of a sailor-scholar. "There is a plaque underneath the statue," I would tell the students. "It quotes Dana declaring this place, what is now Dana Point, the 'only romantic spot' on this coast."

The Winds of Santa Ana

At the end of the channel, we would disengage the prop and slowly glide into the free anchorage below the cliffs. Here in the flat water I would show the students how to release the anchor and how to use the controls for the electric anchor windlass that we will use in the morning. With the anchor down and the engine off, we would all stand at the bow and take in our situation. It is a beautiful little spot. After a minute or two of looking around, I would then set the students to drawing maps of the California coast with its principal rivers and points in their log/workbooks. While they did this, I would cook dinner.

With the dinner dishes put away and an evening chill setting in, we would squish together around the cabin's table to read aloud to each other from *Two Years Before the Mast*. I would set the scene. It is the end of April and beginning of May 1835. Dana, a student at Harvard, has left his classes behind and is trying to figure out who he is and what he is going to do with his life. He is, like my students, about twenty years old. He has been on the California coast since January. Back in New England, he had embraced a lively evangelical faith, but he believed he was losing that faith on this coast. His father had written an essay five years earlier that warned about how easy it was for lively faith to become a lackluster deism. It was now happening to him. He believed he was losing his soul.

At this point I have the students start reading the pages describing Dana's soul being revived here in this anchorage, this same place. Dana helps row the captain and cargo agent ashore beneath the tall cliffs. Dana and other sailors stand at the shore-boat on the beach as their passengers walk south toward the creek bordered by a trail they will take them up to the mission. Dana, beneath the tall cliffs of what will eventually be named Dana Point, writes:

> Not a human being but ourselves for miles; and no sound heard but the pulsations of the great Pacific! and the great steep hill rising like a wall, cutting us off from all the world, but the "world of waters!" I separated myself from the rest, and sat down on a rock, just where the sea ran in and formed a fine spouting horn. Compared with the plain, dull sand-beach of the rest of the coast, this grandeur was as refreshing as a great rock in a weary land. It was almost the first time that I had been positively alone—free from the sense that human beings were at my elbow, if not talking with me—since I had left home. My better nature returned strong upon me. Everything was in accordance with my state of feeling, and I experienced a glow of pleasure at finding that what of poetry

As Refreshing as a Great Rock

and romance I ever had in me, had not been entirely deadened by the laborious and frittering life I had led.[2]

"As refreshing as a great rock in a weary land." What a great line. It comes from a prophecy about future happiness in the Kingdom of Righteousness in Isaiah 32:1–2. Picture the moment, I would tell the students. A young man worries that poetry and romance is being beaten out of him when this rocky point we are now anchored behind, jutting out into sea, offers him refreshment, offers him hope, offers him renewed life. Dana Point is well-named. To anchor here is to be encouraged. This great rock revives lively faith. Poetry is promoted here. This place, given Dana's experience here, promotes a romantic view of the world.

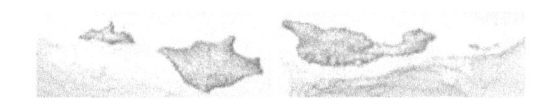

ALLOW ME TO play the history professor and offer the backstory to the evangelical Romanticism that this place revived in the young sailor.

In 1822, when Richard Henry Dana Jr. was seven years old, his mother and his baby sister died. The family was living on the campus of Harvard College in Cambridge, Massachusetts, where his father served off and on as a teacher. The following year, Richard Henry Dana Sr. moved his family into his sister's new house which was just off campus on Quincy Street. This house has since been incorporated into the campus and is today called the Dana-Palmer House. Back in the 1820s and 1830s, during young Richard Jr.'s formative years, leading European and American poets, painters, novelists, theologians, and moral philosophers supped at, or had their letters read out loud at, the Dana's dining room table. Dana's father, Richard Sr., was an influential poet, essayist, editor, and expert on Shakespeare. Richard Sr.'s close friend, and then husband of one of his sisters, Martha, was Washington Allston. At that time, Allston was probably America's most famous painter. He also taught fine art and aesthetics intermittently at Harvard. There is a modern article in *The New England Quarterly* that declares Richard Henry Dana Sr. and Washington Allston to be "America's First Romantics."[3] Growing up in this household, listening at the dinner table

---

2. Dana Jr., *Two Years Before the Mast*, 151.
3. See Hunter, "America's First Romantics," and *Richard Henry Dana Sr.*

to discussions of the new romanticism being developed in Europe and the way romanticism should be understood in America, young Dana could not help but become sensitive to the use of the term "romantic."

More than merely a generic Christian romanticism, the Dana household promoted a particularly biblical and evangelical form of romanticism. During the teenage years of Richard Jr., the Dana household supported the evangelical revivals in the Boston area that were most famously preached by Lyman Beecher. The Dana household along with Allston were opposed to many of the leading figures in Cambridge who were openly antagonistic to the evangelicals. These leading thinkers at Harvard believed the Bible should be re-interpreted in the light of modern rationality, favored Unitarianism, and scorned revivals attributed to the winds of the Holy Spirit. Richard Jr. was thirteen and fourteen years old when the family's local church turned Unitarian and his father and soon to be uncle participated in the creation of a new, evangelical church in Cambridge. Years later after his return from California, Richard Jr. edited and published Allston's *Lectures on Art and Poems* and went out of his way to note that these classroom lectures were delivered by a traditional, Bible-rooted, and Trinitarian Christian.

Richard Henry Dana Sr. wanted an audience beyond the classroom and published essays promoting his Bible-rooted, Trinitarian, type of romanticism. In an essay for a Beecher-funded magazine called *The Spirit of the Pilgrims*, Richard Sr. promoted an evangelical middle way between two dangers. One danger is a spiritualism that stands on no authoritative revelation. The other danger is a narrowly insistent rationalism based on information gained only from the five senses. The former shrouds nature in metaphysical mist and turns nature, itself, into God, while the latter makes human knowledge its God.[4]

When young Dana Jr. in *Two Years Before the Mast* writes of a refreshing rock that revives the poetry in his soul, most likely Richard Jr. is thinking in terms of his father's Bible-rooted romantic poetry. His father wrote often of mountains and sea singing, flowers teaching, birds disclosing, and a brook speaking. The Morning Star bids him to turn his thoughts to God. One whole poem is devoted to moss, humble and lowly, offering consolation to a man. After the man leaves, having been soothed, the moss prays for the man: "Deal gently with him, world, I pray."[5] One poem describes a day of lively pleasure-sailing. Dana Sr. writes of the boat as if she is alive:

4. Dana Sr., *Poems and Prose Writings*, 2.380–89, esp. 386.
5. Dana Sr., *Poems and Prose Writings*, 1.121.

"She smiles; thou need'st must smile on her." At the end of the day: "Careening to the wind, they reach/With laugh and call the shore."[6]

When Dana, having returned from California, was writing *Two Years Before the Mast,* his father read drafts of the book and helped him get it published. At the time, one of the most well-known of his father's published poems was *Thoughts on the Soul: A Poem Delivered to the Porter Rhetorical Society in the Theological Seminary, Andover, September 22, 1829.* In it we can see the similar experience of father and son. Both are in danger of being a "living dead man," and both are revived by the earth:

> Sin clouds the mind's clear vision; man, not earth,
> Around the self-starved Soul has spread a dearth,
> The earth is full of life: the living Hand
> Touched it with life; and all its forms expand
> With principles of being made to suit
> Man's varied powers, and raise him from the brute.
> And shall the earth of higher ends be full, —
> Earth which thou tread'st, — and thy poor mind be dull?
> Thou talk of life, with half thy soul asleep!
> Thou "living dead man," let thy spirits leap
> Forth to the day; and let the fresh air blow
> Thro' thy soul's shut-up mansion. Wouldst thou know
> Something of what life, shake off this death;
> Have thy soul feel the universal breath
> With which all nature's quick, and learn to be
> Sharer in all that thou didst touch or see;
> Give thy Soul air, thy faculties expanse;
> Love, joy, e'en sorrow, — yield thyself to all!
> Knock off the shackles which thy spirit bind
> To dust and sense, and set at large the mind!
> Then move in sympathy with God's great whole;
> And be, like man at first, a LIVING SOUL![7]

Dana Point today, with its name, its statue, and its history, is spiritually entangled with a book and its author. *Two Years Before the Mast* is a coming-of-age memoir of an evangelical Protestant. Deep in it is a motherless young man's appreciation of his father's middle way of evangelical romanticism, a form of evangelicalism neither fully rational nor fully mystical. There is a girl too, Sarah Woods, embedded deep below the surface of the

---

6. Dana Sr., *Poems and Prose Writings,* 1.113.
7. Dana Sr., *Poems and Prose Writings,* 1.93-94.

book. Dana's book is a college gap-year version of Augustine's *Confessions*. Dana wants to live up to the high expectations of those closest to him. He does not want to fall in with the college crowd. He flees, then discovers he wants to return.

Young Dana was a restless nineteen-year old when he boarded the *Pilgrim* on the 14 August, 1834. When he returns on the *Alert* on September 22nd, 1836 he is resolved to embrace the religious and cultural expectations of those he loves. Most distressing, however, he discovers that Sarah Woods has recently died. He had lived with the Woods family in Andover, Massachusetts, for six months when he was sixteen. She was two years younger than Dana and had been infatuated by the family's motherless houseguest. Her father was a dynamic evangelical seminary professor who was involved in a world-wide network of missionaries and a leader in the American Bible Society. His missionary hopes for the people of the Pacific Rim is deep in *Two Years Before the Mast*. Sarah's brother, was Dana Jr's tutor, an inspiring young man who Dana would later say exemplified for him delight "in the beautiful and the good, the strange and the ancient."[8] Woods Jr. taught Dana Jr. to appreciate the aesthetics and ceremonies of European Roman Catholicism, and this appreciation shows up often in *Two Years Before the Mast*. With the empathetic Sarah Woods, teenage Dana shared his struggles with melancholia, his doubts, and his fear that his evangelical faith was not as strong as it should be. Sarah, being spiritually precocious, took upon herself the project of helping Dana anchor himself in his Christian faith. Even after he had left the household, gone back to Harvard for a year, then left again to sail to California, she continued to pray for him. When Dana returns from California and reconnects with the Woods family, Sarah's mother tells Dana that in the delirium before her death, Sarah had spoken his name. The mother told Richard Jr. that in a period of lucidity she asked Sarah why she had called out Dana's name. Sarah responded that she had long been praying for him. Sarah, knowing that she would die soon, told her mother that she hoped that God, when she was in heaven, would permit her to "watch over me, keeping me from sin, & influencing me toward God & holy things." In California terms, she wanted to be Dana's patron saint. Dana Jr. further recorded that "in her very last moments she prayed fervently & impassionedly for me, & the last words that fell from her lips were 'Prepare him for a seat at thy right hand.'"[9]

8. Dana Jr., "Leonard Woods," 143.
9. Dana Jr., *Journal*, 33.

As Refreshing as a Great Rock

All this was in Dana's mind as he began writing *Two Years Before the Mast*. Having returned home, he set himself on a purpose-driven course to be the evangelical-romantic that his family and the Woods family had modeled for him. Today, the words on the plaque beneath the statue of the author, the paragraph about Dana Point being a "romantic spot," should not be taken lightly nor considered narrowly. At this spot on the California Bight, the earth spoke to Richard Henry Dana Jr. The middle-way Christian romanticism he had learned from people who loved him in New England gave him ears to hear such things.

Boethius AND I are still motoring in darkness with a broken boom. I can now see the blinking light on the breakwater of the harbor entrance at Dana Point. Brian Fagan's cruising guide says that sailors should look for the lighted cross of St. Edward the Confessor Catholic Church as a signal above the harbor. NOAA charts show the cross. *Boethius* and I are weary, but a cross will guide us in. The day started with us waking up before dawn anchored off the Malibu Pier in a temporary anchorage called Keller's Shelter. The day before, rough winds with a lot of north in them had pushed us down to Malibu while we were crossing the outer edge of Santa Monica Bay. At dawn, the anchor was up. We were motoring westward toward the islands when I got a text from my wife: "Come home." I pushed the tiller to starboard and pointed us southward, then called Sue. No emergency. Just needed at home. *Boethius* and I sailed first toward Catalina Island, but swerved toward Dana Point when the winds turned charismatic and we were going faster than I had expected. All was going great until we went sideways and the boom broke. Now it is late at night after a long day with a mile or so still to go.

After another half-hour in the dark, close toward midnight, we drop anchor in the lee of Dana's great and refreshing rock. Shore lights illuminate the mess on the deck of *Boethius*. In the cabin I clean up a few things. I loosely push the mainsail forward into the V-berth. I put a bag-salad into a bowl, mix in the dressing, and go up to recline in the cockpit. *Boethius* and I are safe after a long day. I lean further back and listen to the surf break against Dana Point. *Philosophia* appears, stretched out on the opposite side of the cockpit in her jeans and fleece pullover. She smiles at me. We talk for a bit about rocks and whales, their relative qualities as angels. We talk of this coast.

"Kevin Starr, the great historian of California," I tell her, "says that young Dana and his book infused into California a 'Protestant consciousness.'[10] Do you think such a thing can happen, a person and a book can create a consciousness in a place?"

Philosophia smiles, looks at me, and answers: "Places do have souls. Certain places can be deep with spirit. The Acajachemen Indians here told the Franciscan friars that an invisible and all-powerful being created the world and put at its center a black rock called *Tosaut*.[11] The Acajachemen knew the rock. They used fragments of it for tools. The Franciscan friars built a mission here because this rock behind us offered an anchorage to supply ships. It does not surprise me that this rock offered Dana consolation. It does not surprise me that you are guided into the lee of this rock by the cross of St. Edward the Confessor's church. Christianity is strong here. In the Saddleback Valley behind us, the evangelical pastor Rick Warren wrote the amazingly popular and influential book: *The Purpose Driven Life*. It seems appropriate to think certain places like Dana Point can also be *purpose-driven*."

"Dana Point," I say with a smile back to her, "the purpose-driven rock."

"All creation is on pilgrimage," she replies, "rocks too."

"Have you read," I ask her, "Darren Dochuk's *From Bible Belt to Sun Belt: Plain Folk Religion, Grassroots Politics, and the Rise of Evangelical Conservatism*?"

"Do you think I hang out in libraries when not going around the world conversing with readers of Boethius?"

"Well, have you?" I ask.

"Yes, I read it."

"Dochuk," I say, "tells an amazing story of 'plain folk' coming to the Los Angeles Basin, especially Orange County, in the early twentieth century as a driven people creating a driven place famously influential throughout the world for religion and politics. If Kevin Starr is right, maybe we can say that Orange County was prepared in advance for this evangelical migration by Richard Henry Dana Jr. and *Two Years Before the Mast*."

---

10. Starr, *Americans and the California Dream*, 46, the analysis of Dana Jr. runs from 38–48.

11. For the Achjachemen creation story, see Boscana, *Chinigchinich*, chap 3.

As Refreshing as a Great Rock

Philosophia says nothing. She is looking up at the stars. I look up too. Both of us silent. After maybe a full minute, she says: "If we allow ourselves to think in terms of the incarnation of Jesus, the effectiveness of prayers, and the communication of grace in the sacraments, then many things become possible."

"Listen with me," *Philosophia* says while spreading her arms wide, fingers splayed to embrace the sky, "You feel it don't you? Consolation from the rocks, confidence from the stars, affirmation from the waves, encouragement from the wind? We are being formed right now. The potter is at work on the clay."

We both go silent, listening to the waves crashing against the rocks outside the breakwater.

"It is time for you to go to bed," she says.

"I suppose so."

I get up, turn, and look at the broken boom tied down to the deck. I sigh. Then I smile: today I heard a Blue Whale breathe! I take one last look at Dana's rock with the night sky behind it, then fold myself down into the cabin.

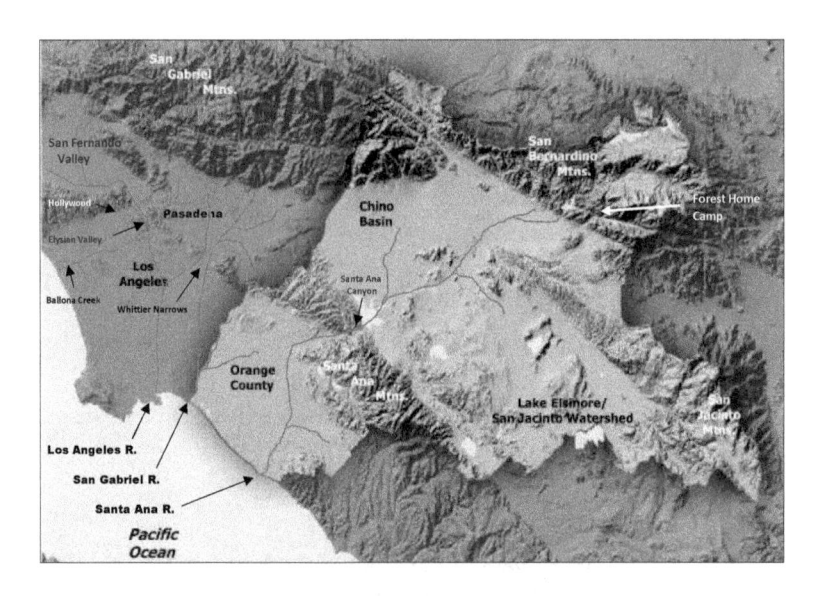

Los Angeles Basin with watersheds of the three major rivers. The routes of these rivers were highly unstable before modern flood control and the Los Angeles River would, at flood, mingle with the Ballona Creek watershed (NASA image, map enhanced by the author with the permission of Sana Ana Watershed Project Authority).

Streams of God, Full of Water, in the Los Angeles Basin

*B*OETHIUS and I are on pilgrimage along the edge of the basin of three rivers. These rivers have not only been used for baptisms, they have experienced their own baptisms. They have suffered but are today being allowed to revive as parks and nature-walks where birds, fish, plants, and humans can be together. They are rivers of hope. *Boethius* and I, from offshore, see the whole Los Angeles Basin as a gift of these three rivers.

An hour or so ago, *Boethius* and I raised anchor near the mouth of the Los Angeles River. At present, we are passing the mouth of the San Gabriel River, headed toward Newport Harbor which is just past the mouth of the Santa Ana River. This coast is long and gently curved. Behind it, grid patterns of lowland suburbs spread over a rich alluvial plain where the waters

Streams of God, Full of Water, in the Los Angeles Basin

of the three rivers formerly spread and mingled. They use to call the lowland around Huntington Beach The Gospel Swamp because of its reputation for tent revivals. In truth, the whole of the Los Angeles Basin can lay claim to being a Gospel Swamp. Today, I have big questions to ask this place, questions about its possible purpose, its role in the world. *Philosophia* is with me in the cockpit. Wedged under my right leg is a topographical map of the area along with a nautical chart of the coast. I am prepared to listen to what this place wants to say about itself.

Having passed the mouth of the San Gabriel River, *Boethius, Philosophia,* and I are sailing large in the middle of the morning with a light westerly breeze a little aft of our beam. *Philosophia* sits next to me. Both of us are on the windward side, wearing sunglasses, looking into the rising sun. We lean back against floatation cushions, both of us wearing wide-brimmed hats and loose long-sleeved shirts. We listen to the gurgle of water along the hull. We follow a course close to shore, parallel to the Pacific Coast Highway. I have sailed and driven this coast many times. In the distance, we see cars stopped at stoplights and clumped in traffic. Unlike those cars, we feel the wind in our sails, and me, a light tug on the tiller. We have passed two river mouths and are headed toward the third.

As we look eastward to the shoreline, I tell *Philosophia* of my embarrassment, more than a decade ago, of running aground in the silt at the mouth of the Los Angeles River. It was a laughable situation. I had rented a big sloop to take some students, along with two of my children, over to Santa Catalina Island for a three-day weekend. We were returning and, in sight of Long Beach Marina, had dropped the sails. I took the helm for the last bit, but then ran us aground. The manager of the boat-rental company had told me that heavy rains earlier in the week had brought a lot of silt into the entry-exit channel. Sure enough, I did not read the channel markers well, got too far to the edge, and we sluggishly came to a stop. We could neither move forward nor backward. The students and kids looked at me with concern. We were in no danger, but I felt like an idiot. A patrol boat happened to be nearby, and two young officers came over at the wave of a couple of our young female crew. They pulled us out of the sludge that vacuum-gripped our keel. After casting off the tow line, we waved to the officers. As I turned to face forward and put the engine in gear, I cursed the Los Angeles River.

I smile at the memory as I finish the anecdote, but *Philosophia* turns with stern eyes to look at me. "You should not curse rivers, especially rivers that bring life to a desert."

Chastened, I sit silent. We both look back toward the shore.

"The Los Angeles Basin," she says, breaking the silence, "is watered by holy rivers watched over by Mary the Queen of the Angels, Gabriel, the archangel of Good News, and Anne, the grandmother of Jesus. These waters have not only nurtured the spiritualities of the ancient peoples of this place, they have come into their fullness by watering the first flowerings of what became in the last century the most vital movements of global Christianity: Pentecostalism, fundamentalism, charismatic Christianity, and neo-evangelicalism. Blessed by these rivers was the first flowering of a new style of worship music that now can be found in churches around the world. Along these rivers, the Signs and Wonders Movement was born. The Los Angeles Basin, this desert watered by three rivers, may be the most influential bit of geography in the history of twentieth-century Christianity."

IF THE LOS Angeles Basin is a basin, it is a basin being tipped toward the sea. The semi-circle of Santa Monica Mountains, San Gabriel Mountains, San Bernardino Mountains, San Jacinto Mountains, and upper Santa Ana Mountains pour their fresh water into the Pacific Ocean. Even when, a few hundred years from now, much of this coast will be under water, the basin will still be tipping and the rivers will still be delivering fresh water from the mountains into the sea. The Los Angeles Basin is not in danger. It is a baptismal basin of hope, and its waters are holy.

The Basin, as with everything called Los Angeles on this coast, traces its name back to the name of its most famous river: *El Rio de Nuestra Señora La Reina de Los Ángeles de Porciúncula*. Contrary to popular notions, the river is named not for angels but for Mary's support of global evangelism, especially Franciscan missionaries. Relics of her were taken to Italy in the 300s where she asked for a chapel to be built on a small portion of land (in Latin a *portiuncula*), next to a small creek. This bit of land was below the hill town of Assisi. Later in the sixth century, the beginnings of the Benedictine Order, the most influential monastic movement in western Christianity,

Streams of God, Full of Water, in the Los Angeles Basin

found support from Mary through this little chapel built next to a creek. Centuries later, the little chapel gave support to the missionary movement that began in Assisi. St. Bonaventure tells us that Francis of Assisi, trying to discern his purpose in life, repaired and restored the building. Bonaventure says of this place below the town with its little creek and tiny chapel:

> This place was loved by the holy man above all places in the world, for here, in great humility, he began his spiritual life; here he grew in virtue; here he attained his happy and perfect end; and this, at the hour of his death he commended to his brethren as a spot most dear to the Blessed Virgin.[1]

While living at this site, this *portiuncula,* Francis had visions and poured forth prayers asking Mary to be his advocate in hope of fulfilling Jesus' command to go into all the world, make disciples of all peoples, baptizing them in the name of the Father, Son, and Holy Spirit. All things named Los Angeles on the Bight, whether basin, county, city, high school, fire department, surf shop, university or sports team are, to some extent, an answers to prayers prayed at the *portiuncula* in Italy. St. Bonaventure, patron of Ventura and namesake of one of Los Angeles's most famous skyscraper hotels, tells us that world-changing events began with prayers spoken long before on that tiny place on the other side of the globe. Small things can matter. On August 2, 1769, two Franciscan missionaries in California asked for Mary, in her connection with a little Italian chapel next to a creek, to bless a relatively dry and unassuming river here on the other side of the world. Their hope was for this bit of land watered by its river to be as evangelistically useful as that place.

William Deverell, the historian of California at the University of Southern California, has written an excellent essay about the Los Angeles River. It starts by noting what Herodotus noted of Egypt: Los Angeles is a gift of its river. He goes on to write that rivers in general are,

> saturated with the past. They can *tell* stories as much as they can *be* characters in stories if listened to and studied carefully enough.... The puny Los Angeles River, so unlike the noble Seine, is also a river in which human memory mingles with water. It is a river all about memory, a place where nature and culture surely flow together.[2]

---

1. Bonaventure, *Life of St. Francis,* 196.
2. Deverell, *Whitewashed Adobe,* 94.

The Winds of Santa Ana

Boethius and I take Deverell at his word. The Los Angeles River has memory and tells stories. The initial pueblo of Los Angeles was prayed into existence on high ground above where the river enters a marshy bottom-land that sprawls down to the coast. A small aqueduct was dug to bring water from upriver down into the new pueblo. Los Angeles was founded as the California Bight's City on a Hill. It was a planned city, planned as a model for future colonizers of the Bight. High-minded and deeply pious politicians, Governor Filipe de Neve and Viceroy Antonio Maria de Bucareli, organized the founding of the pueblo in hope that it would be largely self-governing, economically successful, and centered around a church and school. It would be ethnically diverse. It was built on Indian ground, but was not meant to displace Indians. It was founded in hope that all would flourish. In accord with classical civic values, happiness for all would be pursued, justice would be for all, and the responsibility of rich and strong to care for the poor and weak would not be neglected.

The first citizens were an ethnically diverse group of poor families who first gathered at Mission San Gabriel on the promise of free land and a new start. At the mission, hymns were sung, prayers were offered, and the sacraments were shared. The settlement party were then led to the proposed site above where the Los Angeles River emerges from what today is called Elysian Valley. There a communal plaza and church lot were marked off. House lots were distributed. Farm-lots were also designated to specific families along with the animals, seeds, and tools needed to get started. Sadly, over the next half century, as the population of the pueblo grew and high-minded government weakened, the initial plans ceased to apply. In *Two Years Before the Mast*, Dana described the pueblo as lawless. He exaggerated, but not by far. By the middle of the twentieth century, the Los Angeles River was no longer free; instead, it was channeled in concrete.

Today, *Boethius, Philosophia,* and I sail along the coast from Long Beach to Newport Beach, passing the outflow from massive concrete river-gutters that reach back deep into what use to be a vast floodplain where in winter the Basin's rivers freely mingled. It is hard to image what the Basin looked like before modern flood management. Deverell writes that after the great flood of 1889, a local judge, adjudicating cases of property-loss, decared that the floods of the Los Angeles River "resulted from the whims of the Almighty."[3] Such floods are "visitations whose coming are not foreshadowed by the usual course of events, and must be laid to the account of

---

3. Deverell, *Whitewashed Adobe,* 106.

Streams of God, Full of Water, in the Los Angeles Basin

Providence, whose dealings, though they may afflict, wrong no one."[4] *Boethius, Philosophia,* and I think the judge correct. Floods in the Los Angles Basin signal visitations, divine whims, and acts of providence.

PENTECOSTALISM, TODAY the most dynamic movement in global Christianity, can be said to have begun in Los Angeles on Friday, April 6, 1906. The gift of tongues was given that day to a few people who were fasting and praying in the small home of Richard Asberry on high ground above the floodplain at 216 North Bonnie Brae Street. The Reverend William J. Seymour, born to emacipated slaves in Louisiana, had been teaching his listeners to ask for the baptism of the Holy Spirit, the sign of which would be speaking in a heavenly language. God answered their prayers and began a world wide flood that continues to spread and deepen.

The following year a pastor from Mississippi, Charles Mason, born to a freed slave, came to investigate the rumors of the flood. Seymour was then preaching at a church at 312 Azusa Street, still uphill from the floodplain. After hearing Seymour preach, Mason knelt at the altar and asked for the Holy Spirit to baptise him. He described his experience:

> The sound of a mighty wind was in me . . . . It seemed that I heard the groaning of Christ on the cross dying for me . . . . So there came a wave of glory into me, and all of my being was filled with the glory of the Lord . . . . When I opened my mouth to say glory, a flame touched my tongue which ran down to me. My language changed and no word could I speak in my own tongue . . . . And from that day until now there has been an overflowing joy of the glory of the Lord in my heart.[5]

Mason went home to re-organize the Church of God in Christ into what is now the largest Pentecostal denomination in United States. Ten years later the Pentecostal revivalist and faith healer Amee Semple McPherson built Angeles Temple on the edge of Echo Park within walking distance of Bonnie Brae and Asuza Streets. As the geographical center of the

---

4. Deverell, *Whitewashed Adobe,* 284.
5. Quoted in Bowens, *African American Readings of St. Paul,* 231.

The Winds of Santa Ana

International Church of the Four Square Gospel, Echo Park became and remains a major waypoint on missionary maps of world-wide Pentecostalism.

Today, Pentecostalism is a global phenomenon that reaches into every type of Christian church. Given the global reach of Pentecostalism within one century, Seymour should probably be considered quantitativly and geographically one of the world's greatest evangelist. But he did not need to be a travelling evangelist like Billy Graham. He simply buried himself deep into downtown Los Angeles and let the Basin and its rivers pour the message to the sea. Like all wind storms, the flurry at Asuza Street subsided. Seymour stayed on as preacher to a small black congregation. His ministry, however, transcended issues of race and gender. He preached the Holy Spirit to all people of all types as had been preached in the Bible. In his "Apostolic Address" he declared the following with great generousity considering the racism of his era:

> We want all our white brethren and white sisters to feel free in our churches and missions, in spite of all the trouble we have had with some of our white brethren in causing diversion, and spreading wild fire and fanaticism. Some our colored brethren caught the disease of this spirit of division also. We find according to Gods word [that we are] to be one in the Holy Spirit, not in the flesh; but in the Holy Spirit, for we are one body. 1 Cor. 12:12–14. If some of our white brethren have prejudices and discrimination (Gal 2:11–20), we can't do it, because God calls us to follow the Bible.[6]

When I was young, I went with my father to visit a small, rather poor, black Pentecostal church. My father, as a member of an organization called Gideons, was there to ask for donations to buy Bibles that would be handed out free to people or put in hospitals, hotels, and motels. Dad sat on stage next to the pastor, and I sat in the front pew next to the pastor's wife. My eyes went wide when the service broke into what seemed to be wild gibberish. The pastor's wife next to me jumped up and, with her hands waving high above her head, her eyes closed, and her head bent back, she started speaking in tongues. People all over the room were doing the same. What sounded to me as gibberish loudly filled the room. Not knowing what to do, I looked to my father. He remained seated and had a smile on his face. I remained seated too. When this spasm of worship was over, order was restored by the pastor, and my dad was introduced. He walked to the pulpit and spoke about the power of the Bible to speak for itself without

---

6. Quoted in Bowens, *African American Readings of St. Paul*, 227.

Streams of God, Full of Water, in the Los Angeles Basin

interpetation. The pastor called out "Amen!" People in the congregation called out "Praise God," and the pastor's wife nodded her head next to me saying under her breath "Yes Lord." Then we all prayed for the work of the Gideons. A plate was passed, and I saw people I thought poor opening their wallets.

I have seen and heard people speak in tongues at other times, but that was my first. When I was sixty years old, I was asked to give a short homily on the Saturday before Pentecost at the Jazz service in the small chapel connected to our Presbyterian church in downtown San Diego. As I sat in the front pew, I grew a bit anxious. In the spirit of Jazz, I had written nothing down. This was not smart. When the music stopped. I stood up, walked to the lectern situated in the center aisle, and read from the Book of Acts:

> When the day of Pentecost came, they were all together in one place. Suddenly a sound like the blowing of a violent wind came from heaven and filled the whole house where they were sitting. They saw what seemed to be tongues of fire that separated and came to rest on each of them. All of them were filled with the Holy Spirit and began to speak in other tongues as the Spirit enabled them.[7]

I don't remember well what all I said. Toward the end I recited a verse of Bob Dylan's *Blowin' in the Wind*. I am not sure why. I remember looking down at two women sitting just to my left. Neither of them I recognized. Both were intent on listening to me. I remember then confessing, as I had not planned to do, that I am afraid of the Holy Spirit. I told the congregation I don't speak in tongues and don't really want to. Pentecost scares me. The homily was short. Maybe ten minutes. As I was sitting down, the pianist riffed through the melody of *Blowin' in the Wind*.

When the service was over, the two women came straight at me. Big smiles, both wanted to assure me that it went well. They wanted me to know that I should not be afraid of the Holy Spirit. The two of them were Pentecostals who spoke in tongues. It helps them worship. It helps them pray. They spoke in tongues every day in their private conversations with God. They were much shorter than me and bundled in heavy coats, one woman black and the other white, the two appeared to be from among the homeless people that roam downtown, come to our services, and are fed by our church on Sundays. I remember well the black woman's eyes. She did most of the talking. She obviously loved me. She knew me—or at least my kind:

7. Acts 2:1–4.

timid, constrained, and bookish. She was concerned that my faith be more full. She urged me to allow the Spirit to baptize me. I should not fear the Holy Spirit. I should not be afraid of speaking in tongues. I don't remember what I said in response, but I was deeply moved. Both of them may have been angels in disguise. They were right. I am timid. I have a cruising sailor's timidity. When the wind starts to blow and I am losing control, I shorten sail and look for the lee of a big rock.

Fundamentalism, as a specific name for a twentieth-century biblical-authority movement within Protestantism, has its roots, in the oil-rich soil of the Los Angeles Basin. In 1909, Lyman Stewart, founder of Union Oil, funded publication of *The Fundamentals: A Testimony to the Truth*, a twelve-volume series of book-length journals. The journals were collections of essays written by excellent scholars arguing for the beliefs of Bible-based Protestantism. Three million copies of this journal were sent free of charge to pastors, seminary professors, missionaries, and lay church leaders throughout the English-speaking world.

Stewart's oil money also funded a church and college on the corner of Hope and Sixth Streets called The Church of the Open Door and BIOLA (Bible Institute of Los Angeles). Because the corner of Hope and Sixth is on the rise leading toward the old pueblo, the fundamentalists capitalized on the visibility of the sight by building a huge neon sign that could be seen for miles. The sign declared "JESUS SAVES." BIOLA subsequently moved into the flatlands of the Basin, became a university, and continues to promote Stewart's hope for the global spread of the intellectual fundamentals of Bible-based Protestantism. In 2012, having merged with neo-evangelicalism, BIOLA created the Center for Christian Thought that offers to scholars and pastors "the intellectual and practical resources grounded in thoughtful Christian wisdom, to expose Christ followers to the big ideas that will ultimately lead to personal growth, social good, and the spread of love and biblical *shalom* throughout the world."[8]

Protestant neo-evangelicalism, as a culturally less separatist wing of fundamentalism did not become a global phenomenon until after it was first nurtured in the Los Angeles Basin. Harold Ockenga, one of its founders, traced the beginnings of the movement to his convocational address for the new Fuller Seminary on October 1, 1947 in Pasadena's Civic

---

8. "About," *The Center of Christian Thought*, https://cct.biola.edu/about/.

Auditorium. In the speech he declared, "The hour for the West to enter its maturity theologically has come."[9]

Ockenga is probably right to declare the seminary in Pasadena to be the institutional founding-site of the new Protestant evangelistic movement. Pasadena is on the upper plateau of the Los Angeles Basin and has an outsized cultural influence in the Basin and on Santa Catalina Island. Its waters flow both into the Los Angeles and San Gabriel Rivers. On the other hand, historians with a broader sense of the history of the movement also point other sites and people in the Los Angeles Basin. In 1947, Henrietta Mears was already busy on the upper Ballona Creek watershed and at a Christian camp at the headwaters of the Santa Ana River. In 1949, Mears helped Billy Graham gain nation-wide attention for his tent revival on the corner of Washington and Hill Streets just up from where the Los Angeles River drops into the flatlands of the Basin.

The best biography of Henrietta Mears is titled "The Mother of Modern Evangelicalism." Two decades before Ockenga's speech in Pasadena, Mears came to Hollywood Presbyterian Church as director of Christian education. By the time Ockenga gave his speech, she was the most famous Sunday school teacher in America, publishing her Sunday school lessons with Gospel Light, a press she started in Hollywood which became one of the largest publishers of Christian literature in America, and an owner of Forest Home, a growing Christian conference center along a creek in the mountain watershed of the Santa Ana River. "If evangelicalism is a network," writes Kristin Kobes du Mez, "Mears was the hub."[10] Mears was never the public figure that Ockenga and Graham were, but she influenced the world through mentor-relationships with talented college kids, smart athletes, devout movie stars, and high-minded business leaders. Like Harold Ockenga and Billy Graham, Mears believed that fundamentalism, which was thriving also in the Los Angeles floodplain in the early twentieth century, had become too pugnacious, too anti-intellectual, and too partisan in its political leanings. Mears wanted to encourage a return to evangelical roots and promote something kinder, gentler, and more

---

9. Ockenga states this (wrongly citing 1948) in the "Forward" to Harold Lindsell's, *The Battle for the Bible*. For the correct information and context for the quote, see Marsden, *Reforming Fundamentalism*, 53.

10. Migliazzo, "Introduction," *Mother of Modern Evangelicalism*, ix.

focused on global evangelism. Billy Graham said of Henrietta Mears that, aside from his mother and wife, she had more influence on him that any other woman.[11]

Although Billy Graham is not usually associated with California, it was here in the Los Angeles Basin that he gained confidence in his ministry and first gained fame and popular influence. There is a plaque at Forest Home on a creek at the headwaters of the Santa Ana River commemorating the site where the young and not yet famous Graham prayed on Labor Day weekend in 1949, confessing his uncertainties about Scripture while resolving to believe the Bible and confidently act on that belief. Later in September, after an initial lull, his tent revival at Washington and Hill went viral. The revival was extended, the tent enlarged, and his resolutions about the Bible affirmed. Billy Graham's global ministry was baptized in the Los Angeles Basin.

Charismatic Christianity first became nationally famous after a visit from the Holy Spirit to a group at prayer in the San Fernando Valley, another of the upper plateaus of the Los Angeles Bight. The Los Angeles River first gathers on that plateau before dropping through the Elysian Valley into the floodplain of the basin. Charismatic Christianity is a somewhat broader, more gentle, less insistent form of Pentecostalism. In the Spring of 1960, the Rev. Dennis Bennett of St. Mark's Episcopal Church in Van Nuys and some parishoners, urged by study of scriptures and the history of the early church, prayed for the baptism of the Holy Spirit. They then began speaking in tongues. Within the year Bennett was being interviewed by national magazines. Using the model of Bennett's experience, Episcopalians, Roman Catholics, and Protestants of every type all over North America soon experienced similar charismatic revivals.

Philosophia, Boethius, and I, travel with sails wide to a consistent breeze from the northwest. From offshore we look eastward over the coastal flatlands back to the arc of mountains behind, contemplating the global significance of The Los Angeles Basin. We ponder the liveliness of Christianity on this coastline: the beach bon-fires of church youth groups over the last hundred years, the surf-ministry pastors who since the 1970s proliferate here, and the barefoot songwriters here at the end of every day, sitting cross-legged in the sand, with guitars, listening for the Creator to speak in the crash of a wave or the silence of a sunset. Having passed Sunset Beach, off Seal Beach, heading toward Huntington Beach, *Philosophia,* still

---

11. Migliazzo, *Mother of Modern Evangelicalism,* 198.

seated, stretches out her arms toward all that we can see, splays wide her long fingers, and calls out to me, boat, sky, sun, surf, and whoever is listening: "Behold! This is a place where the Creator baptizes creation. Rivers of life pour down into wetlands mixed with high tide then out into the Bight. Here, waters cover the sea. Here, waters mingle as sign, symbol, and sacrament."

AFTER A PERIOD of silence following *Philosophia's* outburst, I ask: "Can the California Bight be a Holy Land, a distinctive place set aside for a particular purpose? Think of the Christian extremists who have thrived here as rabid culture-warriors, self-aggrandizing spiritual entrepreneurs, and promiscuous promulgators of detailed time-lines describing the End Times? These rivers and this lowland empower wackiness as much as holiness. This place nurtures industrialized pornography, racism, and materialism. I suspect the oil extracted from the ground here has funded more evil than good. Isn't it dangerous to link the Los Angeles Basin too closely to the Holy Spirit? Don't you think when Jesus comes back he will treat this place the way he treated the tables of the temple money changers?"

"You assume Holy Lands are utopias?" She asks this as she turns towards me with exasperation. "All creation is fallen," she says as she turns back again to look at the coastline. "It is a blessing when anything good comes of it." After taking a deep breath, she says "Have you not read D. J. Waldie's *Holy Land* about Lakewood, the suburb out there behind Long Beach?" She points to the northeast. "Waldie is wise. He has low expectations. But he still finds holiness."

I have read the book, and we chat about its pleasant mix of memoir, geography, history, and philosophy. He writes of the troubles of living in a flatland between precarious rivers. He writes of looming problems such as salt water incursion, sea level rise, and the inability of the region to sustain itself. Waldie grew up Roman Catholic in Lakewood and is serious when he writes of his flatland suburb as a Holy Land.

"My favorite line in the book," I say to *Philosophia* is: "Sometimes I think the only real forces here are circumstance and grace."[12]

---

12. Waldie, *Holy Land*, 138.

In silence we sit for a while listening to the gurgle of water along the hull. We stare off into the lowland distance. *Philosophia* says Waldie's line again, slowly: "Sometimes I think the only real forces here are circumstance and grace."

"St. Bonaventure," she says after a pause, "advises us to be on the lookout for signs, symbols, and sacraments. Waldie identifies the sacramental in the Los Angeles Basin."

"Freeway signs too," I say with a smile. "The 405 North has signs advising cars to stay in the center lanes for Sacramento."

She smiles too, but then turns quiet again. Water continues to gurgle along the hull. Then she again speaks softly. "We who are from old Ethiopia, remnants of the ancient kingdom of Axum, are like the people of the Los Angeles Basin. We also depend on our rivers for life. Egypt is the Gift of the Lower Nile, but we of the high deserts above the upper Nile are the gift of what we call wadis, fickle rivers, often dry, but they often they flood. From ancient times, we have been taught by our rivers to be stubborn and pugnacious. We are a chosen people on a chosen land. Judaism first, then Christianity, thrived. Our hold to the scriptures is strong. Our land and our people have a special duty. We are charged with protecting the Ark of the Testimonies. We are charged with protecting the wisdom of the ancients. Ethiopia is a Holy Land, historically, geographically, and culturally distinct. So too is the Los Angeles Basin."

"Peter Brown, the great historian of late antiquity in North Africa," I interject in the standard manner of my profession, "calls Ethiopia a 'micro-christendom.'"[13]

Philosophia smiles. "Holy Land or micro-christendom. The terms say the same thing. A place set aside. A place and people with distinct calling and purpose. A place historically, geographically, and culturally significant to the story of creation's hope. Neither term means utopia. Neither means a good place. Both terms signify a historically, geographically, and culturally identifiable pilgrim-place, a purpose-driven place, a sacramental place."

We sail further down the coast. She leans her head back to soak in the noon sun. Me? Under a broad hat, I stare off into the middle distance, thinking. Lakewood is, as Waldie says, a type of neighborhood holy land where circumstance and grace meet. But what we are talking about is larger. Lakewood is part of the Los Angeles Basin which is part of the California Bight. It is the California Bight that is distinct. Lakewood is just a part. So

13. Brown, *Rise of Western Christendom*, 218.

too is the Los Angeles Basin. I think, if Peter Brown were sailing with us, he would classify the California Bight as a micro-christendom somewhat like Ethiopia. If we are then, in academic parlance, a micro-christendom, I agree with *Philosophia* that we should just call the California Bight a Holy Land.

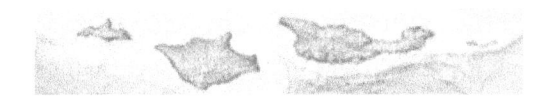

WE HAVE BEEN sailing southeastward off Bolsa Chica State Beach, a continuation of the marshy estuary behind a strand topped by the Pacific Coast Highway. The winds are now moderately Presbyterian from the west. These winds have rounded Point Conception as strong northwesterlies, swung westward toward the coast, and diminished in power to the north of Santa Catalina Island. As we sail further down this coast, *Boethius* and I expect the winds to twist a bit in the shadow of the island and become northwesterly again. The water in which we sail is relatively shallow. We have been running parallel to the shore with a consistent eight to ten fathoms of water underneath us.

To make a sandwich, I leave the tiller to go below. *Philosophia* doesn't steer, so I trust *Boethius* to go it alone. The boat can't steer herself with the wind over the stern quarter, so I angle her out into the channel to a broad reach. I loose the line that lets the centerboard under the keel drop so as to give *Boethius* some extra grabbing power in the water. I leave the main out wide. When the mainsail starts spilling wind, I pull in the jib sheet till the foresail is properly trimmed. With these adjustments the jib is doing most of the work. At this point the tiller neither tugs nor pushes my hand, which is its way of telling me that wind, water, hull, and sails are balanced for self-steering. I sit for a minute to watch our progress, making sure *Boethius* is now in complete control. We lose some speed, but *Boethius* is happy. I sense her contentment. Confident, I step forward into the companionway, look around one last time for anything that might come at us in the next ten minutes, then duck below to make a sandwich. I sit at the table, reach into storage bags and into the ice box, and proceed to make lunch. From my seat in the cabin I can see *Philosophia*, long thin legs stretched athwart the cockpit, bent at the knees. She is looking intently out over the eastern coast of the San Pedro Channel.

The Winds of Santa Ana

Back in the cockpit with a turkey sandwich and a less-than-cold can of amber ale, I eat silently while *Boethius* continues to steer. There are few things better than a lunch at sea with *Boethius* steering herself. After a quick clean-up, I grab the tiller, loosen the jib sheet, pull up the line linked to the centerboard, and point us down toward a large oil rig named "Eva."

This coast use to be populated by a dense forest of ugly oil derricks. Today, the shoreline is empty of the oily wooden towers. A few offshore rigs with helipads and living facilities now do the work of extraction. Up ahead, Emmy and Eva were built in the early 1960s, close in, on state-controlled waters. The newer and bigger rigs are further out into the channel in federal waters. In the early 1970s, after the debacle of the Santa Barbara Oil Spill, California created a Coastal Commission that keeps watch over the preservation and beauty of the shoreline along with insisting on public access to the beaches. Oil companies were forced to build in deeper waters.

Boethius and I appreciate the dignity of the strong, tall, complex, offshore platforms. They are, in their own way, like lighthouses. Their form follows function. At night each is a Christmas-tree of lights. Underneath the surface of the water, each is a commonwealth of teeming sea life. Like so much of the Bight, they are a drab above but full of color underwater. Each rig has a name, most have personal names. Down here off the coast of LA and Orange counties, the oil derricks have feminine names that start with E: Esther, Eva, Emmy, Edith, Ellen, Elly, and Eureka. Off Ventura they are Gina, Gale, Gilda, and Grace. The one's off Santa Barbara don't have personal names, but the rig furthest north, just outside of the Bight and close to Point Arguello, is "Irene."

Streams of God, Full of Water, in the Los Angeles Basin

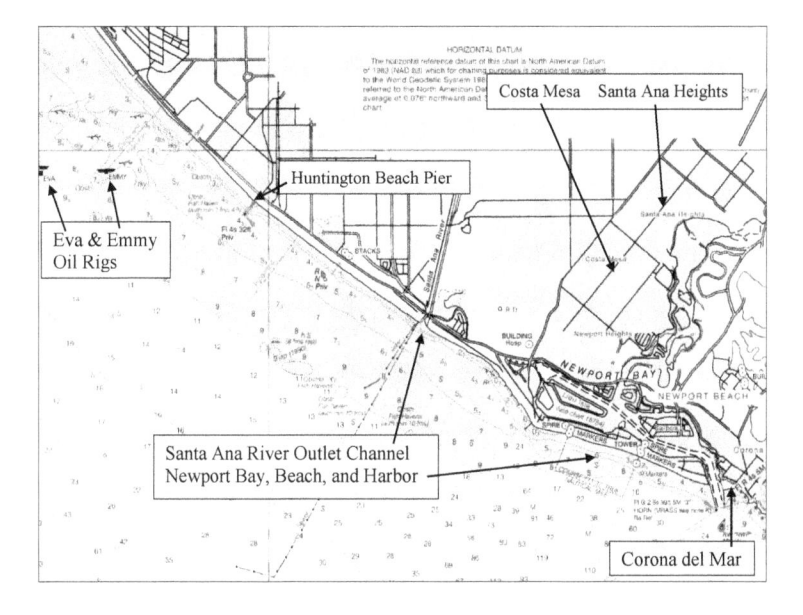

Coast of Orange County from Oil Rigs Eva and Emmy to Newport Bay. Note Costa Mesa and Santa Ana Heights above the overflow wash of the Santa Ana River that separate the river from Newport Bay. (NOAA.)

As we approach the large and looming Eva, having decided to pass outside of her, I ask *Philosophia* whether oil rigs have soul. I am feeling good after the sandwich and beer and am ready to be optimistic.

"All living things have machine-like qualities," she says, "and all machines have life-like qualities."

"You chided Boethius long ago for being too quick to say something is inanimate. You said rocks have a will and flames have desires."

"Yes," she smiles, looking up at the oil derrick. "Is anything gained by thinking of life as limited?"

We both laugh as we continue talking about this. Neither of us insists on systematic definitions or hard-and-fast understanding.

"Some wooden boat owners say fiberglass boats don't have soul."

"Shush!" she whispers. "You will offend *Boethius*."

"Up there," I point inland in a southeasterly direction, "up the Santa Ana River a bit, that is where *Boethius* was built." I then pat the boat lovingly with the flat of my palm. "Fiberglass was new and the boat-building industry boomed on this coast from the late 1950s through the 1970s. More family-style boats were built here in this region than anywhere else in the world. Land along the Santa Ana River was cheap back then. Boat builders moved in after the war and made yachting accessible to people who could never afford a wooden boat."

"*Boethius* and I have a bond with Santa Ana," I say with the palm of my hand still rubbing the boat's fiberglass. "I lived here as a baby. My mother brought me and my older brother by train to Los Angeles from Kansas in 1958. Dad was in the Navy and had arranged a cheap apartment for us in Santa Ana. As for *Boethius,* she is a transplant too. John L. Shumaker Jr., the founder of Yankee Yachts, brought the design of *Boethius* from the East Coast to Inglewood near the Los Angeles airport, but soon moved boat production to Santa Ana where *Boethius* was built in the winter of 1969–70. We are of one piece, *Boethius* and me. We are of the middling sort, the Santa Ana sort, the kind who benefit from the development of fiberglass."

Philosophia laughs. Sitting next to her, she places a palm on my leg and places her other palm on the fiberglass coaming behind her. Then looking up to the sky, she calls out to Santa Ana using old Latin to start: "*Ora Pro Nobis Sancta Anna!* Pray for us Saint Anne! Commend us to Christ, the one who holds all things together. I commend these two into your care. You might have forgotten them. They were under your care long ago but had to leave your town. They have not forgotten you. Please do not forget them, especially when they sail in your winds along your coast."

She pulled her hands back, sat up straight, looked at me, and smiled. "There. That will help. May St. Anne and her husband St. Joachim keep watch over both you and *Boethius.*"

I tell her thanks for the prayer and blessing. I tell her about a striking picture I saw in the autobiography of Fr. Francis J. Weber who was both chaplain of the chapel on Santa Cruz Island and the long-time archivist for the Roman Catholic Diocese of Los Angeles. In the picture, the archbishop of Los Angeles, standing inside the newly remodeled diocesan archives at Mission San Fernando Rey, is praying a blessing over a bunch of file cabinets.[14]

"See!" she laughs. "There is nothing than cannot be blessed: file cabinets, oil rigs, even fiberglass boats. Life abounds. Everything created has soul, and at some level, and in some way, is blessed with hope. Life is relentless. This is the deepest meaning of baptism. We are dunked in, poured over, or sprinkled with waters of life that symbolize a temporary death. Life

---

14. Weber, *Memories of an Old Country Priest,* 278.

Streams of God, Full of Water, in the Los Angeles Basin

is in everything. As the Bible says, "Through Jesus all things were made; without him nothing was made that has been made. In him was life."

We are now in close to Eva. *Philosophia* and I stoop to look up from underneath the boom at the three-level conglomeration of metal stairways, shipping containers, and pre-fabricated work and storage rooms. In one corner, hanging off the edge and looking like a tree fort, are offices and living spaces surmounted by a helipad. Looming over everything, as if on a bad-hair day, are three massive cranes poking out in different directions. *Philosophia* and I smile at it. Silently, we both give it our blessing.

HAVING PASSED EVA, *Boethius, Philosophia,* and I are now off Huntington Beach and can see the hills behind Newport Harbor in the distance. Huntington Beach has a bit of a rise under it as the lowland around it stretches wide for miles. The outlet of the Santa Ana River is barely discernable in its flatness. At the southern edge of the Santa Ana River washland is the tight rise up to Costa Mesa and Santa Ana Heights. As sea levels rise, the central part of Huntington Beach will be an island and the Santa Ana River may flood over into Newport Bay. Today Newport Bay is separtated from the Santa Ana River by this low rise. The bay's water comes from creeks descending out of the hills behind the bay named for Santa Ana's husband, Joaquin. From *Boethius* we can clearly see the Huntington Beach pier where every year an interfaith group performs "The Blessing of the Waves." *Philosophia* and I sit with our backs to Santa Catalina Island, our legs braced against the leeward cockpit seat. The sun is behind us now and we talk of the Jesus People and Signs and Wonders Movement.

The Jesus People of the 1970s are most commonly associated with the ministry of Pastor Chuck Smith who was born under the patronage of San Buenaventura and thrived under the patronage of Santa Ana. Born in Ventura in 1927, he died in Newport Beach in 2013. After pastoring several churches in Orange County, he and his wife settled into a small church called Calvary Chapel on the flatland border between Costa Mesa and Santa Ana in 1965. Along the way he had realized that he only wanted to preach and teach from the Bible. Nothing fancy. At first, his church services remained small, but his neighborhood Bible studies grew strong. In his autobiography, Smith praises Bill and Nancy Younger, owners of a home in suburban Newport Beach who hosted increasingly large gatherings of seekers. I met the Youngers a few decades later when they were elderly members of First Presbyterian Church, San Diego. Nancy, who speaks in tongues, told me the Holy Spirit made it plain to her and her husband that they should buy the house because Pastor Chuck could use the wide-open downstairs room for his group Bible studies.

At Calvary Chapel, the suburban members embraced the rootless youth on the beach in the later 1960s. Smith tells of driving with his wife Kay, the two of them worrying about these unkempt kids hanging out in town, when Kay announced: "We have to meet a hippie." Soon after their daughter brought home a college friend named John who was a student at the Christian college in Costa Mesa that is now named Vanguard. Kay asked the young man to introduce her and her husband to a hippie. "Within a couple of weeks," writes Smith, "John was driving down Fairview Street in Costa Mesa when he spotted a hippie hitchhiking and noticed he was carrying a Bible. John pulled to the side of the road, picked him up and said, 'There's someone I would like you to meet.'" The hitchhiker was Lonnie Frisbee. Smith wrote of Fisbee, who was born in Costa Mesa in 1949 and died in Orange County in 1993:

> Kay and I were really taken by Lonnie. He had a charismatic presence that came across as gentle and kind, yet firm. The way he talked about Jesus was like he had just come from a meeting with Him—not the way some believers tend to trap Jesus in history or doctrinal concepts. Lonnie was a student of the Gospels and he lived in the same spiritual environment where demons plagued humans and angels came to their assistance.[15]

Eventually, Pastor Smith and Lonnie Frisbee amicably parted ways. Lonnie's demons were real and unrelenting. Lonnie wanted Calvary Chapel to embrace the ancient Christian gifts of healing and exorcism in ways that crossed a line that Pastor Smith thought inappropriate. Around 1980, Lonnie left the Calvary organization along with a nearby congregation led by John Wimber. That congregation dropped Calvary from its name and became the Anaheim Vineyard Christian Fellowship.

John Wimber was born in Missouri but raised in Whittier on the Los Angeles County side of the San Gabriel River. In 1962, not a Christian but a talented pianist and singer, Wimber joined up with some Orange County

15. Smith, *Memoir of Grace*, 175.

musicians to form the band that became "The Righteous Brothers," best remembered today for the 1964 hit "You've Got that Lovin' Feeling." Wimber had his own demons back then. Much troubled, he started, cold, reading the Bible without any guidance. In 1963, he converted to Christianity, left the band, and enrolled at Asuza Pacific College in the San Gabriel Valley as a Biblical Studies major. By 1983, Wimber was the lead pastor of a network of forty churches with his own church in Anaheim pushing upwards of three thousand members. In 1982, he was invited to teach a class at Fuller Seminary in Pasadena, the seminary that Ockenga was the founding president. That class quickly became famous as MC510 "Signs, Wonders, and Church Growth." In 1986 he published the story of his conversion and his belief that too many churches had turned their back on the power of the Holy Spirit—especially the powers of healing as it is expressed in the New Testament. He called his book: *Power Evangelism*. The book, which sold more than a million copies, was named in 2006 by *Christianity Today* as number twelve in a list of the fifty most influential books that have shaped evangelicals. Jack Hayford and David Moore in their excellent book *The Charismatic Century: The Enduring Impact of the Azusa Street Revival* describe the appeal of Wimber and the Vineyard Movement to suburban folk of the middle class.

> His balanced approach to healing and his concerted effort to ground spiritual gifts theologically helped him gain a large audience among mainline Protestants, and strategically among evangelicals as well. The years of teaching the MC510 course helped Wimber articulate an approach to spiritual gifts that congealed better with evangelical theology. Wimber never emphasized either Spirit baptism or speaking with tongues; instead, he put the emphasis on what he called 'power evangelism,' declaring that healings, miracles, and spiritual gifts made people more ready to receive the gospel of the kingdom of God.[16]

Still at sea, *Philosophia* and I talk about these matters as we approached Newport Harbor. As we get close, I decide to tug the outboard to life and take down the sails. I see other boats sailing down the channel into the harbor and consider for a second or two whether we might also sail in. I decide against it. We are not locals, and Newport is a busy, even chaotic, harbor on a pleasant afternoon. I don't want to be dropping sails by myself and get in the way of someone.

---

16. Hayford and Moore, *Charismatic Century*, 264–65.

With the outboard in gear at slow throttle and *Boethius* pointing into the wind, I step over *Philosophia* to get up on the cabin roof. When I turn around at the mast to loose the jib halyard, she is gone. I smile. We had a good day together.

Sails flaked and tied, I swing the bow toward the entry channel. There is a free anchorage deep in the harbor. We will be there soon. We putter slowly behind the breakwater and turn down the channel. To starboard is what has to be the most famous baptism site in America. I have friends and students who have been baptized here. Thousands of people, maybe even a hundred thousand, have been baptized at this little side-beach along the channel at Corona del Mar. It is most famous for mass-baptisms of Jesus People (you can see them on YouTube). In general, ever since the entry channel was dug before WW II, this protected bit of water has been a perfect place for regional churches to do ocean baptisms. There is no surf. If you want to be baptized in waves, you have to go somewhere else. Here on the edge of the San Joaquin Hills, close to where the Santa Ana River meets the sea, flat water and soft sand call sinners to repent.

As we putter into the harbor, I take in the harbor life of Newport Beach and think about our day. The whole fallen earth as depicted in the Snake Path of La Jolla is being daily baptized along this coast. Hope abounds! Baptism is the most abundant and mysterious of sacraments. Christian theologians have never agreed upon what is happening in baptism, how to do it, and what restrictions there should be on it. Readers of the Bible only agree that it is commanded. Just do it. Baptism is the most democratic, optimistic, and hope-filled of sacraments. Midwives can baptize a dying newborn in the intimacy of a bedroom. Baptism in one type of church generally counts for baptism in all types of churches. Baptism is all about life being relentless, even after passing through death. The Los Angeles Basin is a baptismal bowl being tipped into San Pedro Channel and Santa Monica Bay. Three rivers watched over by Mary, Gabriel, and Anna supply most of the water. Here, motoring into Newport Harbor, *Boethius* and I pretend to no understanding, but after a day of sailing along the coast and now being at this famous baptismal site, we sense something grandly geographical and spiritual happening on the California Bight, something sacramental.

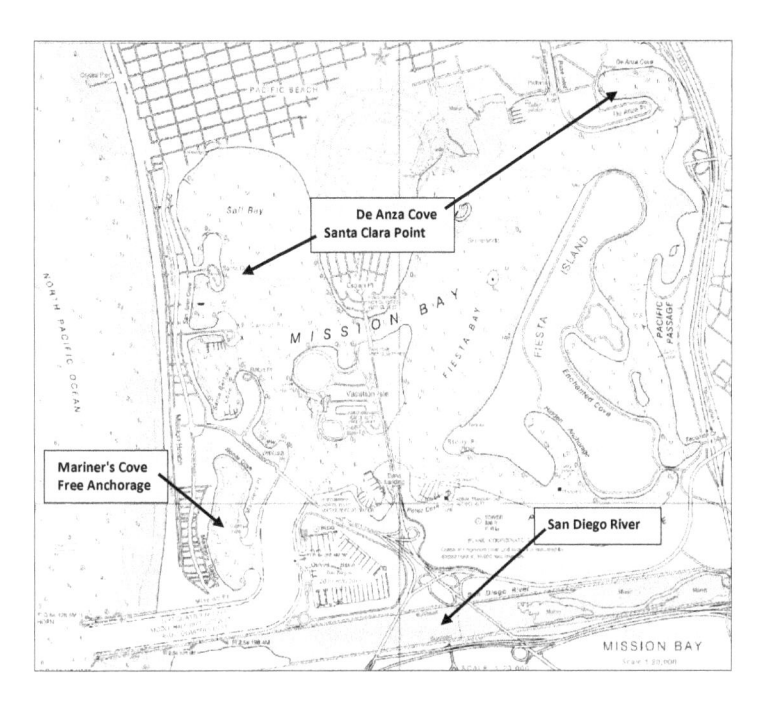

Mission Beach and Mission Bay, San Diego. (NOAA charts.)

Mission Bay Baroque

My mother tells me that my first excursion to Mission Bay was in 1959. The Navy brought our family to live on Point Loma for a few months after living first for a few months in Santa Ana. She tells me of a Sunday car-excursion, driving around San Diego seeing the sights, me on her lap, my father driving. No car seats back then. I doubt the car had seat belts. My older brother, who was about three years old, stood on the back seat with his elbows resting on the front seat between our parents. Even though my family is Protestant, I now assume St. Diego of Alcalá, patron and guardian angel of the city, kept an eye on us. St. Diego had been a missionary to the Canary Islands. Back then, he, like others of great humility and piety, tended to levitate when he prayed. A historian at Yale, Carlos Eire wrote a good article on levitating saints: "The Good, the Bad, and the

Airborne: Levitation and the History of the Impossible in Early Modern Europe." In 1995, my wife and I moved our young family to San Diego. Even though we kept our children safely strapped in car seats when we would take them for drives around Mission Bay, I still assume San Diego the Levitator kept an eye on us.

There is probably no another major city in the United States that promotes evangelistic Christianity more than San Diego. The place celebrates its historic mission and cheers with abandon at its professional baseball team—the Padres—led by a missionary-mascot named "The Swinging Friar." Only those with plugged ears can live in San Diego and not hear this place celebrating Spanish evangelism and encouraging more evangelism in the world. Mission Bay is at the mouth of Mission Valley on the inside of Mission Beach. To enter Mission Valley from the west on the 8 freeway requires passing between monuments majestically perched high on cliffs, one a Roman Catholic university and the other the tower of a museum dedicated to St. Junípero Serra. When driving north on the 5 freeway, after passing between the statue of Mary atop the dome of Church of the Immaculata and Mission Bay, a driver is confronted, straight ahead, high above the freeway, with the huge cross of Christ on top Mount Soledad. When *Boethius* and I turn northeast in San Diego Bay toward our mooring or eastward into the channel of Mission Bay, straight ahead, prominent on the edge of a mesa, guiding us in is the tall cross-surmounted tower of the Church of the Immaculata.

San Diego, as a European settlement, was founded by a saint: Junípero Serra. The whole Bight was unified, culturally and politically, by this evangelist-saint. Born about the same time as Benjamin Franklin, Serra first lived the easy life of a university professor on an island off the coast of Spain. The easy life, however, was not his calling. He was fifty-six years old, limping on a leg that would never heal, when he arrived here. He was not an easy man to love, and the love he had for others often caused them problems. He had all the worst qualities of a university professor. He was elitist, authoritarian, and given to talking, not listening. His piety and tenacity, however, inspired many. A statue of Serra represents California in the United States capitol.

The San Diegan most influential in American culture during my lifetime, until his death in 2016, was the evangelical Baptist pastor Tim LaHaye. From Shadow Mountain Church, which is up the San Diego River through Mission Valley, LaHaye led a megachurch, founded a college, and wrote (usually with ghost-writers or co-writers) best-selling Christian therapy books, a marriage/sex manual, cultural commentaries, and apocalyptic novels, the most famous of which are the *Left Behind* series of mega-sellers. Larry Eskridge of the Institute for the Study of American Evangelicals rates LaHaye behind only Billy Graham among the most influential evangelicals in America during the last quarter of the twentieth century.[1] In San Diego, LaHaye led the founding of the Institute for Creation Research which became the focal-point of anti-Darwian and Young Earth educational literature for schools across America. LaHaye's *The Battle for the Mind* (1980), *Battle for the Family* (1981), and *Battle for the Public Schools* (1982) are founding books for what came to be called The Culture Wars between traditional and progressive intellectual methods and values.

From the coming of St. Junípero Serra through to the career of Pastor Tim LaHaye, San Diego has been at the forefront of evangelical-style Christianity in North America. San Diego was founded as an outpost on a mission field and continues to promote the Good News of Santa Cruz. This has not been easy for the city or the California Bight. Jesus tells us he did not come to bring peace to this world. He came to save it.

Boethius and I often sail back and forth between San Diego Bay and Mission Bay. These are our home waters. Anchored for the night in Mission Bay we usually do not feel the contentious presence of St. Serra or Pastor Tim. Instead, we feel the presence of two of westward Christianity's most pleasant evangelists: Mary, the mother of Jesus, and St. Francis of Assisi.

Mary, as Our Lady of the Immaculate Conception, oversees Mission Bay from the top of the huge dome of the Immaculata Church. Francis, has his backed turned to the bay at the Joan B. Kroc School of Peace Studies on the campus of the University of San Diego. He is the most pleasant of all evangelists. The statue's face is a mixture of humility, kindness, purpose, and sadness. His body bows slightly in deference. He is neither triumphant nor pugnacious. He has the look of a celibate friar at a wedding banquet—music is playing while he asks a young girl to dance with him. To stand silent in front of this statue with Mission Bay and the Pacific Ocean in the background, knowing the statue of Mary is also overlooking the same scene, is to feel in the overwhelming goodness of this evangelical-oriented coast.

---

1. Eskridge, "Most Influential American Evangelical is . . . ."

The Winds of Santa Ana

St. Francis of Assisi by Giacomo Manzu, 1988, at the Joan B. Kroc School of Peace Studies on the campus of the University of San Diego. Mission Bay and the Pacific Ocean are in background (author's photo).

When I was a boy, sometime around 1965, Mission Bay became one of my family's favorite places to sail. We were living in Salinas near Monterey Bay when my father decided that sailing was to be the family sport. With three sons, he got excited about teaching each of us to sail. At first he borrowed a ten foot mahogany pram called a Melody from an older relative. When we boys showed interest, he bought a used eight foot pram called an El Toro, built another El Toro from a kit, then borrowed two more. He designed a rack for the family station wagon to carry four boats at a time. We had family friends with whom we sailed who lived on the Santa Ana River in Riverside. Dad joined the Riverside Sailing Club so that we could attend their weekend outings in San Diego at Mission Bay. Eventually our family started coming on our own. We would camp on De Anza Point in the northeast corner of the Bay and picnic every day on Santa Clara Point. Eventually, my grandparents moved to Southern California, and throughout the 1970s and on into the early 1980s, sailing on Mission Bay held together an extended network of family and friends.

Two or three times a year during my high school years, we would line up a fleet on the beach at Santa Clara Point: two sixteen-foot Hobie Cats, a 16' scow, a 17' plywood sloop with a cuddy cabin, and at least four El Toro prams. My future wife got her first long look at my family while on a sailing trip to Mission Bay. She was, and still is, a good sailor, but the seeds of why I mostly sail alone were sown on a family trip to Mission Bay in 1978 or 79. She and I were happily sailing one of the Hobie 16s, slicing through flat water at upwards, I suppose, of fifteen to twenty knots. The windward hull was lifted slightly out of the water. To balance the boat, we were both sitting with our butts hanging off the edge of the windward rail. I was steering. I leaned toward her and told her to take her feet out of the harness on the trampoline stretched between the two hulls. A trusting soul, she did this. I then reached under her knees and flipped her off the boat. When I brought the boat around and came back to get her, I thought she would be laughing and telling me that I am the most fun person she has ever met. She wasn't, and she didn't. Over forty years later she still prefers for me to sail without her.

Mission Bay today is a favorite pilgrimage destination for *Boethius* and me. We leave our mooring on Friday afternoon, sail south out of the bay, then tack up northward along the outside of Point Loma's kelp forest. We usually arrive at the entry channel for Mission Bay a little before or after sundown. In the declining light, we see the tower and dome of the Church of the Immaculata. It is usually dark when we motor into the free anchorage at Mariner's Cove.

Today, *Boethius* and I are anchored after just such a pilgrimage. I am stretched out in the cockpit with family memories of this bay circling like eddies in my brain. I remember fondly a time when my daughter anchored here with *Boethius* and me. She was maybe eight years old. After checking her lifejacket twice, I put her in an inflatable dinghy so she could learn how to row a boat. I stood on the cabin top of *Boethius* acting with my arms to show her the circular motion of manipulating the oars. She is coordinated and learned quickly. We laughed and had fun as she rowed around *Boethius* with me spinning on the cabin top. Later I cooked dinner while she sat at the table drawing in the log book. Now she is into her twenties and living far away.

I took to sailing from the start. As a kid, sailing turned me into a captain of my own ship. My dad, friends, and brothers had their own ships when we were down here in Mission Bay. As a fleet, we would gather off shore, holding our boats together, plan an adventure to some part of the bay, haul in our sails, and the wind would take us. My father, who had grown up on a farm and had been a meteorologist in the Navy, loved teaching us the mechanics of sailing. He would point and tell us the types of clouds above us. He would stick his right index finger in his mouth, draw it out, hold it up in the air, and tell us the direction of the wind. He would sail his pram up alongside me or my brother and give us advice on sail position. On one of these adventures, I remember him, almost six feet tall, scrunched up on the floor of an eight-foot dinghy, beginning to sail past me. Seeing that I was going slower than I should, he slid his hull over close to mine and matched my speed and course. "Let your sail out a bit till it begins to luff," he said. "Then bring it in just a smidge. You'll go faster." I scowled at him. I am captain of my ship. No way was I going to take his advice about sail trim. It was the late 1960s. Question authority! I told him to let me be. I will sail my own way. He did not get angry with me. He just slid his boat away from mine to give me some space. After trimming his sail as he had told me to do, he then steadily moved ahead of me.

The author sailing an El Toro pram c. 1967–1968. (Author's collection.)

Sailing, for a cocky little boy, is humbling. Fifty and more years of sailing works against a person's natural hubris. Dad was right. I needed to let my sail out. I needed to adjust for the wind. Sailing is an obedience-skill. The goal is not to triumph over the elements. The goal is to find one's proper place within them. My father, I suspect, knew if he made me captain of my own little ship, I would learn not to trust myself. I would learn the social arts of faith, hope, and love. Boat, wind, and water would teach me ancient traditions of dancing with the much larger forces of life. Tacking and gybing are types of allemande left or allemande right. Sashay with the swells. A tiller should be held lightly. Boats should be allowed to guide as well as be guided. Wisdom is not marching to one's own drummer. Wisdom senses when to submit and when to assert, when to be passive and when to act, when to add on sails and when to shorten, reef, and hunker down. Sailing is more like dancing that even dancing is like dancing. Land-dancers assume that the floor will stay put. In sail-dancing the floor undulates, walls sway, and you have to duck at the right time or you will be hit in the head by the boom. To sail is to slouch, twist, and lean in relation to multiple centers of wavering gravity. To sail is to dance with multiple partners, always moving in relation to each other. There is no sailing "my own way." There is only submission to the music of the spheres.

ST. FRANCIS OF Assisi was a sailor-dancer. The patron saint of Ventura tells the story of how the Franciscan Order began with Francis's trimming his sails to the winds of the Holy Spirit. Francis was in church when he heard the priest read the story of Jesus sending missionaries out into the countryside. Francis immediately realized he should be a missionary. Rallying some friends to a similar desire, Francis said "We must ask God's advice about this." The group said some prayers, then, in Trinitarian fashion, Francis opened the Bible three times to random passages, asking God each time to speak to them. The first passage they opened to was the command of Jesus to rich young ruler to go, sell all that you have, and give it to the poor. The second passage they opened to was Jesus's command to his apostles to "take nothing on your journey." The third passage was Jesus' call: "If anyone wishes to come after me, let him deny himself and take up his cross and follow me." After reading these three passages, Bonaventure tells us Francis immediately looked up to his friends and declared: "This is our life and our rule."[2]

My great appreciation of Boethius, the person not the boat, comes in part from his view that spontaneous and willing belief is often an indicator of truth. He would not criticize Francis in the above story for deciding too quickly what God would have him do. Boethius, in his logic textbooks, taught that a person's whole self is a generally reliable truth meter. If we hear something that makes immediate sense, then it is likely to be true. Of course, humans are fallen creatures so nobody should over-rely on this. On the other hand, when it works, it works, and it tends to work more often than not. Aristotle and Boethius taught that truth is stronger than error and generally, in the long run, makes itself known to people. Often it makes itself known by an immediate and spontaneous belief. This is not a license to think for oneself. Boethius agreed with Aristotle that humans think best in groups, not as individuals. When trying to discern what God is telling you, a spontaneous and willing belief that fits within a strong tradition has a high probability of being true.[3]

Like many kids, I went off to college listening for a call. I wanted a vocation not just a money-making career. I never thought I would hear anything so grand as an audible voice directing me to a career choice; however, like a compass that registers communications from the earth, I expected to sense my calling and recognize it as an answer to prayers. As a freshman, I was in college in San Luis Obispo with a vague notion that I could be a singer-guitarist of the folky, one-man band, sort. Living in a college town back in the day when there were many open mic nights, I gave it my best, playing guitar to sparse audiences at coffee houses and bars. One weekend in the spring of 1977, my roommate and I took our motorcycles on a road trip to a Christian music festival at Magic Mountain up the Santa Clara River near Santa Clarita. We rode south over Gaviota Pass, down to, then along, the waters of the Santa Barbara Channel. My roommate was on a Suzuki 500, and I was on a Honda 360. Camping gear was tied to the seat behind each of us. We were kids, and we were free. Following the coastline eastward, the sky was blue, the islands clear and distinct, and the weather perfect. When we saw in front of us the freeway climbing up into the west end of the Santa Monica Mountains, we exited and squeezed between the mountains and the sea, passed inside of Point Dume and outside of the

---

2. Bonaventure, *Life of St. Francis*, 200–1.
3. See Kennedy, *History of Reasonableness*, especially chapter 3, and "Educating Bees."

campus of Pepperdine University, then pulled off the highway to eat dinner in Malibu. After dinner, we found an unobtrusive place on the beach to lay our sleeping bags. The next morning we got up early so as to head up over the hill into the San Fernando Valley and make it to Magic Mountain when it opened.

At the entry gate my roommate and I split. I went directly to catch the morning set of a singer-songwriter named Randy Stonehill. The venue could hold, probably, five hundred people, but there were only maybe thirty or forty people in seats with me. On the big stage, Stonehill, who was tall and skinny with wildly long hair, gave it his all, standing alone with his guitar. He was both funny and profound. I loved it. When the set ended, I felt the need to talk to Stonehill. I had never done anything like this before, but I stood up, walked down the stairs, went around to the side of the stage, climbed the stairs, and wandered backstage. There were no security guards. Stonehill was sitting in a room with a couple couches. I knocked at the open door, and he invited me in. I told him that I wanted to have a career like his and needed some advice. He was kind, and we chatted a bit. I even picked up his guitar—which I think now was a rude thing to do—and played him a bit of a song I had written. I was anxious that he know I had some skills. He listened. Then he asked what I would do if I could not be a folk singer. I answered without much thought: "A history teacher." He stood up, walked me to the door to usher me out and said, "The world needs good history teachers more than it needs folk singers."

Later that afternoon, riding our motorcycles down the Santa Clara River Valley toward Ventura, I knew that I should be a history teacher. I had a "spontaneous and willing belief" that Stonehill had spoken truth. Stonehill was an angel to me that day. Playing folk guitar was not to be my vocation. A course correction was in order.

Driving our motorcycles westward along the coast, with the islands off to my left, I asked the loveliness of the earth, asked the loveliness of the sea, asked the loveliness of the sky, and all agreed that my vocation was to teach history. Had the sovereign Trinity, creator and sustainer of the universe, sent a low-level recording artist to Magic Mountain for the purpose of pointing me to my vocation? Maybe. I simply entrusting myself to spontaneous and willing belief. Further inquiry over the next forty years has affirmed the call and only increased the wonder. On the long ride back to Gaviota Pass, we passed inside of UC Santa Barbara, Storke Tower prominent against the late afternoon light. Not long after, I applied to UC Santa Barbara as a transfer student and soon moved to the California Bight.

Willing and spontaneous belief is not unreasonable. Thinking is like dancing. Even more so, it is like sailing. I have a sextant on board *Boethius*. In a celestial navigation class, I learned how to use it. One of the first lessons was about the difference between the true and personal time a sextant tells and the abstract standard time told by watches and clocks. Noon, for example, is when the sun is at its highest angle over us. When sailing with *Boethius* and the sun is approaching noon, I set the rigging for the boat to sail itself, retrieve the sextant from the cabin, calibrate its gauges, and start taking sights of the sun's angle above the horizon. The angle keeps increasing with every sight. Then, when the angle being measured by the sextant is neither increasing nor decreasing, that is true noon for *Boethius* and me. It does not matter what my watch says. In the great age of sailing, an officer would set a ship's hourglass every day to the boat's own, personal, true noon. Back then noon was when the sun was highest in the sky. Today, noon is a political abstraction. It is an international agreement that has no interest when the sun is highest over an individual boat and its sailors. As I sit in *Boethius* on Mission Bay, I worry about the way my watch separates me from direct communication with the cosmos. I worry about the way we are taught to set aside our own senses and conform to standardized notions of what we should experience.

In sextant class, we also learned how to match untrue time to an untrue earth. Every child learns in school that the earth is not a sphere and wobbles, but in navigation class we are taught to pretend that the earth is a sphere with poles, north and south that are stable and do not wobble. Celestial navigation is that art of taking a spontaneous and true experience and fudging it into a standardized system of faked lines of latitude and longitude. A three dimensional experience must be made two dimensional.

Boethius and I dance between reality and abstraction. Those of us who go down to the sea in sailboats, who have learned to dance on great waters, know the weaknesses of our gear, worry about abstractions and standardized beliefs. Those who have learned on Mission Bay how to sail-dance in the manner of St. Francis of Assisi have learned how to be reasonable, not necessarily rational.

Mission Bay Baroque

To LIVE ON the California Bight is to be constantly evangelized. Christian history, patron saints, stories of signs and wonders surround us. After the many crosses, the Santa Cruzes, the second most common Christian icon on the California Bight is probably the image of Our Lady of Guadalupe. Catholic tradition tells stories of Mary as a westward-moving evangelists. She appeared in Italy and encouraged the Franciscan missionaries. Princeton University has recently published *The Miraculous Flying House of Loreto* by Karen Veléz about Mary's role as a westward missionary. To live in Southern California is to live north of the city of Loreto, a memorial to the flying house, and to be surrounded by the image of Mary as Our Lady of Guadalupe, the most famous western apparition of Mary.

As Our Lady of Guadalupe she offered an image of herself, painted on a cloak or *tilma,* to a Nahua Indian named Juan Diego in 1531. Her appearance demanded leaders of Spanish colonization to recognize Indians as their brothers and sisters and know that God's plan for the Americas included the poor, weak, and those who lost in the fight for political control. She appeared to a Christian Indian and eventually sent him to the local bishop with her image on his *tilma.* Go anywhere on the California Bight and you will see road-side murals, storefront posters, paintings in restaurants, statues on dash boards, and decals on car windows that depict Mary as she depicted herself in 1531. Citizens of Mexican descent use the image to evangelize those of us who belong to the culture that took California away from Mexico. The only known relic outside of Mexico City of Juan Diego's actual *tilma* is a tiny cutting from the original cloth in the stunningly modernistic Chapel of Our Lady of Guadalupe in the Cathedral of Our Lady of the Angels. To live on the California Bight is to be regularly evangelized by the Mary who traveled west in order to reach out to the Indians who first lived here.

Growing up Protestant, I assumed it was best not to think too much about Mary. At best she makes messy the communication of grace in the incarnation, and at worst, some people seem to worship her almost as a fourth member of the Trinity. I began to start thinking of her more when I was teaching at Indiana University Southeast in the early 1990s. Mary was, at that time, appearing regularly at Medjugorje in what was then Yugoslavia. A student came to my office to tell me he was quitting school to go live with a community in Italy allied with the Marian apparitions in Yugoslavia. He was adamant. I knew very little about Marian apparitions but worked it out for him to finish his degree by correspondence. In Europe, he would read books about the history, cultural anthropology, and theology of alleged Marian events and send me his thoughts about each book. Because a teacher has to read what a student reads, I set to work studying Marian apparitions to keep up with him. A month or two into this, I got a letter from him that included a sealed piece of oiled cloth that had been, in some way, blessed by Mary in an apparition. I was in my small office on the second floor of the Social Science building. I looked at the cloth and wondered what to do with it. I could not just put it in my desk drawer. So I unwrapped it, wiped it on my forehead in the shape of a cross, and prayed for Mary to watch over me and my family. No kneeling. No emotion. Pretty boring. I then tossed the cloth in the waste basket.

A few years later, back in San Diego, I noticed more than ever the many images here of Our Lady of Guadalupe. She demands consideration. Eventually, I got a chance to go on pilgrimage to see the *tilma* in Mexico with a small group sponsored by an academic organization called The Conference on Faith and History. We spent a week in Cholula, Puebla, and Mexico City visiting centuries-old Franciscan churches and schools. We ended the week with a subway pilgrimage out to the Basilica of Our Lady of Guadalupe on the edge of Mexico City, the most visited pilgrim-site in the world. My daughter and daughter-in-law were with me, and we first went to mass and saw the *tilma* as part of an assemblage next to a huge cross and above a high altar. We were sitting toward the back of a huge congregation. Hundreds of newly arrived pilgrims re-fill the church every hour all week long, all year long. After the mass we followed the pilgrim trail around to the back of the building. We followed people down a walkway that runs low behind the altar to where a pilgrim can look up at the *tilma*. I took a picture, then went round a second time to say a prayer in its presence, a petitionary prayer for wisdom and belief. I prayed for belief, in part, because there had been talk among us academics questioning whether the story of the *tilma* was true, even whether Juan Diego, the Nahua Indian actually existed.

We were crammed tight on a small bus in the mountains between Puebla and Mexico City when, over the roar of the engine, one of the scholars said, rather casually, Juan Diego never existed. "Stafford Poole," he went on, "pretty much proves this in his book." Several of us jumped at the bait. As pilgrim-historians on our way to see Juan Diego's *tilma* should we so easily give up on the existence of Juan Diego?

Stafford Poole was born 1930 on the California Bight near Ventura. At nineteen, he took his vows as a Vincentian Father, and in 1961 earned a doctorate in Latin American history at Saint Louis University. Later in the decade he became a leading advocate for reforming Catholic seminaries by bringing them more in line with modern universities. In 1971, he returned to California to serve at Oxnard's St. John's Seminary College. From 1980–84 he was president of the college. Along the way he became a well-respected historian and has been for the last forty years the most visible, articulate, and adamant professional academic writing in English against the canonization of Juan Diego—even after canonization was bestowed by John Paul II on 31 July 2002. In *The Guadalupan Controversies in Mexico*, published in 2006 by Stanford University Press, he criticized the Vatican for academically irresponsible bias.

In an interview conducted in 2012, Poole succinctly described the core of his argument against the Vatican's belief in Juan Diego:

> Between 1531 and 1648, in all the documents that were published in Spanish and Nahuatl, there is not one mention of Juan Diego. There is of course [mention] of the shrine but never the apparition . . . . That silence, together with the silence of . . . [those] who would have been expected to comment on such a wonder, is a powerful argument against the historicity of the Guadalupan tradition.[4]

After I got home from Mexico, wanting to believe, I went on a reading spree of professional literature about Marian apparitions. The best of these was by Timothy Matovina, a professor at Notre Dame University. His *Theologies of Guadalupe: From the Era of Conquest to Pope Francis* and "A Response to Stafford Poole" in *The Catholic Historical Review* defended the historical reliability of accounts of Juan Diego. Matovina notes that Poole has been widely influential among academics, but shows that Poole's arguments are weak. Poole adamantly assumes that there *should be* written evidence, but he can find none. Matovina counters Poole by noting that non-existence of written evidence is not really, itself, evidence. Matovina goes further by offering evidence of a local oral tradition gradually evolving in the first decades after the encounter between Juan Diego and Mary. This oral tradition, Matovina asserts, is evident in transcriptions, dismissed as unconvincing by Poole, of testimony from elderly witnesses interviewed in 1665–1666.

I take comfort in Matovina's scholarship and his arguments in favor of belief. Poole describes scholars like Matovina as "baroque" and lists three

---

4. Schroeder and Poole, "Seminaries and Writing the History of New Spain," 247.

thinking-rules characteristic of baroque thinking in the Roman Catholic Church. As a card-carrying elder in a Presbyterian church, I find the traditional wording of each of these maxims overstated; however, as a sailor-pilgrim trained on Mission Bay to sail-dance below the statue of St. Francis of Assisi, I embrace these baroque methods. To do otherwise would be to refuse to listen to what the California Bight wants to teach.

The traditional Latin, as Poole gives it, for the three rules of the dance are:

1. *Traditio est, nihil amplius quaeras*—It is a tradition. Seek no further.
2. *Potuit, decuit, ergo fecit*—God could do it, it was fitting that God do it, therefore God did it.
3. *Roma loquta causa finite*—Rome has spoken, the case is closed.[5]

As for the first, the rule has deep classical and Christian roots. Essentially it is a burden-of-proof rule. Baroque scholarship puts the burden of proof on new arguments. Poole, as a progressive thinker, wants to put the burden of proof on old traditions.

The second can be called the "It is fitting rule." The great church historian Jaroslav Pelikan referred to this rule as "maximalism" and writes that it was first codified by Duns Scotus in support of the doctrine of Mary's Immaculate Conception.[6] Essentially the rule supports a methodological principle that "it is better to believe too much than too little." In jurisprudential terms, it is a rule about who gets the benefit of the doubt. This rule can be easily softened and understood as an intellectually generous guideline similar to the courtroom rule that a defendant is "innocent until proven guilty."

The third rule of baroque historians is *Rome has spoken, the case is closed*. Here again, although worded in a way that sends shivers down a Presbyterian's spine, this guideline is actually, in practice, not too different than the jurisprudential role of an appellate court when it declares settled the historical facts of a case. Reasonable people allow authorities, in most matters, to decide matters of fact for us. Pope Benedict XIV (1740–58) established a system of investigative commissions to review alleged Marian apparitions. The Roman Catholic Church does not rush to judgement on

---

5. Poole, *Our Lady of Guadalupe*, 127–55. See also *Guadalupan Controversies in Mexico*, 173.

6. Pelikan, *Mary Through the Centuries*, 196. See also *Christian Tradition*, 67–73, 166–74.

such matters. Investigations of Juan Diego by highly educated and conscientious experts occurred over the course of two centuries before John Paul II, a highly intelligent, ethical, and responsible man, relying on the counsel of his scholar-bureaucracy, declared Juan Diego's story of the *tilma*, settled.

Boethius and I are happy to be baroque. Anchored under the stars in Mission Bay, water lapping against the hull with wind-driven rhythm, I imagine myself a dancing scholar. I image myself on the dance floor with Timothy Matovina, with Pope John Paul II, and with a bunch of scholar-bureaucrats from the Vatican. The dance floor gets crowded with Juan Diego dancing with Mary, Bonaventure with Monica, San Francisco with Santa Clara. San Diego starts levitating. Santa Catalina, Santa Margarita, and Santa Barbara step back, laughing, to give him room. I smile at the thought, then go below to get some sleep. As I wriggle into my sleeping bag, I worry that my university colleagues and I don't offer enough dance instruction. We too often are too much like Stafford Poole. I lay in the bunk and put my ear over close to the hull. I hear the water lapping at the side of the hull and feel blessed.

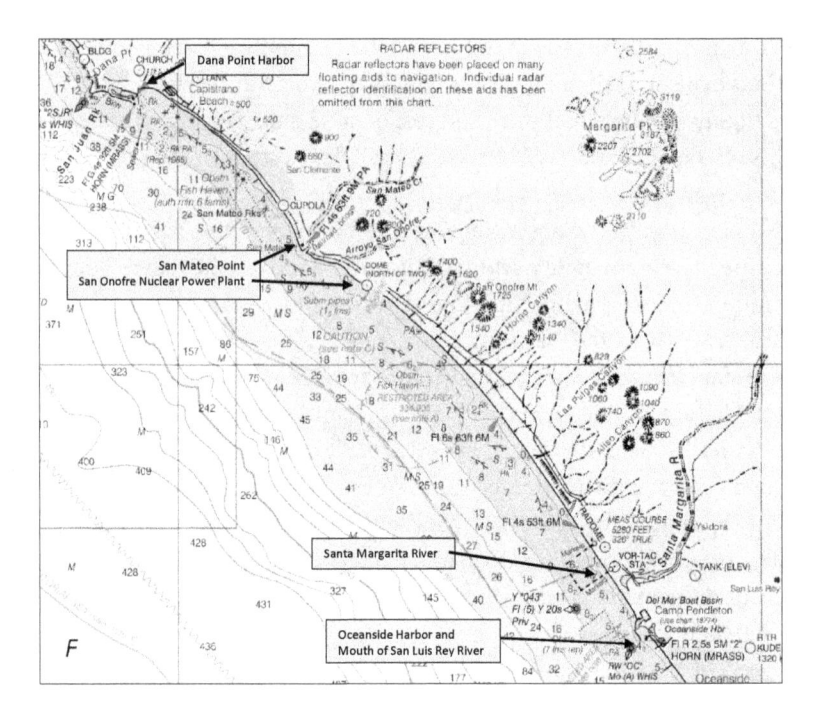

The Gulf of Santa Catalina from Dana Point Harbor to Oceanside Harbor. (NOAA)

The Rivers Santa Margarita and San Luis Rey

*B**OETHIUS* and I are trying to sail south after a night at anchor in the lee of Dana Point. The day is blustery. The sky ranges from grey to dark grey. Southerly winds have so much south in them that they will not allow us to sail toward La Jolla Shores. We angled southeast toward San Mateo Point, tacked back out, and now are angling southeast again toward the mouth of the Santa Margarita River. The Santa Ana Mountains loom large behind surf-beaten cliffs. Viewed from several miles offshore there does not appear to be much evidence of human habitation—aside, of course, from the railroad, freeway, nuclear power plant, and the practice buildings for teaching urban warfare. Our sails are in tight. I work the tiller at the crest of every swell to nudge the bow as high into the wind as possible. If sailing is

The Rivers Santa Margarita and San Luis Rey

dancing, this is a rough dance. If the ocean is sign, symbol, even sacrament of divine presence, today is troubling. Today is one of those passages in the Bible you wish were not reading. In a few hours we will have to tack back out to sea in order to set up a final tack into Oceanside Harbor at the mouth of the San Luis Rey River.

We sail with no recourse to a motor. At dawn I had tugged the outboard to life, but it soon made a clunking sound then died. Further tugs did nothing. A slight breeze carried us to the fuel dock where a kind attendant and the manager joined with me in trying to get the motor going. But nothing came of it. They suggested I sail *Boethius* around the corner to the boat yard. Needing to get home, however, we decided to sail to Oceanside Harbor and try to make San Diego on the following day. We left Dana Point under looming clouds with light winds blowing out of the south. As we sailed toward San Mateo Point, I kept hoping for winds to swing so as to come from the west, but they didn't.

Now it is middle afternoon, the wind is strong and there are intermittent chops at the bow that sometimes erupt into spray sweeping back over the cabin top. I sit athwart the cockpit, back to starboard, with my legs spread apart, feet braced against the upper edge of the seat opposite me. Ahead, beyond the Santa Margarita River, I see the notch in the mountains through which runs the San Luis Rey River. *Boethius* is equal to the push. I have dropped her centerboard to help her point high into the wind. I only lightly hold the tiller as we rise to the top of a low, white capped, swell then, when the sails are close to luffing, I give a tug and we push forward into the next oncoming swell. *Boethius* and I stretch, twist, and lean while all the lines hanging from the spars swing wildly from port to starboard then forward to aft. There are moments at the top of the larger cresting swells when *Boethius* rises high and gravity seems to lose its hold on us. The sails flop inward. All the normal forces of nature go slack for a moment. Then the bow dips, the stern rises, and the sails fill. Gravity and inertia become laws again.

Geologists say that the California Bight was born along this part of the coast when a ridge that ran north-south broke off, twisted sideways, then became the top of the Santa Barbara Channel. Look at a topographical map of the western coast of North America, and it is all too evident that something weird happened to form the California Bight. The coastline and mountains run north-south, but then at Point Conception they run east-west. Hard to grasp. Point Conception and Santa Cruz Island were born along this southern coast. Hard to believe. But then, much goes sideways in history. *Boethius* and I try not to expect history to run smooth. We try to take things as they are.

This is a dangerous coast, a lee shore. On the north side of San Mateo Point is the Western Whitehouse where the presidency of Richard Nixon ran aground. On the south side is the defunct San Onofre Nuclear Generating Station where engineering hubris is falling into the sea. This is also a missionary coast. When Richard Henry Dana sailed along here, he wrote of seeing the missions, San Juan Capistrano and San Luis Rey, midst the treeless hills. When he sailed here there was also an Indian pueblo visible named Las Flores. It, along with other planned Indian pueblos up and down the coast, was supposed to be the fulfillment of the promise of Spain and Mexico to return control of the land back to the Indians. Governor Figueroa, at that time, affirmed Mexican policy that the Indians were the ancient owners of California and, having shared in the work of the missions, were now to be treated as full citizens of the republic, encouraged to thrive in self-governing pueblos. Sadly, the greed of large land owners twisted the hopes of Las Flores and the other Indian pueblos.

Boethius and I now sail along Camp Pendleton, a Marine Corps base stretching south from San Mateo Creek to the San Luis Rey River. Although this coast is mostly a wide-open, long, sloping grassland, with cliffs at the water's edge, it does not allow us to forget that it is a military reservation. Heavily weaponized helicopters fly overhead, sometimes so low that we feel the beat of their rotors. Along this coast, *Boethius* and I have watched hovercraft, surrounded by billowing spray, race from out here directly toward shore so as to practice discharging troops. I feel like Ezekiel as we sail off this coast. Storm winds, dark clouds, metallic forms, flying wheels, and angelic four-winged creatures with four faces making unearthly movements.

These are bellicose waters. Santa Margarita Peak rises above us in the northeast. Up ahead to the southeast, the Santa Margarita River empties into the Pacific. Santa Margarita is one of the patron saints of this coast. The story of Margarita is that she was about to be raped by the Devil. She fought back and got the best of him. She pushed him to the ground, planted her right foot on his head, and said: "Lie still at last, proud demon, under the foot of a woman!" The Devil cried out: "O blessed Margaret, I'm beaten! If I'd been beaten by a young man I wouldn't mind, but a tender girl!"[1] The serpent depicted in La Jolla is vanquished. The cross on Mt. Soledad and

---

1. Jacobus de Voragine, *Golden Legend*, 369.

The Rivers Santa Margarita and San Luis Rey

the island of Santa Cruz mark the high tide of victory. The war ebbs, but it continues none the less. We fool ourselves if we think we can let down our guard. This coast upholds the example of Santa Margarita, a young woman who was not complaisant. It also upholds the example of San Luis Rey, the saint-crusader-king of France.

Boethius and I plunge forward, angling across on-coming seas. Two military helicopters fly low overhead. *Boethius* vibrates with the beat, and I feel pounding in my chest. Images of Santa Margarita and San Luis Rey appear in my mind with their armor, swords, and spears. *Boethius* and I are sailing in rough waters on a militarized coast. What does such a coast want to teach us? I sense an affirmation of war, war against evil. Should we be passive? Santa Margarita says no. San Miguel Island is named for the sword-wielding archangel who leads the host of heaven. When I was a grad student, my wife and I worshipped at the Episcopal mission church to UC Santa Barbara named for the archangel Michael, leader of an angelic army. At the entry of the church hangs a bell made out of the metal nosecone of a Cold War-era missile.

THIS IS A crusader coast. It has cultural roots in the Spanish Empire. For better and for worse, the Spanish Empire was for three centuries probably the most spiritually zealous, missionary-minded, empire on earth. Although violence and the pursuit of wealth undermined much of Spain's history in the Americas, in many ways, the settlement of our coast exemplifies Spain's highest hopes. To live on the California Bight is to be entangled in Spain's best sense of itself as a missionary empire, spreading the gospel in preparation for the return of the true king.

The gospel was first preached in Spain by St. James, the disciple of Jesus, the brother of John. This is the story told at the pilgrim-site of Santiago de Compostela. Soon after James, St. Paul preached the gospel in Spain. This is the story told first by St. Clement of Rome, the namesake of the Bight's island and town of San Clemente. Spain, as a land and a people, a church and a state, very early on embraced its role in the Great Commission, to spread the gospel around the globe. Its particular mission, Spain believed, was to take the gospel to the Pacific Ocean. The appearance in Mexico of Our Lady of Guadalupe affirmed its belief. God was closing the circle on this the far side of the world. Spain was moving westward after the Jews had already moved eastward. Many believed Solomon's navy had sailed out of the Gulf of Aqaba on the Red Sea and reached the Pacific after passing through the Indian Ocean. The Solomon Islands in the western Pacific were named in 1567–1569 by Álvaro de Mendaña y Neira as a way of saying that Spain was picking up God's global plan that had begun in the Old Testament. Spanish missionaries, especially the Franciscans in the Americas, believed they were participating in the last days of God's global plan. A popular book written in Peru by a Franciscan named Gonzalo Tenorio declared that American Indians would be the first to enter Christ's new kingdom because the last shall be first and the first shall be last. Readers of Tenorio spread rumors the Pope might remove himself from the Vatican and make himself ready for the second coming by living in Lima, Peru.[2]

Between the time of Santiago de Compostela and Our Lady of Guadalupe, Spanish hopes for themselves were upended by the Muslim conquest of the Iberian Peninsula. But Spanish hopes were revived by the *Reconquista,* the recapture of the Iberian Peninsula, as the most successful result of the crusades against Islamic civilization. On the California Bight, two famous saint-kings, upholders of the highest missionary values of the Crusades, have been prayed down upon us as patron saints: Louis IX of France, the namesake of the river and mission San Luis Rey, and Ferdinand III of Castile, the namesake of the valley and mission San Fernando Rey. Our name, "California," refers to an Amazon queen who, in a popular novel, joins a Spaniard in crusade against Islamic civilization.

The coast of California was first settled by Spain in the evangelical optimism of the *Reconquista.* Our first missionaries hailed from Mallorca, an island believed to have a special role in the Great Commission to spread the gospel throughout the whole world. James I of Aragon, the re-conqueror of the island, in his autobiography tells of a divinely ordained wind that guided his fleet to the best port from which to conquer the island. Soon after, Ramon Llull, the greatest scholar in Mallorcan history, received a vision on a hill outside the city of Palma. He was told to write a book that would unite all the people of the world in a single form of right-thinking. This right-thinking would unite people in the truth of Christianity. Aside from inspiring the creation of a Llullian university on the island, Lullian

---

2. See Eguiluz, "Father Gonzalo Tenorio," and Phelan, *Millennial Kingdom of the Franciscans.*

The Rivers Santa Margarita and San Luis Rey

thought spread throughout Spain and helped inform the mystical architecture of the Philip II's royal palace-monastery, El Escorial. For good and ill, a Llullian spiritual optimism, built upon the crusades and *Reconquista,* came to the coast of California, a spiritual optimism sure of divine purpose and backing.[3]

Junípero Serra, the founder of a unified Spanish culture on the California Bight, before becoming a missionary, was a philosophy professor at the Lullian University in Palma. One of Junípero Serra's specific duties at the university was to teach the thought of John Duns Scotus, who like Llull, was amazingly optimistic about the power of the human mind to unify our thoughts in line with God's thoughts.[4] Scottus promoted a term, "univocity," to describe how God and humanity could speak with one voice, think unified thoughts, and understand each other. Univocity does not promote humility. We do not know how much Serra agreed with Scotus's univocity; however, we do know he tended to believe, that since he acted out of love, God approved of his actions. When California Indians or Spanish politicians did not agree with him, Serra's mind tended not to compromise, adjust, or accommodate.

Most of the initial missionaries to California were educated at the Llullian University in Mallorca. Many of the indigenous people Serra and the other missionaries encountered felt their love, accepted Christ, and freely became members of the mission system; on the other hand, humility was in short supply among the missionaries. Serra and most of his fellow missionaries treated the Indians as children. The stories today told against the Spanish missionaries, their harsh punishments, insistent work ethic, and extensive restriction of Indian freedoms, arise out of misguided love. The term "univocity" does not appear in the colonizing records, but it appears to have been part of the mystical architecture of California's settlement. Serra, when founding the mission system of California, was too sure he was doing what God wanted.

---

3. See *Ramon Llull: A Contemporary Life*, Barber, *Raymond Lull: The Illuminated Doctor*, and Mourelle, *Every Knowable Thing*.

4. Beebe and Senkewicz, *Junípero Serra*, 49–52, 372.

I GLANCE TO leeward and *Philosophia* has appeared. We are still sailing southeastward through rough waters toward the mouth of the Santa Margarita River. *Philosophia* is opposite to me, wedged into the cockpit corner, blocked from most of the wind by the aft end of the cabin. She is wearing foul-weather gear. The collar is turned up high on the coat so as to keep spray off her neck.

"You lament the history of the California missions?" she asks me, apparently having read my mind.

"Yes and no. I am happy that maritime California was first united as a missionfield by a man now recognized as a saint. I lament the bad that happens when we Christians try to do what Jesus asks us to do."

We are silent for a bit, looking at each other. The hull then reverberates with a pounding sound as the bow shoulders its way into an extra-steep on-coming swell. Water splashes back over both of us.

"Given the loss of Paradise depicted in the *Snake Path*, we Christian historians are surprised when anything goes right."

"It is good to lament," she eventually replies. "When in the Old Testament Joshua leads the Hebrew tribes violently into the Promised Land, I do not think readers are supposed to feel good. The triumph of Jesus on the cross does not call forth a cheer. World evangelism is often not a heart-warming story."

Philosophia, after looking up into the darkening sky, continues: "St. Paul said we creatures see though a glass darkly. Jesus told his disciples, their evangelism will have disturbing consequences. 'I did not come to bring peace,' Jesus said."

"Junípero Serra came here out of love." I say. "He was doing what Jesus asked him to do. But many Indians suffered. Many of the Indians who embraced him and converted to Christianity also contracted syphilis."

Philosophia and I talk about this for a while. In the 1770s, syphilis spread rapidly wherever the Spanish went on the Bight. Although most often thought of as sexually transmitted, syphilis seems to have spread mostly through contact directly with open sores or even clothing and blankets. Any sort of health care involving close contact spread the disease. Midwives spread the disease. Tattooing, which was much practiced by the Indians, spread the disease. Syphilis, which is not usually deadly, wheedled its way throughout the culture and debilitated society, especially at the missions. James Sandos in *Converting California: Indians and Franciscans in the*

The Rivers Santa Margarita and San Luis Rey

Missions offers a powerful chapter on the ravages of syphilis.[5] By the time Serra died in 1784, the Franciscans knew Spain's colonization was the cause of an uncontrollable epidemic. Sandos notes that Indian girls and women suffered disproportionately more than men from the new diseases. The missionaries felt a special duty to protect the health and well-being of girls and young women and set up women's dormitories for them, but in trying to help them, the missionaries hurt them all the more. Marriages at the missions were encouraged but pregnancies declined. Of the pregnancies that did occur at the missions, many failed to reach full term. Many babies died soon after birth. The joy that the Franciscans promoted was undermined by widespread suffering. In 1806, the unhealthiness of the missions exacerbated a measles epidemic spreading along the coast and among the islands. Here, on the California Bight, one-third of Indian children under five died. The syphilitic debilitation of society did not begin to decrease until around 1810, long after Serra died in 1784.

The wind is getting colder and the sky is darkening. *Philosophia* squeezes her arms around her legs and pushes herself even tighter against the leeward cabin wall to get out of the spray. "Do you think missionaries should not have come to California?" she asks.

I stare forward for a short while, then respond. "I wish the process had been less of a political-military expedition. I wish Serra had been less sure of himself, less sure that he knew the mind of God, more willing to listen to the Indians here."

WE SEE BREAKERS crashing under the cliffs up ahead. Dark clouds loom above us. Intermittent spray continues to splash back from the bow into the cockpit. Time to tack back out to sea. As the boom swings, the port gunwale rises, and the starboard gunwale goes awash. I stand and duck as I loose the jib sheet on the port and winch it in on the other side. As we list now to starboard, *Philosophia* unfolds and scooches over to wedge herself into the new leeward cockpit corner. *Boethius* is now headed west into the Gulf of Santa Catalina. The wind is charismatic but not so strong that we need to shorten sail. We ride heeled over, but *Boethius* is designed to ride at

---

5. Sandos, *Converting California,* 111–27.

an angle like this. We continue to angle across short steep swells that chop at us, but as we get further from shore, randomly it seems, tall swells hit us hard from a direction we do not expect. As an image of God, the seas today offer no solace. *Boethius* regularly scoops water out of the steep face of an oncoming swell, stalls, then surges ahead as water washes aft over the whole length of the boat. At times, *Boethius* is lifted from behind at an angle that twists her into a trough. I push away on the tiller, then pull back hard. Several times over the next hour a rogue wave pounds flat against our beam sending shivers through the whole boat. Rain begins to fall intermittently. I zip my coat more tightly at the neck and tighten the chin-strap on my wide-brimmed hat.

I glance leeward at *Philosophia* who has folded herself even more tightly into the cockpit corner, clinging with her left hand to the top of the sheet-winch and her right to a cabin-rail. She is wet and not smiling. She has the hood up and draw string pulled tight of her yellow foul-weather coat. I tell her loudly that we need to stay on this tack for about an hour. She nods. We have to get far enough out into the gulf so as to be able to make only one tack back into Oceanside harbor.

As we pound, drop, rise, and crash through the increasingly chaotic waters, sometimes seemingly tossed into the air, we call to each other, using short, staccato sentences.

"No easy yoke today!" I yell. "No, 'My burden is light.' No happy Jesus."

Philosophia looks at me with no consolation.

"It seems counterproductive!" I declare as I switch my left hand off the off the tiller, twist, and point with my finger back toward San Mateo Point and the town of San Clemente. "Back there is the 'Cristianitos' exit sign on the freeway that is supposed to remind the millions of commuters who drive under it about the baptism of two sick and dying little Indian children. The freeway sign declares the good heart of Spanish evangelism in the midst of the suffering of Indians. Would a good God really have evangelism combined with suffering?"

"You, Boethius, and Serra," says *Philosophia* looking disgusted.

"Me, Boethius, Serra, and all the world!" I respond too quickly.

"You think like Scotus, not St. Francis and St. Bonaventure. You say: Wouldn't it be nice if we all lived in peace. Wouldn't it be nice if the Crusades and *Reconquista* were not violent. Wouldn't it be nice if Europeans never intruded into the Pacific and all the people here got their own revelation.

The Rivers Santa Margarita and San Luis Rey

You are a historian. You know there is no wisdom in singing 'Wouldn't it be nice.'"

Feeling a bit mean, I snap back: "Was Boethius actually consoled by you telling him, as he waited to be executed, that a good God holds the tiller of the cosmos?"

In a calm voice, barely loud enough to be heard above the turbulence of wind and water, she responds, "What are these waters teaching you right now? Are they telling you that the Creator-God of Love does not hold the tiller of the cosmos?"

"I have many friends who insist that a sovereign God would not let the world be as it is. The history of this coast teaches, they say, that God is not in charge. God is not sovereign. God is subject, along with all creation, to the mysterious procession of time."

At that point, *Philosophia* and I duck and turn as a several buckets of water fly over the deck and splash across our backs. We both come up dripping.

She then looks strait at me as the boat goes bow-down into the trough of a wave and digs into the face of the next, water then rushing over the bow and out the scuppers on the side of the boat. "God is always responsible. Your friends want to protect God. As the preacher says: 'Who can straighten what God has made crooked?'"[6] With that declaration, she lets go of the boat for a couple seconds, spreads her arms wide, turns her palms upward, raises her face into the rain, and with a laugh yells "Sailing!" The bow then drops, and she quickly re-grabs *Boethius*.

We both quickly look southward when a bolt of lightning flashes. *Philosophia* starts singing, and I join in. We sing the *Navy Hymn*, a hymn of proper fear, proper attitude, and proper action in a cosmos created by a sovereign God. We sing, not with the slow beat used at Navy funerals; instead, we sing in the robust manner of sailors working their way through a heaving sea. We both sing loudly, loud enough to hear each other over the blowing wind. *Philosophia* sings with her knees tight to her chest, hands clutching the boat. I look forward as I sing, feet spread wide for balance, right hand on the tiller. My students and I use to sing this every day when learning California History on a boat.

> Eternal Father, strong to save,
> Whose arm hath bound the restless wave,
> Who bidd'st the mighty ocean deep

6. Ecclesiastes 7:13.

Its own appointed limits keep;
Oh, hear us when we cry to Thee,
For those in peril on the sea!

O Christ! Whose voice the waters heard
And hushed their raging at Thy word,
Who walkedst on the foaming deep,
And calm amidst its rage didst sleep;
Oh, hear us when we cry to Thee,
For those in peril on the sea!

Most Holy Spirit! Who didst brood
Upon the chaos dark and rude,
And bid its angry tumult cease,
And give, for wild confusion, peace;
Oh, hear us when we cry to Thee,
For those in peril on the sea!

O Trinity of love and power!
Our brethren's shield in danger's hour;
From rock and tempest, fire and foe,
Protect them wheresoe'er they go;
Thus evermore shall rise to Thee
Glad hymns of praise from land and sea.[7]

Lightning, again, flashes in the distance. "Tell me!" I call over to *Philosophia* in a loud voice as we finish singing. Water splashes, again, high off the bow and falls back on us. "Are you the kind of apparition that helps out in a crisis?" I say this because Joshua Slocum was helped when he was sailing around the world alone by a man he took to be the navigator of the *Pinta,* one of Columbus' boats. Ernest Shackleton, trying to save his crew who were stranded in the waters off Antarctica had an extra someone help him rescue his crew. There is a whole book that has gathered reports of apparitions who help adventurers in tight situations: *The Third Man* by John Geiger.

"Me?" she responds, a bit astounded. "Help? No. I am not that kind of angel. I am a wisdom-angel. I am not here to help you and *Boethius* in dangerous situations. Long ago, Boethius wanted me to help him get out of prison, but I am not authorized for such work."

"Bummer," I reply. "You are an angel, though, right?"

---

7. Whiting, "Eternal Father, Strong to Save."

The Rivers Santa Margarita and San Luis Rey

"Sort-of. I am not one of "The Angels" created by God who are above humans in the hierarchy of creation. I am an angel outed by a book."

"Are you merely in my mind?"

"I would not say 'merely.' You want to talk. I am sent."

"I also have a guardian angel, right? A different angel, someone assigned to me who does actually help me in dangerous situations?"

"Oh, yes. People have guardian angels, often a patron saint."

"Does mine know how to sail?"

She laughs. Then leans toward me. "You are in the Gulf of Santa Catalina. She likes to look after boaters in these waters. The mountains range above the coast is the Santa Ana Range. You are in good hands."

I look over my shoulder back toward Oceanside harbor. Estimating we had sailed far enough away from the coast, I call out, "Helm's a lee!" while pushing the tiller to starboard. The bow swings toward the coast. I twist around in the cockpit as I trim the sails. Oceanside is ahead. I sit down on the new windward side and look for *Philosophia*. She is gone. For an hour or so *Boethius* and I chop through more turbulence. Rain still comes down intermittently and lightning sometimes flashes. We have a metal pole stuck in the air, so I worry about the lightening. Out loud, I say a prayer and sing again, under my breath, the "Navy Hymn." The flashes continue but stay far to the south. As we sail through another hour, the winds begin to diminish and the seas are less chaotic. Eventually I am confident that the white line of splashing waves I see in the distance is where the Oceanside breakwater shelters the entrance to the harbor. After another half hour I start thinking seriously about how to approach the harbor entrance.

Boethius and I have been in and out of Oceanside Harbor enough times to feel confident, but we have not come in from the northwest when a storm is coming up from the south. Also, we have no working motor. Modern harbors on the Bight are all built tight with the expectation that boats use motors to drive in, out, and around in them. Brian Fagan's *Cruising Guide to Central and Southern California*, which I had brought up from below and laid open next to me, warns that the approach to this harbor is dangerous in strong southeast conditions. Today we have southeast conditions—not necessarily "strong" but certainly not light. As we get closer to the crashing of waves against the breakwater, I watch several small fishing boats enter and leave the opening of the channel at the south end. If they can do it, *Boethius* and I can do it. I trust *Boethius*. Even though she is small, she has a design that encourages confidence. We need to swing to the south of the breakwater on a starboard tack, gybe, then run north before the wind up into the flat water behind the rock wall. Unless some rogue wave breaks at the opening of the channel entrance, all will work out fine.

So with heightened sensibility to wind direction, water movement, and boat momentum, *Boethius* and I ride past the outer edge of the boulders at the south end of the breakwater on a starboard tack. We are close hauled at first but then shape the sails into a beam reach as we turn fully eastward heading straight at the beach. We keep on that ominous course for what seems a long time. Then, when a swell lifts us to its crest and starts to roll under us, I yell to the wind "Don't abandon us now!" I then push the tiller windward with my lower leg so as to start the bow swinging northward. At the same time, I grab with both hands all the mainsheet lines coming down from the boom-block, pull the boom over my head to gybe the sail, reach down to give out more mainsheet, lean to my left to set loose the jib sheet from the rising port winch, bring the tiller to center line with my leg, cross over to lean out over the falling starboard side of the boat to grab the now leeward jib sheet, give it a couple of turns on the winch, yank it partly in, sit back down, look back to the breakwater to assess our position, then, with both sails full of wind rushing now over the port quarter, we run into the flat water behind the breakwater. I say a quick prayer of thanks. I laugh, feel proud of myself, then stupidly look around to see if anyone is watching.

Next, we park the boat. The wind is seldom favorable for sailing into Oceanside's guest slips. As noted earlier, the smaller modern harbors are not designed for sailboats under sail. The designers of Oceanside Harbor offer no free and open anchorage in which to glide in, luff-up, and drop anchor. The designers expect all vessels to be motorized. So as we come down the entrance channel at a fast pace under full sail, I spy an open slip at the guest dock. We sail high into the turning basin then round into the wind. With the boat stalled, I go up to the cabin roof to take down the mainsail, all the while letting the jib wildly flap about. Back in the cockpit, I pull in the jib sheet just enough to get us moving toward the cement and wood of the guest dock. Once we have enough momentum, I let the jib again flap violently as we coast forward. At the last moment before hitting the dock, I run forward and jump over the bow to guide the boat into the slip. If *Boethius* were any bigger and heavier, or me older and weaker, we would not have been able to make this maneuver. With *Boethius* secure, I take a walk over to what is now the walled-in mouth of the San Luis Rey River. Oceanside Harbor is dug out of what use to be the wide estuary of the river.

The Rivers Santa Margarita and San Luis Rey

After returning to the boat, I make dinner then stretch out in the cockpit to read. Later, I contort myself into a sleeping bag in the quarter berth and lie awake listening to late-night harbor sounds of sea lions barking in the distance, wavelets lapping against the hull, and loose halyards slapping gently against metal masts.

IT WASN'T TILL 1798, fourteen years after Serra had died, that the Spanish finally decided that a mission should be established in this region between the port of San Diego and anchorage at San Juan Capistrano. According to Fr. Crespí who had met the Indians living here twenty-nine years earlier, the Quechla name of the river valley that opens up here is *Jatir Jo*. The Spanish name for the new mission here was chosen by the viceroy of Mexico: *San Luis, Rey de Francia,* the French saint-king, warrior in the crusades, and staunch supporter of global evangelism. St. Louis, Missouri is also named for him. In 1798, the river's name was changed to conform to the mission.

The ceremony naming San Luis Rey as patron was conducted by the father-president of the missions, Fermín Francisco de Lasuén. All who met Lasuén, even the scientific-minded explorers of the Pacific who generally disapproved of missionaries, were impressed by the friar's intelligence and goodness. The English explorer, George Vancouver, in honor of Lasuén, gave the missionary's first name "Fermín" to the point that juts out into the Pacific on the southern corner of Palos Verdes, just above San Pedro. At the ceremony on the banks of what was now called the San Luis Rey River, Lasuén was an impressive man leading an impressive ceremony. Quechla families in the crowd were so moved by the man and the ceremony they offered fifty-four of their very young Indian children to be baptized that day. Seven older boys and twelve older girls also requested baptism, but Lasuén explained to them that older children need first to be instructed in the Catholic faith. Indians of age should be fully cognizant of what they were getting into before they joined in the fellowship of the mission. When the naming ceremony was done, the building of the new mission began.

Two friars, ten or so soldiers, four elected Indian officials, along with a multitude of Indian managers of farms, ranches, and kitchens worked together to create what was one of the most extensive and probably one of the happiest missions in California. The lead friar who served here for thirty-two years, Fr. Antonio Peyri, was by all accounts a pleasant and moderate priest, less authoritarian than most of the missionaries. Under his leadership, the mission was run rather loosely with no insistent centralization. By 1820, there were upwards of three thousand Indians associated with the mission. Although syphilis spread here as it did at other missions, San Luis Rey was a relatively healthy mission because the *Luiseño* were widely spread to the north up the Santa Margarita River, to the south up the San Dieguito River, and far up among multiple independent villages along the San Luis Rey River. With the Indians spread widely, a large amount of responsibility fell on the Indians themselves to run the multiple farms and ranches that fed into the mission. Fr. Peyri and his colleague missionaries were primarily concerned with teaching the catechism, leading the choir and orchestra, and offering mass. Every month or so, one or the other of the priests would travel north, south, and upriver to offer mass and conduct marriages and funerals. Spanish law required that every mission have four Indians elected by Indians, two to serve as *alcaldes* (executives) and two as *rigidores* (advisors to the executives). Within six months of the founding, the Indians held their first election. The friars at San Luis Rey, as best we can tell, worked well with the mission's Indian leadership. Because Fr. Peyri's patron saint was Anthony, every year, when the Catholic calendar came round to the day dedicated to San Antonio, the mission went into high fiesta and the Indians gathered from far and wide. Ball games were played. Dances were danced. Indian choirs and orchestras blended the music of various cultures. A *Luiseño* boy named Pablo Tac wrote an essay about life at San Luis Rey. As a Quechla Indian, targeted by Peyri for further education and sent to Mexico City, then on to Rome with the goal of ordination and return to California, Pablo Tac represents the highest ideals of the Spanish mission.

Given that this mission was one of the most stable missions in California, it makes sense that here on this isolated coast, beginning in 1825, the Mexican government pushed for redistribution of land back to Indian families and the creation of Indian pueblos. In 1833 Governor José Figueroa in a published *Manifesto* made it clear that he considered the Indians of California as "proprietors" of their ancient lands. There was a sneaky move afoot to designate the Indians as "colonists," thereby implying that the Indians should receive allotments of land as if they were immigrants. But Figueroa was adamant. He wanted to support the highest ideals of the Mexican constitution with more than just talk. Under Figueroa, three official Indian

The Rivers Santa Margarita and San Luis Rey

pueblos were established on the remains of what were called *estancias*, the semi-independent ranches and farms that had long functioned under Indian leadership while formally being under the jurisdiction of the mission. The most successful of these new pueblos, probably because it was the most isolated, was at San Pasqual high up in the backcountry. Another was to the south on the San Dieguito River. The most prominent, least isolated, and most contested was Las Flores just north of the Santa Margarita River. Las Flores was an obvious choice to become an independent pueblo because it had recently been raised to the status of *asistencia* with the construction of a sub-mission chapel building. The pueblo at Las Flores was established but soon faltered. Governor Figueroa died in 1835, and the redistribution of land associated with mission San Luis Rey came under the control of a local land-grabber, the greedy, unscrupulous, and misnamed Pío de Jesús Pico. He wanted Las Flores lands and the chapel building built there for himself. The Indian *alcalde* at Las Flores complained about Pico to officials in San Diego and Monterey but little happened until 1839 when Governor Alvarado sent as visitor-general Guillermo Arnel (often called by his pre-Mexican name, William Hartnell) to review the Indians' complaints.[8]

At Las Flores, Arnel found thirty-three married Indian couples with forty-six children, ten widowers with ten children, and six widows. Together these families wanted their rights according to Mexican law and Spanish tradition. But Pio Pico had many political allies. Pico eventually became governor himself. He continued to insinuate himself into the ongoing decommissioning of the San Luis Rey mission and into the politics of the region. By the end of the 1840s he owned the whole of what he called *Rancho Santa Margarita y Las Flores*. The Indians were forced to leave or become laborers on his rancho. He and his family appropriated the chapel building at Las Flores and expanded it into one of his personal residences.

Pio Pico, along with complicit supporters, destroyed the highest of the Spanish and Mexican hopes for the region. Arnel, as Visitor-General of the Missions for Governor Alvarado, tried to uphold Indian rights; however, as we are told by his sister-in-law, Arnel "realized all his efforts were in vain, and disgusted, he resigned."[9] About the same time, in Italy, small pox killed Pablo Tac at age nineteen before he could return to California as its first native-born priest. No California Mission Indian became a priest, and what

---

8 See Farris, "Jose Panto," 149–61; Englehardt, *San Luis Rey*, 104–15; Dakin, *William Hartnell*, 214–24, and Gray, *Forster vs. Pico: The Struggle for the Rancho Santa Margarita*.

9. Beebe and Senkewicz, *Testimonios*, 254.

was left of Figueroa's *Luiseño* pueblos failed to survive the legal system of the United States after the take-over in 1848. In 1942, the U.S. government bought *Rancho Santa Margarita y Las Flores* from the heirs of Pico and created Marine Corps Base Camp Pendleton.

In October of 2007, a wild fire powered by Santa Ana winds rushed through the small reservation of the Rincon Band of Luiseño Indians, one of the up-river villages that can trace its history back for thousands of years. Among the buildings burned was a tiny chapel built in the 1930s by the congregation with funds solicited through the *Indian Sentinel,* a national magazine that kept Roman Catholics abreast of evangelistic needs. The tiny chapel took the name "St. Bartholomew" because a church of that name in Oceanside gave them pews. During WWII the *Indian Sentinel* reported the Christian resilience and stability of the Indians at Rincon seems quite remarkable considering that priests had long been scarce among them.

St Bartholomew's Chapel, Rincon Band of Luiseno Indians. Designed by Kevin deFreitas. (Harrison Photographic with permission of Kevin deFreitas)

In 2007, an architect-sailing friend of mine, Kevin deFreitas, designed the replacement chapel and took me with him to the chapel's consecration ceremony. The bishop was there along with several priests. Members of the Rincon congregation opened the service with dancing and singing in ancient dress. During the service, George Arviso, a grandfatherly member of the Rincon and key liaison for the design of the building, spoke to the packed congregation with a voice full of wisdom, love, and piety:

> I want to say first: all praise and honor to our heavenly father for this house of prayer and worship. God's hand has been in it from the beginning since we lost St. Bartholomew's in the fire. Without

The Rivers Santa Margarita and San Luis Rey

hesitation our heavenly father and his son Jesus began touching hearts. I would like to thank our former tribal chairman who has passed on, Vernon Wright. He stepped forward right away and said the tribe would rebuild the chapel and from that moment the rebuilding began . . .

We wanted the church to honor our people. From the beginning, before the missionaries came to evangelize us, we knew the Creator, and we wanted to recognize that in the building itself, his house. Of course we prayed a lot on this and out of those prayers comes the wampkush wall. In our Indian religion, the wampkush was a gathering place for our sacred ceremonies, not all ceremonies, but sacred ceremonies. In essence, it was the church, a gathering place for rituals and for the people to come and honor the creator. So this wall behind the altar and the walls back by the front door represent the wampkush. As you walk around the building you will find that the circle continues from the wampkush wall inside to the walls outside and ties into the front walls and you're just encircled in a circle of God's love. This represents the wampkush in our religion. We wanted this to honor our people from the very beginning because it was God the creator, Jesus, who put us here and gave us the gift of the land, to the people who live here, the Rincon people. We wanted to honor that . . . .

If you look at the ceiling you might say "What is that?" You see the perforations but if you look closely it forms a cross from the doors to the altar because it is through the cross that we are saved . . . .

There is much symbolism in the building, and we have a pamphlet that we put together that explains most of the symbolism. It all ties together in our Catholic Christian faith. The spirit is alive in our Indians. When you meditate on that spirit you know there is only one creator. He created us all. We just need to respond to him and seek to do his will . . . .

The baptismal rock comes right here from Rincon, back in the canyon. It turns out the rock that Ed Read picked is a very rare rock for the area. When it was at the stonecutters being cut a couple of geologists came by and said "Where did you buy that rock? It is rare to the area." We said 'We did not buy it. God provided it' . . . .

I don't want to fall into that sin of pride, but I am really proud to be part of this, along with our committee and community. It is our hope and our prayer that God's house will not be a house of division. We all know how the Devil likes to get in our hearts and tries to lead us astray. Today is a day of joy. We celebrate that.[10]

---

10. Arviso, "Consecration Speech," Feb. 14, 2010.

In Oceanside Harbor, lying inside *Boethius*, listening to the harbor sounds, I think of George Arviso's speech as a blessing to all on this coast. A friend, Rick Pointer, who teaches at Westmont College near Santa Barbara, writes in *Encounters of the Spirit: Native Americans and European Colonial Religion* about the "religious hybridity" of both Indians and whites on the frontiers of North American evangelism.[11] The encounter between Indians and missionaries can end in relationships that are "fundamentally reciprocal and often mutually transformational." I am happy Christianity came to this coast. I lament the troubles. *Boethius* and I believe that all is working out for the good.

---

11. Pointer, *Encounters of the Spirit*, 7, 8.

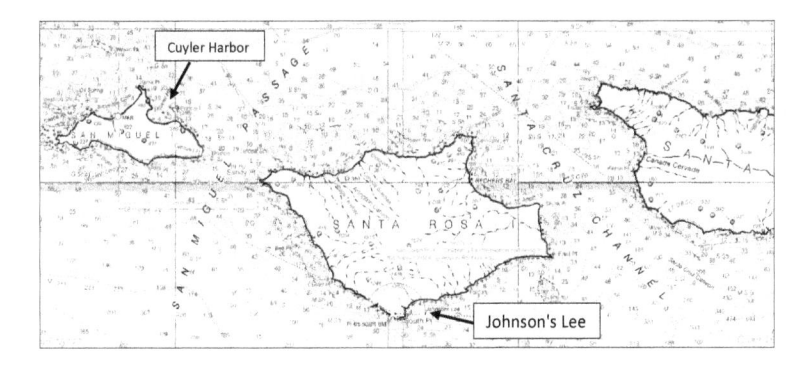

San Miguel, Santa Rosa, and Santa Cruz Islands. (NOAA)

The Point of Immaculate Conception and the Wedding Banquet in Santa Barbara

A PILGRIM-STUDY of the California Bight, based out of San Diego Bay, requires a there-and-back-again to Point Conception at the Bight's northwestern corner. The point's full name in Spanish is *Punta de la Limpia Concepción* and is named for the doctrine of the Immaculate Conception of Mary. In the intimacy of Santa Ana and San Joaquín, Mary was conceived miraculously without sin. The name of the point signifies both the final act of the family-story at the core of God's restoration of fallen creation and points toward Mary's primacy of place at the final great wedding and banquet when Christ marries the church and all creation is made new.

The story of Mary's birth is not in the Bible, but Santa Ana and San Joaquín appear as her parents in the early literature of the church. The theological idea of her Immaculate Conception did not appear until the middle ages and was heavily promoted by Franciscans interested in End Times. St. Bonaventure was not in favor of the doctrine. He was willing to think Mary was sanctified in the womb of Santa Ana by God, but he thought it best not to think of her conception as sinless. On the other hand, Ramon Llull and John Duns Scotus, two Franciscans with direct influence on St. Serra and the Mallorcan missionaries on this coast, promoted it as fitting for apocalyptic balance: just as God created two sinless people in the Garden of Eden, Eve and Adam, so too would God begin the new paradise with the birth of two sinless people, Mary and Jesus.

In 1602, when Point Conception was named, the Immaculate Conception was not an official doctrine of the church. Nor was it in 1787 when the near-by mission on the Santa Ynez River was consecrated as *La Misión de la Purísima Concepción de la Santísima Virgen María*. St. Serra, however, California's founder, promoted the doctrine in Mexico and on this coast. He is believed to be the author of a short *Novena a la Concepción Inmaculada de Maria* and offered this as a model prayer:

> O most brilliant Lady of the Angels, Refuge of Sinners, I come before you as a sinner, humbled to the depths of my nothingness. I praise the Holy Trinity for the singular graces and prerogatives with which He has adorned you from the moment of your Immaculate Conception. I also wish to thank Almighty God for all He has given me through your intercession, not the least of which is this period of prayer.[1]

The Santa Barbara Channel preaches the story of salvation from beginning to end as a family story of births, weddings, and fellowship. San Miguel Island reminds boaters of the archangel who ushers in the second coming. The namesake of Santa Rosa Island married herself to Christ in order to focus on embracing the poor and outcast in Peru. Santa Cruz Island celebrates our fellowship in Christ's suffering. Refugio State Beach remembers Mary as a refuge to us sinners, a mother-figure who gathers us all in her embrace. Richard Henry Dana seems to have heard the message of this channel deep within his soul. The most famous story in *Two Years Before the Mast* is a grand wedding followed by three days of fiesta-fellowship. Dana's account is filled with signs and symbols of the gospel. Everybody gets an invitation. The bride and bridesmaids enter the mission church dressed in black and come out in white. A three-day fiesta results. He closes his account with the dance of a girl named "Holy Spirit." Like Dana, deep in my soul, I hear the call of family love and fellowship when I am sailing on the Santa Barbara Channel or driving its coast. I live in San Diego but Santa Barbara has my heart.

---

1. Serra, *Marian Novena*.

The Point of Immaculate Conception

BACK IN 2003, I tried and failed to get students all the way to Point Conception. We sailed on the schooner *Californian* as educational cargo, the boat being owned and operated by the Maritime Museum of San Diego. The plan back then was to sail from the San Diego Bay to Ventura Harbor then out among the islands before going up to Cojo Anchorage. I brought with us copies of diary entries from the Portolá/Crespí expedition when it camped at Cojo along with a Coast Survey chart drawn in 1852. The students and I would use these to help us walk the grounds of the ancient Indian village, find the site of the pioneer observatory built by the Coast Survey, and wander over to the lighthouse.

That was the plan. We did not make it to Point Conception. The captain, Chris Welton, a young man with a grizzled look and bushy mustache, called for me to come talk with him down below when we were anchored in the windy, desolate, and wide-open bight on San Miguel Island called Cuyler Harbor. We sat at the end of a long center table in the schooner's main cabin with a chart laid out between us. He recommended that we not try to make it all the way to Point Conception. We had lost a day earlier in the trip when, after a shackle high in the rigging let loose and fell on the deck with a big thud, we spent the following day in Ventura Harbor frapping wire onto the bolt of every shackle and checking all the rigging for any weaknesses. As a college-level class reading Dana's *Two Years Before the Mast*, we were happy to share in the work, but this put us late into the islands. Now, anchored at San Miguel Island, we had only two days to get to Santa Barbara. The captain, drawing on the chart with his finger, recommended two beautiful days of easy sailing off the wind, first across the top of Santa Rosa Island to anchor in Bechers Bay, then a final day crossing the channel to Santa Barbara. To press further to Point Conception would mean an unpleasant day motoring up into wind and waves, leaving us almost no time to explore on shore before leaving early the next morning for a long day that would get us late into Santa Barbara.

The captain's plan was, of course, best. It was merely a courtesy that he asked my opinion. I was disappointed because it meant not reaching Point Conception, but the next two days the weather for sailing was glorious. The following morning, after a good breakfast, we first raised our sails and let the bow point into a late-morning breeze. Then, with fifteen of us lined up on deck heaving on the thick anchor rode, we raised anchor. Up forward, a couple of crew pulled foresail sheets inward to catch the oncoming breeze. The bow swung to leeward as a couple of other crew hauled in the other sails. As pretty as can be, we then sailed out of the bay. Running eastward across the top of Santa Rosa Island, we rounded Carrington Point and anchored in the late afternoon in an empty Bechers Bay. Next morning, after another pleasant breakfast, we again lined up to raise anchor. We motored out this day because there was no wind. We pushed our way into the Santa Barbara Channel on one of its famous crystal-clear days with no cloud in sight. Angling northeastward, up ahead were the Santa Ynez Mountains that rise steeply behind Santa Barbara. Sailing at this angle, later in the afternoon we would have a good view of Storke Tower at UC Santa Barbara. I can't help but be anxious to see UC Santa Barbara and the scruffy student-community called Isla Vista next to it. I moved there as a kid and left nine years later with a wife, the beginnings of a personal library, and a sense of calling and community. If *Two Years Before the Mast* tells Dana's coming-of-age story, UC Santa Barbara and Isla Vista tell mine.

That morning, without any wind yet, the captain gave me permission to climb the mast—as long as the second mate went with me to keep me safe. High up, standing on a topsail spar, I saw the channel stretching far into the distant east and west. Up ahead, were water, mountains, and sky, but I could not yet see the town of Santa Barbara. To the north, the Santa Ynez Mountains lined the channel like a fortress wall. On the south side were the islands, east to west: Anacapa, Santa Cruz, Santa Rosa, and San Miguel. The heights of Santa Cruz Island filled my view to starboard. To port, slightly aft of the beam, I could see, clear and distinct, where the land tapered down from the mountains into a smooth lowland. At its tip, Point Conception jutted into the blue as the gate into and out of the California Bight. I clung to the swinging mast. The schooner's deck was far below. We were powering through swells, bow waves spraying out to port and starboard, white with froth against the dark sea. I was forty-five years old back then. I remember the moment well, high up in the wind, boat surging below. At that point in time and space, I became a full sea-brother to Richard Henry Dana Jr. whose book I was teaching to the students below. He had sailed these waters into Santa Barbara. He had seen and felt what I was seeing and feeling. I was thwarted from reaching Point Conception, but I could see it in the distance. High in the rigging, I sensed creation's embrace. Most particularly, I felt the

The Point of Immaculate Conception

channel's love. It swaddled me in beauty. Immaculate Conception to the northwest. Santa Cruz to the southwest. Santa Barbara ahead. San Miguel and Santa Rosa behind. I spontaneously and willingly accepted my position in the world. I am a child of this coast, these islands, and these waters. The Mexican *Californios* called themselves *Los Hijos del País,* Children of this place. Sailing across the Santa Barbara Channel I embraced my home. I am a child of this coast and these islands, *Un Niño de la Costa y las Islas.*

Author and students up in the rigging of the schooner *Californian,* Ventura Harbor, 2003. (Author's collection.)

Ever since not getting there on the *Californian*, Boethius and I have felt the need to sail the full extent of the Bight from San Diego Bay to Point Conception. Fifteen years later, we have an opportunity. We sail north through the Gulf of Santa Catalina, then up along the eastern side of San Pedro Channel, and on the third day across the outer edge of Santa Monica Bay to the Malibu coast, anchoring in Paradise Cove to the lee of Point Dume. Sunrise over Los Angeles is behind us on the fourth day as we weigh anchor. Today, we head west into the islands. Captain Ann, the owner of Seabreeze nautical bookstore in Point Loma, recommended tacking up to Santa Barbara harbor then sailing along the north coast of the Bight as the best way to get to Point Conception. While crossing over to Anacapa Island, I choose not to tack up to Santa Barbara. Instead we sail westward

The Winds of Santa Ana

under Anacapa and Santa Cruz islands and plan to round up to the anchorage at Bechers on Santa Rosa Island. My plan for tomorrow is to pull up the anchor in Bechers before dawn, motor early around Carrington Point and head northwest into the Santa Barbara Channel before any winds developed. We can then ride the afternoon winds into Cojo Anchorage in the lee of Point Conception. From our anchorage in Cojo, I can row the dinghy ashore and walk over to the lighthouse.

As it turns out, *Boethius* and I should have followed Captain Ann's advice. The moderate conditions at this end of the channel will not be what we experience at the other end of the channel.

Today, we are now south of the Anacapa Island lighthouse. We are lighthouse hopping. Having left behind Point Loma light we have sailed past the lighthouses at Point Fermin and Point Vicente. Now we are in the lee of Anacapa light. If the Franciscan missions of the Bight — San Diego, San Luis Rey, San Juan Capistrano, San Gabriel, San Fernando, San Buenaventura, and Santa Barbara—mark an *El Camino Real,* the Spanish King's Highway, the lighthouses mark a parallel maritime highway created later by the United States Coast Survey. As with most everything depicted on the nautical charts of this coast, the lighthouses are best thought of as alive, personal, and communicative in many ways. Each has both a name in the common tongue and a technical name in chart-language. Sailing within sight of Anacapa light, I loose the mainsheet a bit and let go the tiller so *Boethius* will steer herself. I go below, grab a couple of nautical charts, and return to my seated position athwart the cockpit. I spread the charts on my lap and search out the chart names. Anacapa light is named "Fl (2) 60s 277ft 14M Horn." The name means that she declares herself to boaters at night from two hundred and seventy-seven above standard sea level, declaring who she is with two flashes every sixty seconds to anyone within fourteen nautical miles. In fog, she will call out with a horn. Point Vicente lighthouse at the southern tip of Santa Monica Bay is named "Fl (2) 20s 185ft 24M Horn" which means she declares who she is with two flashes, one hundred and eighty-five feet above standard sea level, every twenty seconds. Continuing south, Point Fermin's lighthouse is "Fl 10s 120ft 13M" and Point Loma's "Fl 15s 88ft 14m Horn." These lighthouses flash in the night and call out in a fog, identifying themselves to anyone trained in the grammar of nautical charts. *Boethius* and I are anxious to see and hear Point Conception declare her name to us: "Fl 30s 133ft 26M Horn."

The Point of Immaculate Conception

At dusk, we anchor in the lee of Santa Cruz Island at Yellow Banks anchorage. This afternoon there are only a few boats anchored nearby. One boat drops two kayaks in the water. I wave when two young people paddle by, and they wave back. In the morning, *Boethius* and I raise anchor and continue our pilgrimage to Point Conception. By early afternoon the wind is blowing charismatic. When we try to turn up into the passage between Santa Cruz and Santa Rosa islands conditions have become Pentecostal. Wind-driven waves chop at the bow. *Boethius* shoulders into them, but we are not allowed any progress into the passage. I take down the jib, tug the motor to life and twist it to full throttle, cinch the mainsail in tight and try to point into the passage between the islands. The wind and waves still beat us back. Unable to reach up to the anchorage at Bechers, I raise the jib, turn off the motor, loosen the mainsheet and swing the bow down for a run underneath Santa Rosa Island. In the island's shadow, the winds are Presbyterian and the waters calmer. *Boethius* and I relax.

By the late afternoon, *Boethius* and I make it to the south end of the passage between Santa Rosa and San Miguel Islands. Here we hope to do what we couldn't do earlier. We have more room here to sail far to the west, then tack high up into the channel where we can then bring the wind to starboard for a run westward into the wide cove called Culyer Harbor. But Pentecost hits again, harder this time. We are unable to make even westerly progress. Waves larger than before chop at the bow, and winds stronger than before simply will not let us go where we want to go. If we could sail west, we might be able to do our planned tack northeast, but the best our bow will do is point west-south-west. We expected a rough time. Every boater knows that late afternoons at this end of the Bight can be wild. But what we thought we could handle is now obviously impossible for *Boethius*. With the ocean spraying horizontal off the bow as we crash up and down across waves, the music of the spheres has given way only to a pounding timpani. With nothing to do but bring the wind across our stern and retreat, we run due east back to the south side of Santa Rosa Island where we swing up into the flat water of Johnson's Lee. With sails luffing wildly, we let the wind slow us. Having left the tiller and untied the anchor from its harness, I hold it while standing at the bow. I wait, wait a bit more, and when all forward motion ceases, I drop the anchor into about twenty-five feet of water. The wind now pushes us sideways and backward as I pay out one hundred and seventy-five feet of chain and another one hundred and seventy-five feet of rope.

The wind is still blowing strong, but the water is flat. With sails flogging, I stand at the bow, a bare foot on the anchor rode feeling for any signs of slippage. Heavy seas and winds are in the distance to the south and southwest. This is August, high season for sailing, but only one boat is at the other end of the anchorage. It soon leaves. Loud construction sounds, a random low clunking noise, reverberates through the anchorage. I initially think that a crew might be working among the remains of military barracks on the barren hill above a long beach. But there is no evidence of people up there. The loud clunking sounds must be coming from the clusters of elephant seals on the beach. Anchored safe with wind and water raging out beyond, I lower the jib, then the main, tugging the mainsail's luff to get the wrinkles out as I flake it onto the top of the boom. I use three gaskets to hold the bundle of sail tight against the boom. *Boethius* is now floating calmly in flat water. I stand in the cockpit, arms crossed in front of me as I lean on top the boom and mainsail, contemplating the late afternoon light on the island's brown landscape. Both *Boethius* and I breathe easy. This place is beautiful. We smile at the wonderfully weird chorus of elephant seals.

JOHNSON'S LEE IS the site of an ancient village named *Nilal Ihuya*. On the other side of this island, the north side that receives the full brunt of the winds and surf of Windy Lane, is an archeological site called Arlington Springs where in 1959 two human femur bones were discovered that date back some 13,000 years. They are among the oldest human remains found in North America. Archeologists think settlers first came here by way of a "Kelp Highway" along the edge of the coast. The First Peoples rounding Point Conception were a maritime people who had boats capable of handling the channels rough waters and reaching these offshore islands.

The earliest boats were probably made of reeds tied tightly together. At some point, using the tar that oozes beneath our sea floor as a sealant, the Indians invented a new type of sturdy sewn-together plank canoe. Two versions of the canoe were developed. *Tomols* plied Santa Barbara Channel, and *ti'ats* worked Santa Monica Bay and the San Pedro Channel. It is not easy to cut planks and sew them together into a boat with high-capacity for people and cargo, so it is fair to say that *tomols* and *ti'at* are monuments to

The Point of Immaculate Conception

our fore-parent's resourcefulness and dedication to maritime life. Jeffrey Altschul and Donn Grenda in *Islanders and Mainlanders: Prehistoric Context for the Southern California Bight* report "ethnographic data suggest that plank canoe owners were men of wealth, prestige, and economic power." These men apparently wore distinctive, "short, waist-length capes of fur"— not unlike, I suppose, the commodore and vice commodore of modern yacht clubs. Altschul and Grenda further report that in the Santa Barbara Channel, boat owners banded together as a "Brotherhood of the *Tomol*."[2]

There is a maritime brother-and-sisterhood that continues on the Bight. I think we can all get along. The most famous story of maritime friendship between Indians and Spaniards on the Bight is Francisco Palóu's account of the naming of Santa Cruz Island. The *San Antonio,* one of the first three packet-boats purchased by the Pious Fund, an endowment specifically collected to support evangelism of Baja and Alta California, was on its first trip up from Mexico carrying supplies to San Diego. Palóu tells of *San Antonio* tacking far out to sea until the boat reached the latitude of Point Conception. The packet-boat then tacked eastward toward the point in order to enter the Santa Barbara Channel. Now sailing easy and needing fresh water, the *San Antonio* anchored on the east end of the largest island. Good anchorages attract boats and boating-minded people. The islanders welcomed the crew of the *San Antonio.* While Indians helped the shore crew fill water casks, the two missionaries on board—Franciscans always come in twos—engaged the islanders in rudimentary sign language. After a few hours, the *San Antonio* weighed anchor and headed south toward Point Loma. The wind, however, soon calmed as darkness fell. The *San Antonio* had not traveled far when the missionaries realized that they had left a staff topped with a cross on shore. The friars assumed they would never see the staff again because the cross on top "was iron, and it was known how the Indians coveted this metal." Lo and behold, after wallowing in light winds all night, the next morning an Indian *tomol* approached them. The Indians, thinking that the friars would want it, had the lost staff with its cross. "For this reason," Fr. Palóu writes, the island is named "Holy Cross (Santa Cruz), and as such it has been known ever since."[3]

Second in command on the *San Antonio* that day in 1769 was Juan Pérez. He would quickly become captain and, until his death in 1775, was the most active of the Spanish ship captains who plied the California Bight.

---

2. Altschul and Grenda, *Islanders and Mainlanders,* 54–55.
3. Palóu, *Historical Memoirs of New California,* 16–18.

He is remembered fondly by both Fr. Palóu, who was in charge of the missions in Baja California, and St. Serra, who was in charge of the missions in Alta California. Pérez was another of those on this coast from the island of Mallorca. The Spanish missionaries had access to a rich endowment called *The Pious Fund for the Californias* that had first been created to support evangelism in Baja California. This endowment paid for the purchase of boats, the hiring of captains and crew, and the building of a port at San Blas to service the coast of Alta California. Palóu tells of a plan to have the *Pious Fund* pay for a college in San Blas to teach Indians the navigational arts of Europeans similar to the way the *Pious Fund* later paid for Indians to attend a liberal arts college near the mouth of the Salinas River. For about fifty years, the Spanish packet boats, along with their crews that serviced the mission anchorages and missionary travels on the California coast, were a specialized boating fellowship paid for by an endowment started with money donated by families in Europe who wanted to help Indians in California become Christians. Juan Perez was exactly the kind of good-hearted captain hoped for by those who administered the *Pious Fund*.[4]

Here at *Nilal Ihuya* on Santa Rosa Island, there was in the 1770s, 80s, and 90s a thriving fishing community. Standing with my elbows out on the boom and mainsail, I imagine a time when maritime empathy, boater hospitality, and mutual appreciation for messing about in boats thrived here. The missions and presidios were far away on the coast. Out here on the far side of this island, it is easy for *Boethius* and me to imagine the *San Antonio* anchored here at Johnson's Lee. Up in the village a couple of the Majorcan friars would be using sign-language to tell the chief about the Creator of the seas and all it contains while down on the beach Captain Pérez and a group of sailors would be swapping gear and information with the captains of several *tomols*. I see Pérez stooped down with a couple of *Roseño*, communicating in nautical pidgin and sign language, about the use of local tar to fill the spaces between the planks. It is highly likely that Indians would have shown Pérez how to use the tar to caulk Spanish boats, and Pérez would have given Indian captains some of his rope-like oakum to experiment with in the seams of their *tomols*. Given the goals of the missionaries, it is easy to imagine Pérez bringing rope, fishing, and boating gear to the *tomol* and *ti'at* captains of the Bight as gifts. It is likely that *tomol* and *ti'at*

---

4. See Castor, "The Last Days of Don Juan Perez;" Thurman, *Naval Department of San Blas*; Weber, "Pious Fund for the Californias." For the college, see Palóu, *Historical Memoirs of New California*, 76.

The Point of Immaculate Conception

builders, along with Spanish sailors, experimented with sailing versions of the canoes. There is every reason to believe the local Indians of the Bight went day-sailing and voyaging on Spanish boats as both passengers and crew. Like me on the schooner *Californian*, Chumash sailors would have been anxious to learn the ropes and climb the mast of a strange ship. There is also every reason to believe, that Spanish sailors stood in line for an opportunity to be taught by the Indians how to paddle a *tomol*.

Sad to say, the boating fellowship of the Bight also helped spread syphilis to the islands. In 1806, with a population apparently weakened by syphilis, there was a massive dying on the islands during a measles epidemic. Franciscan plans for missions to be built on Santa Cruz and Santa Catalina Islands were abandoned as the cultural stability of those two islands dissolved. By 1815, the islands of the Santa Barbara Channel were empty of people. Islanders moved to the coast, amalgamating themselves into pan-Indian identities delineated by mission jurisdictions. What had been a larger diversity of islanders merged more narrowly into the *Ventureños, Barbareños,* and *Gabrieleños.* The last of the island Indians—made famous by local novelist, Scott O'Dell in his classic *Island of the Blue Dolphin*—lived on San Nicholas Island. The boating fellowship of the Bight kept watch to bring her to the mainland, but she hid from attempts to help her. It wasn't until after eighteen years, she showed herself to an otter hunter named George Nidever. He and his wife took the Lone Woman into their home in Santa Barbara, but she died soon after.

We historians use to teach only about the dispossession of Indians and destabilization of their cultures. We promoted the myth of dying ways of life. Truth is the Indians of the Bight remain active and creative. In the 1970s when I first came to live on the Bight, the Indians began to take control of their narrative and began to promote their living culture. *December's Child: A Book of Chumash Oral Narratives* was newly out when I first began studying California history. The book recorded the story of Point Conception and saved oral stories of island life, particularly the stories of María Solares, who lived at Mission Santa Ynez, and Fernando Librado, who was born on Santa Cruz Island and later lived in Ventura. Solares remembered stories of Point Conception as a place long called Humquq:

> It was said that the spirit of the dead before leaving for Similaqshua [the Land of the Dead, across the sea] went to Point Conception. That was a wild stormy place.... It was called Humqaq.... There the spirit of the dead bathes itself and paints itself and then it sees a

light to the westward and goes towards it and thus reaches the land of Similaqshua, going through the air—not the water.[5]

Librado had learned the art of building a *tomol* and remembered stories and village names of both the islands and the coast. Since the 1970s, people with Indian heritage have rallied to the name Chumash and have gathered many more stories and traditions that have come to light. During my lifetime on the Bight, being Chumash has become a unifying identity and a dynamic way to participate in the creation of public policy. Many Chumash today are embracing their heritage as a maritime people. Techniques for building *tomols* have been improved and the Fellowship of the *Tomol* is reviving in more democratic ways than its former brotherhood. Since 1979 the Chumash have been devoted to conservation of the land and waters around Point Conception/Humquq. Since 2015 they have been proposing to the government a Chumash Heritage National Marine Sanctuary along the coast above and below Point Conception, reaching into the Santa Barbara Channel toward Refugio State Beach. The Chumash are already working as partners with the National Parks Service in protecting the Islands and waters on the south side of the Santa Barbara Channel.

Fellowship of the *Tomol*. (Photo: Robert Schwemmer/NOAA)

Anchored here with *Boethius* on Santa Rosa Island, the *tomols* are gone along with the ancient village. As I stand in the cockpit looking toward shore, *Boethius* and I would like to be considered fellow travelers with the Brother and Sisterhood of the *Tomol*. We want to identify with the boater fellowship that has plied these waters for thousands of years. We

5. Blackburn, *December's Child*, 98.

want to share in the legacy of *tomols, ti'ats,* captains such as Juan Perez, and Point Conception's role as a gateway between worlds. We, who live in and love this place, hear the California Bight calling us together for the great wedding banquet that will come.

LATE IN THE NIGHT, I climb the short ladder up out of *Boethius'* little cabin, step further up onto the cockpit seats, and walk forward across the cabin roof to stand on the bow facing into the wind. In the dark I try to judge whether there is any decline in its force. If there is any lessening, I can't sense it. What matters more is whether the choppy wind-waves out in the San Miguel Passage have flattened. *Boethius* and I can negotiate with wind, but we can't win any progress to Point Conception against steep waves coming straight at us. Out loud I ask *Boethius* if we should go out and see what it is like in the passage. We need to anchor in Cuyler tonight, rest three or four hours, then launch ourselves at dawn into the channel. Given a morning calm, we will be able to cross most of the way over to Point Conception before any big afternoon winds develop. *Boethius* seems anxious to go. I go back to the cabin, put on my coat, life jacket, and harness. I turn on our running and steaming lights. At the stern, I tug the motor to life and let it idle in neutral. At the bow, hand-over-hand I strain to retrieve the anchor rope and chain. When the anchor lifts from the bottom, we blow sideways and start skittering uncontrolled out of the anchorage toward wide-open waters. I stay at the bow dropping chain into its locker and securing the anchor. With *Boethius* cockeye to the wind, I carefully make my way back to the cockpit, attach my harness to the line that ties me to the boat, put the motor in gear, and swing the bow all the way down and around on a course that will take us out into the passage where we hope to turn northwest toward Cuyler Harbor on San Miguel Island.

Our exploratory trip is short. Once into the passage the full force of the wind hits as hard as before and steep waves chop at the bow like they did earlier. I do not even try to put up sails. After about ten minutes of listening to the motor wail at full throttle, with no forward progress to San Miguel Island, I push the tiller to port, swing the bow to starboard, and race back to the anchorage with waves rocking us sideways, water sometimes splashing over our beam. Back behind Santa Rosa Island, having again dropped the anchor, I stand on the bow and watch moonlight shimmer off the flat water in Johnson's Lee. We will try again early tomorrow morning.

Before dawn I wriggle out of the quarter-berth, put the kettle on the burner, and turn on the VHF weather channel. I stand on the ladder with my head sticking out above the cabin roof. The wind is still Pentecostal. The electronic voice on the radio tells me that what is hitting us at this end of the Santa Barbara Channel will continue for several more days. I climb out and up onto the cabin roof in order to see out into the passage between San Miguel and Santa Rosa islands. I see the tops of waves in the distance spewing white. There is no way we are going to get to Point Conception this trip. I climb back down and hunker into the cabin, make a second cup of coffee, and spread the NOAA chart on the table. I smile in relief. We may not be able to go to Point Conception, but going to Santa Barbara harbor will be a sleigh-ride in this kind of wind. The plan is to sail east under the island then turn northeast to pass between Santa Rosa and Santa Cruz Islands on a beam reach. Once in the channel we will loose sails into a extra-broad reach. We should have a great, all-day run, to Santa Barbara. If the sky clears, as it usually does later in the morning, we shall have a glorious day. Dinner tonight will be at Rudy's Mexican restaurant, only a short walk inland from Santa Barbara Harbor.

With the sun rising, we raise anchor and sails. The anchor chain gave me some trouble halfway into the uptake. My best guess is that a big halibut or large manta ray spent the night sleeping on top of it. I tugged and yanked, tugged and yanked, then tugged and yanked some more. This was not a kelp or rock problem. Something was on top the anchor chain. Elephant seals don't sit on the ocean floor, do they? Yank, yank, yank, then finally, something big down below decided to swim away. All came up fine after that.

Mid-afternoon we are more than two thirds of the way across the Santa Barbara Channel. In the far distance, I can see Storke Tower on the campus of UC Santa Barbara. I smile. I spent nine years with Storke Tower, like a compass, orienting my life. It is the architectural center, the symbol, of UC Santa Barbara. Of course, as students, we all thought of it as an erect penis. Any student with a normal education learns Freudian interpretation of architecture. St. Bonaventure would agree that sexual interpretation is appropriate, but better with broader context. Signs and symbols are everywhere. Our environment is constantly talking to us. Schools are supposed

The Point of Immaculate Conception

to teach people how better to listen. The Bible was teaching this long before Freud. Christian architecture was especially influenced by Song of Solomon and the conversation between Jesus and Nicodemus about the need to be born again. Church doors were designed to reference vaginas, church interiors reference wombs, and church facades with two towers reference breasts. For Christians, sexual iconography is not modern psychology; rather, it is the ancient and medieval Christian vocabulary of the Creator's plan for creation to participate in creation.

As we near the entrance buoy to Santa Barbara Harbor, I can see the famous façade of Mission Santa Barbara halfway up the back of the amphitheater. Generally regarded as the most beautiful of the Spanish missions, with her two domed towers and grand entrance, she is certainly the most feminine of the missions. She is one of this coast's most popular wedding sites.

The most famous wedding and wedding feast in Santa Barbara—there is a plaque downtown celebrating it—is the marriage in 1836 of Alfred Robinson to Ana María (Anita) de la Guerra, daughter of Jose de la Guerra, a man Dana describes as "the grandee" of Santa Barbara, "head of the first family of California."[6] *Two Years Before the Mast* describes the wedding as a great unifying event in Mexican California. At other places in the book, Dana is wary and critical of Mexican rule and culture in California, but those feelings do not appear in the pages about the wedding. The wedding does for Dana what all weddings are supposed to do: lift us out of this world of sin into a world of hope, love, and covenant. Weddings are supposed to point toward the ultimate wedding when all will be born again.

Dana's wedding story begins with rounding Point Conception in the *Alert* with a boat load of people from Monterey headed to the wedding. The groom was with them, as were also, most likely, Don Guillermo Arnel (William Hartnell) and his wife, the bride's older sister, Teresa de la Guerra. The groom and his soon-to-be brother-in-law, had been immigrant outsiders, Protestants from Boston and England, but were now embraced as *Los Hijos del País*. Each had willingly joined the Roman Catholic Church and had become citizens of the United States of Mexico. A decade earlier Teresa and William had also been married here in Santa Barbara. Their home up near Monterey Bay was the site of *El Colegio de San Jose*, California's first academy/college where Guillermo and an Irish priest were the first faculty. That year, thirteen Mexican and six Indian boys were enrolled. Teresa was

---

6. Dana Jr., *Two Years Before the Mast*, 258.

probably pregnant on the boat trip down the coast given that she gave birth at least nineteen times in twenty-six years. The extended de la Guerra family represented the highest hopes for Mexican California.

After the *Alert* was anchored, Dana, as deckhand, helped transfer passengers and wedding supplies to the beach through the rough surf Santa Barbara is famous for. For the next three days, the crew of the *Alert* helped prepare for the big event. On the morning of the ceremony, Dana helped row his captain ashore then returned to the *Alert* which was anchored beyond the surf but close enough in to see easily the two towers of the mission and the large door between. Dana writes: "Our guns were loaded and run out, men appointed to each, cartridges served out, matches lighted, and all the flags ready to be run up. I took my place at the starboard after gun." They watched, he writes, the bride, dressed in "deep black" process into the mission where the wedding would take place. They waited, staying close to their posts because timing was crucial. Inside, he knew the groom and bride would be offering their confession. The ceremony would be long because there needed to be allowance, after the confession, for the bride to change into a white dress to signify absolution of her sins. "Nearly an hour intervened," Dana writes:

> When the great doors of the mission church opened, the bells rang out a loud, discordant peal, the private signal for us was run up by the captain ashore, the bride, dressed in complete white, came out of the church with the bridegroom, followed by a long procession. Just as she stepped from the church door, a small white cloud issued from the bows of our ship, which was full in sight, the loud report echoed among the surrounding hills and over the bay, and instantly the ship was dressed in flags and pennants from stem to stern. Twenty-three guns followed in regular succession, with an interval of fifteen seconds between each when the cloud cleared away, and the ship lay dressed in her colors, all day. At sun-down, another salute of the same number of guns was fired, and all the flags run down. This we thought was pretty well—a gun every fifteen seconds—for a merchantman with only four guns and a dozen or twenty men.[7]

A beautiful day! Bride and groom were born again through the doors of mother church. Bells rang. Cannons boomed. Flags were let fly. A great event had occurred, a wedding, one of the most vivid in the history of North American literature. After their salute to the new couple, Dana and

---

7. Dana Jr., *Two Years Before the Mast*, 259.

The Point of Immaculate Conception

the crew of the *Alert* go ashore, dressed in their best, to join in a three-day fiesta at *Casa de la Guerra*.

Dana describes the wedding fiesta as a great success. The de la Guerra house, which still stands, low and U-shaped around a large courtyard, is open to what is now de la Guerra Square. Dana describes the house, with a tent in the courtyard, embracing several hundred people. "As we drew near," he writes:

> we heard the accustomed sound of violins and guitars, and saw a great motion of the people within. Going in, we found nearly all the people of the town—men, women, and children—collected and crowded together, leaving barely room for the dancers; for on these occasions no invitations are given, but everyone is expected to come, though there is always a private entertainment within the house for particular friends. The old women sat down in rows, clapping their hands to the music, and applauding the young ones.[8]

The whole town is together with people from up and down the coast. The music would have been excellent because the missions imported instruments and encouraged diverse music for all occasions. Dana describes Don Jose de la Guerra, the father of the bride, waltzing for near half an hour with his oldest daughter, Angustias, alone in the center of the courtyard, her name signaling the anguish of Christ on the cross. Dana describes her as "a handsome women and a general favorite." The father and daughter were "repeatedly and loudly applauded, the old men and women jumping out of their seats in admiration, and the young people waving their hats and handkerchiefs." Writing two years later, Dana thinks back fondly on the scene: "Indeed, among people of the character of these Mexicans, the waltz seemed to me to have found its right place."

The great amusement of the evening, he goes on to say,

> was the breaking of eggs filled with cologne, or other essences, upon the heads of the company. One end of the egg is broken and the inside taken out, then it is partly filled with cologne, and the whole sealed up. The women bring a great number of these secretly about them, and the amusement is to break one upon the head of a gentleman when his back is turned. He is bound in gallantry to

---

8. Dana Jr., *Two Years Before the Mast*, 259.

find out the lady and return the compliment, though it must not be done if the person sees you.[9]

Dana, apparently smitten by Angustias, describes her sneaking up behind one of the great landowners, knocking off his hat with one hand while with the other breaking one of the eggs, called *cascarones,* on his head. She immediately springs back, disappearing into the crowd.

> The Don turned slowly round, the cologne, running down his face, and over his clothes, and a loud laugh breaking out from every quarter. He looked round in vain, for some time, until the direction of so many laughing eyes showed him the fair offender. She was his niece, and a great favorite with him, so old Don Domingo had to join in the laugh. A great many such tricks were played, and many a war of sharp maneuvering was carried on between couples of the younger people, and at every successful exploit a general laugh was raised.[10]

Dana's description of the wedding is lengthy. It is one of the best-told stories in the book. The narrative has a political quality. It paints a picture of Mexican California at its best: diverse, happy, and fulfilling. There is also has a prophetic quality to the three days of the wedding fiesta. Beauty, joy, and love are announced by canons and flags following confession of sin and prayer for redemption. There is mysticism in the historic event. The Holy Spirit was there, it seems, signaling the future. Dana writes:

> Another singular custom I was for some time at a loss about. A pretty young girl was dancing, named, after what would appear to us the sacrilegious custom of the country — Espiritu Santo, when a young man went behind her and placed his hat directly upon her head, letting it fall down over her eyes, and sprang back among the crowd. She danced for some time with the hat on, when she threw it off, which called forth a general shout; and the young man was obliged to go out upon the floor and pick it up. Some of the ladies, upon whose heads hats had been placed, threw them off at once, and a few kept them on throughout the dance, and took them off at the end, and held them out in their hands, when the owner stepped out, bowed, and took it from them. I soon began to suspect the meaning of the thing, and was afterward told that it was a compliment, and an offer to become the lady's gallant for the rest of the evening, and to wait upon her home. If the hat was

9. Dana Jr., *Two Years Before the Mast*, 261.
10. Dana Jr., *Two Years Before the Mast*, chap. 27, 261

The Point of Immaculate Conception

thrown off, the offer was refused, and the gentleman was obliged to pick up his hat amid a general laugh. Much amusement was caused sometimes by gentlemen putting hats on the ladies' heads, without permitting them to see whom it was done by. This obliged them to throw them off, or keep them on at a venture, and when they came to discover the owner, the laugh was often turned upon them.[11]

BOETHIUS AND I tie up to the Harbor Master's dock, and I go up the stairs to the office to pay for one night in a slip whose usual occupant is gone. Anxious for a shower, I steer *Boethius* down the fairway, turn first into our assigned row, then into our assigned slip. Thirty minutes later, happily showered and in clean clothes, I step off *Boethius*, quickly make sure all is secure, and head up the dock, looking to the right and left at beautiful yachts. The reflections of harbor lights are beginning to shimmer on the water between the boats. Halyards lightly slap against their masts. There is laughter in the distance from the open deck of Brophy Brothers seafood restaurant. It is a joyful end of a beautiful day.

---

11. Dana Jr., *Two Years Before the Mast*, chap. 27, 261–62.

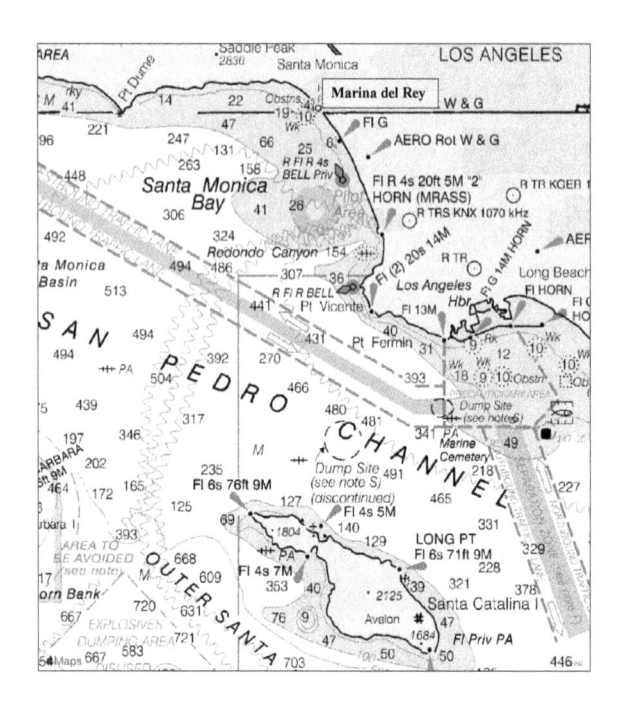

Marina del Rey to Santa Catalina Island. (NOAA charts.)

The Alexandrian Waters of San Pedro and Santa Catalina

THE best sailing route from the mainland to Santa Catalina Island is a southward beam reach from Marina del Rey, surging past the lighthouse on Point Vicente, then sledding across San Pedro Channel to any anchorage along the northeastern side of the island. On a normal day, all creation favors sailor and sailboat. The sky is blue, the wind full, and the water lively. In the channel, wind and water conspire to lift and press the boat forward toward the island through pods of frolicking dolphins and past long undulating lines of pelicans. All nature sings on a beam reach to Catalina, and round the sailor rings the music of the spheres.

Sailing this route has a Dante-esque quality. In *Paradiso*, Dante, the pilgrim who has seen the layers of hell and purgatory with Virgil, is met

The Alexandrian Waters of San Pedro and Santa Catalina

by the beautiful Beatrice. Leaving Virgil behind, the two then board a boat that sails toward islands, inward and further inward, toward the center of Heaven. (Many a scholar has compared Dante's Beatrice with Boethius's *Philosophia*.) At the end of his epic poem, what does Dante find embedded in the light and love of the Trinity at the center of Paradise? A book!

> I saw that in its depth far down is lying
> Bound up with love together in one volume,
> What through the universe in leaves is scattered.[1]

Boethius and I read the California Bight in the way literature professors read *Huckleberry Finn* and *Moby Dick*. We look for deep messages. Jesus, talking about his parables, said that nothing is hidden except to be revealed. But unlike *Huckleberry Finn* and *Moby Dick*, the Dante-esque ride from Santa Monica to Santa Catalina Island is not increasingly reckless and fraught with dangers; instead, there is a library-like, Presbyterian decency and good order to both the passage and the island itself. The patron saints of the passage—Monica, Pedro, and Catalina—first lived on the African side of the Mediterranean and, in their second lives, bring a North African quality to this part of California's version of the Mediterranean Sea. Monica was the domineering mother of St. Augustine, who watched over the young man, his friends, and her grandchild, making sure decency and good order prevailed among them. When she died in Ostia, the port of Rome, these young men mourned the loss, then sailed back to what is now Tunisia where they became influential bishops in the upper-management of the Christian Roman Empire. In Alexandria, a city famous for its library and lighthouse, Pedro was a bishop-martyr and Catalina was a scholar-martyr. To sail from Santa Monica Bay through San Pedro Channel to the Island of Santa Catalina is to be watched over by saints who have an appreciation of education, stewardship, and holistic health, both physical and spiritual.

TODAY'S PILGRIMAGE TO Santa Catalina Island, although usually bright and encouraging, will be under a darkened sky. The VHF says rain is a possibility. Instead of the usual northwesterly, a southwesterly wind is predicted.

---

1. Dante, *Paradiso*, 85–87.

As *Boethius* and I motor out of Marina del Rey, the tall spire of the Loyola Marymount University Chapel gives us its blessing while also reminding us to keep our thoughts heavenward. Our plan is for one long close reach to Gallagher's Cove which is south of Long Point and just up from Avalon on southeastern side of Santa Catalina Island. Since 1951 Gallagher's Cove and the canyon behind it has been an InterVarsity Christian Fellowship camp. Back in 1975, when I was seventeen, my church youth group spent a week at the camp. Every day we mixed Bible study with snorkeling, and I have tried to keep the two mixed ever since.

InterVarsity is a university-oriented Christian fellowship with a reputation for devotion to Bible study. Although international, this small camp has a distinctive role in the history of the organization because it was out on this island that a local leader from the University of Southern California named Paul Breyer invented what is called the Mark Study, a distinctive Bible study method that is still widely taught within InterVarsity in an expanded form called the Inductive/Manuscript Bible Study Method. Breyer, out on the island, gave college undergraduates a portion of the Gospel of Mark printed on the left half of sheets of paper without any chapter or verse designations. Every student was given colored pencils and access to a Bible dictionary. The goal for the students, in concert with their group leaders, was to "mark-up" their Gospel of Mark with multi-colored schematics that linked subjects to predicates, identified adjectives and adverbs, connected recurring nouns and verbs, and noted distinctive actions, ideas, and dialogue. The objective back then and ever since has been a grammatical dive into understanding an ancient text that is God-breathed. The goal is philology, not philosophy; reading well, not theological speculation.

Given that St. Mark was a writer and the first Christian missionary to Alexandria in Egypt, *Boethius* and I find it appropriate that the Mark Study was first promoted on an island next to these waters. As usual on the Bight, cartography, history, and Christianity entangle. When Sebastián Viscaíno explored the Bight in 1602, he, his chaplain, and his crew anchored in the lee of what is now Point Fermin on November 24, the feast day of St Peter of Alexandria. There they prayed and asked San Pedro (locals say "Peedro") to oversee what would later become the Port of Los Angeles. On the following day, the feast day of St. Katherine of Alexandria, they prayed for the patronage of Santa Catalina on the island that still bears her name. *Boethius* and I don't dismiss such prayers as random, nor do we think it

The Alexandrian Waters of San Pedro and Santa Catalina

a coincidence when three scholars of the Alexandrian church have their histories entwined with these waters.

San Pedro is not a famous saint. We have very little biographical information to work with. Tradition has it that he was a scholar-bishop after being scholarch (headmaster) of a very early Christian academy in Alexandria. The best book about him is Tim Vivian's *St. Peter of Alexandria: Bishop and Martyr.* Tim wrote the book when he and I were graduate students together in Santa Barbara. I think the Bight was working on us back then. We were both members of St. Michael's and All Angels Episcopal Church in Isla Vista, a tiny mission church under the same patronage as San Miguel Island. In *St. Peter of Alexandria,* Tim put a nice note in the acknowledgements about the two of us in Isla Vista often discussing how, as Christian scholars, we straddle churchly-belief and university-skepticism. Both of us in our different ways have spent our teaching careers trying to walk the line between belief and skepticism.

Santa Catalina is one of the most popular saints in Christian history. The earliest written sources for her story have long been lost. What we are told is she was the daughter of a North African nobleman living late in the 200s. She was highly educated in a city famous for its high regard for education. She fits a pattern of highly educated women in Alexandria that includes Cleopatra and Hypatia. She got into trouble, however, when she argued with a pagan official of the Roman Empire and tried to convince him of the error of paganism. The official, not being as astute as she in the arts of dialectic and rhetoric, called for government-sponsored orators to meet with her in formal debate. Fearless, smart, and well trained, she bested these orators to the extent that they converted to Christianity and were willing to die for their new faith. The official then sent Catalina to prison where she received encouragement from an angel and food from a bird. When the Roman official's wife came to visit her, Catalina's presentation of the reasonableness of the faith convinced the woman to become a Christian. In the end, the Roman official ordered both his wife and Catalina to be executed. Catalina's execution was botched. She was supposed to die on a torture device involving a wheel—thus she is often depicted in Christian iconography with her hand on a wheel—but she endured. Finally, the governor had Catalina's head cut off. Subsequently, angels carried her body to be buried at the base of Mount Sinai.

The best book on Santa Catalina is Christine Walsh's *The Cult of St. Katherine of Alexandria in Early Medieval Europe.* "Cult" in this title is not negative. Catalina inspired people. Her story gave license to girls who sought to be bookish. Aside from depicting her at a wheel, paintings of Katherine usually show her with a book. Her tomb at the base of Mount Sinai became a center of biblical scholarship where a monastery and a library grew around her tomb, eventually becoming a major pilgrim-destination. It has been designated a UNESCO world heritage site. Geographically, the site combines the story of Catalina with the story of the Burning Bush and the Ten Commandments. Catalina and Moses are celebrated together on Mount Sinai as writers and patrons of libraries. The monastery of Santa Catalina on Mount Sinai houses what many think is the oldest continuously run library in existence today. There is evidence that the collection of manuscripts dates back to the century following Santa Catalina's angelic journey there.

When I give walking tours on the island to students, I take them to the church in Avalon dedicated to *Catharina Alexandrina*. I encourage my students (who are mostly female) to ponder the long Christian tradition of female scholarship that is affirmed on the California Bight. We identify the iconography of her as scholar with a Bible when we look up to the tower-statue and inside the front doors at another statue. We also enjoy the stain glass window above the entry door that depicts her in California with her "wheel," not depicted as a torture device, but a ship's helm.

St. Catherine of Alexandria, Roman Catholic Church, Avalon (author's photo).

The Alexandrian Waters of San Pedro and Santa Catalina

The California Bight is not open ocean. Like the Mediterranean Sea, it is an eddy tucked away from the principal forces of the earth's oceans. Nautical charts of the Bight beg for readers to sense a thick geographical relationship with lands surrounding the Mediterranean Sea, a dense historical, literary, and spiritual relationship that reaches through time and across space.

AFTER LEAVING MARINA del Rey and motoring for an hour, *Boethius* and I raise sail. We pull our sheets tight then loosen them, allowing the leech of the mainsail and jib to spoon with each other in two shallow curves. We are pointing high into a light southwesterly wind on a starboard tack. I can see the Point Vicente lighthouse, small, in the distance ahead. Right now, it appears we will pass it with plenty of room. But a sailboat cannot go in a straight line. There is always leeward motion that accompanies forward. My head and gut do some instinctive calculations. I think we can make it. *Boethius* will do her best.

The chart folded on the cockpit bench opposite me declares, in bold type, we are in Santa Monica Bay. Most of the shoreline is not very pretty and the jets leaving alternately from the parallel runways of LAX do not encourage productive pondering. But Santa Monica is here—as is the memory of her son. Santa Monica Bay, since the 1920s, has been host to many script-writers, song-writers, novelists, poets, actors, artists, and musicians. Thomas Mann in Pacific Palisades, Robinson Jeffers on Hermosa Beach, Joan Didion in West Malibu, Bob Dylan on Point Dume, and thousands of other important writers have walked the surf-line of Santa Monica Bay. The great life-themes of love and death, family and freedom, good and evil, science and faith, sin and redemption have been written up in myriad ways and laid down in popular songs, movies, and TV shows. I suspect, during the decades between the 1920s and 1980s, there was more concentrated literary activity between Point Dume and Point Vicente than anywhere else in the world.

We approach noon. The wind is picking up. *Boethius* is heeling to leeward. I have lowered the centerboard below the keel. Now and again the gunnels go awash. Our goal is Santa Catalina Island, but first we want to pass outside of the buoy off Palos Verdes Point named Fl R 4s BELL. After passing that, we will stay wide of the lighthouse then bring the wind a little more toward the stern and head more southward into the San Pedro Channel. Normally at this time of day, on this part of the bay, there is a light Presbyterian wind from the northwest, and we sail large, meaning our sheets are eased and the sails are deep-curved with feminine grace. Today, a strong stable wind comes at us out of the southwest. I tug on the sheets to flatten sails even more. *Boethius* is running like a thoroughbred, neck outstretched, waterline lengthening as she tips leeward, bow slicing through moderate swells and small wind-waves. Even though the sky is ominous, the day is glorious. *Boethius* was born for this kind of sailing.

Having past the buoy and the lighthouse and entered into the wide Alexandrian waters of San Pedro Channel with the island profile in full view, we ease our sheets, allow a little more curve to the sails, and allow our thoughts to turn to St. Katherine's scholarly presence on the Bight. The first girls boarding academy on this coast was named St. Catherine's. It still thrives in Anaheim as a school and orphanage. Boys could attend during the day and were taught in a military tradition, but girls were boarded and given more attention. Recently, a new university has been founded under the patronage of St. Katherine of Alexandria. It started on the coast in Encinitas but has moved inland into hills named for the other Alexandrian, San Marcos. The motto of the new university is "Inquiry seeking wisdom." The principle founders are members of the Antiochian Orthodox Christian Archdiocese of North America, a branch of Eastern Orthodoxy with surprisingly extensive roots in the California Bight. Jon Braun, one of the principal founders of the California branch of this church and St. Katherine's lived down the street from my wife and me in Isla Vista. Before coming to Isla Vista, Braun had been an evangelist employed by Campus Crusade for Christ, an evangelical organization with its roots in Hollywood Presbyterian Church. When I moved to Isla Vista, Braun was the leader of a group of mostly young evangelicals who were creating a new church called the Evangelical Orthodox Church (locals called them the Evee-Orthos). Later, after my new wife and I had bought a tiny house on the same street as the Brauns, I joined a group of neighbors in the Braun living room to learn about the new church. Peter Gillquist, another founder who was in and out of Isla Vista, tells the story we heard in the Braun living room in *Becoming Orthodox: A Journey to the Ancient Christian Faith*. Gillquist says the founders of the new church, wondering how their church should be

The Alexandrian Waters of San Pedro and Santa Catalina

organized and what its theology should be, divvied up research duties. "Let me do the church history," Braun requested of his co-founders, "I want to get hold of the historic continuity of the Church—who the right Church is, who the wrong church is, and how she stayed on track or went off track."[2] Braun's research led him to Eastern Orthodoxy, the wing of Christianity that traces itself back to the earliest bits of what we know about the Greek-speaking churches, especially the church in Alexandria, the home-church of St. Katherine and St. Peter.

In the backyard of my house, Tim Vivian and I talked often about the hopes and ideals of the Evee-Orthos. We appreciated their desire to follow ancient traditions but did not see the need to create a new church. Back in those days, no historic Eastern Orthodox tradition wanted to adopt them and they seemed to be floating alone in the world. We made our choice for St. Michael's Episcopal Church in Isla Vista. In the late 1980s, however, the Evee-Orthos were welcomed into the Syriac Orthodox Church with its long tradition that reached back to Alexandria's sister-city, Antioch. The Book of Acts says followers of Jesus were first called Christians in Antioch.

Today, as *Boethius* and I sail in Alexandrian waters, I think myself blessed to have been in Isla Vista with a new-born church down the block. That church is now flourishing as part of the world-wide fellowship of Eastern Orthodox churches and supporting a growing university here on our coast. I suspect San Pedro and Santa Catalina were watching over them back then and continue to encourage them today.

HUNGRY FOR LUNCH, I adjust the sails so that *Boethius* can steer herself. I watch for a few minutes to see how well we keep our course, then go below. As I rummage for sausage, cheese, crackers, and a beer, I look out the tiny cabin window above the port-side galley sink. The hull is down and the water is rushing white just a couple of feet from my face. I love this. With most of my body below waterline, I am one with the forces of wind, water, and boat. I smile. Why is life so good to me? Joy incites a quick prayer of thanks. I reach up through the companionway to place my lunch against the leeward side of the cockpit and grab my water-stained copy of the Loeb

---

2. Gillquist, *Becoming Orthodox*, 24.

edition of Boethius' writings that is on a shelf within arm's reach. Stepping up the short ladder and twisting to get myself athwart the cockpit, I wedge myself into the low side of the boat and push my feet against the high windward seat. Still letting the boat steer itself, I cut the sausage and cheese into small chunks and position the opened can of beer in a secure spot. Thus situated, I open the book with one hand and feed myself with the other. I note on the flyleaf at the front of the book: "From Sue, Christmas 1981." Sue, me, and this book—we go back. We all are having a good run.

Instead of reading from *The Consolation of Philosophy*, I turn to Boethius' *De Fide Catholica*, a title which meant for him "The Universal Faith." The *Consolation* is not specifically Christian in that it does not mention Christ or make reference to the Bible. Boethius' other writings are more specifically Christian, and since today *Boethius* and I are feeling sort-of Club Med, I turn to *De Fide Catholica*. Boethius wrote during the century between the fall of the Roman Empire and rise of the European Middle Ages. He lived among the ruins of ancient Rome and worked for a Gothic king who was not of the Trinitarian faith. For Boethius, everything he believed in was falling apart. His calling, in the midst of this chaos, was to write short, helpful, books and essays on how to think things through. C. S. Lewis in *The Allegory of Love* calls Boethius "the divine popularizer."[3]

Boethius' first sentence in *De Fide Catholica* is "The Christian Faith is proclaimed by the authority of the New Testament and of the Old."[4] He goes on to say that churches are not unified on all matters of faith; however, all true churches fit the following: first, they believe what is clearly taught in the Scriptures; second, they believe the creeds agreed upon by all the churches; and third, those churches that teach some additional things peculiar to their church, those additional teachings should be appropriately grounded in the Bible.[5]

Boethius believed that Scriptures are the divinely-given earthly foundation of right thinking. Reading can be tricky, however, so Boethius agreed with Santa Monica's son, San Pedro, and Santa Catalina on the importance of a liberal arts education that teaches how to read the Bible. In textbook fashion, *De Fide Catholica* teaches readers of the Bible to sort what they read into three categories: history, allegory, and a combination of the two.[6]

---

3. Lewis, *Allegory of Love*, 46.
4. Boethius, *De Fide Catholica*, 53.
5. Boethius, *De Fide Catholica*, 71.
6. Boethius, *De Fide Catholica*, 59.

The Alexandrian Waters of San Pedro and Santa Catalina

This is one of the reasons why I named the boat *Boethius*. I have used this three-part way of reading as foundational to our pilgrim-understanding of the California Bight.

By "history" Boethius broadly means "the facts." For example, Herod, Pilate, and Jesus lived in Palestine and did the things the Bible says they did. Jesus's resurrection is a historical fact because it is presented in the Bible as an event attested by eyewitness testimony. The facts of the Bible include God created both heaven and earth, all creation shares in the sin of Adam and Eve, and all sorts of bodily, often invisible, beings are active in the cosmos. Boethius believes it is historical fact that the death and resurrection of the God-man Jesus accomplished redemption and salvation. It is also a fact that someday there will be a bodily second coming of the God-man Jesus and what is corruptible will be made incorruptible. History, for Boethius, is a comprehensive category of assertions by the Bible about what happened, what will happen, and who was, is, and will be involved.

"Allegory" is different. It is poetry to history's prose. Allegory includes all sorts of figural language. For Boethius, the Bible often teaches using allegories that should not be confused with "facts." For example, Jesus' parables are figural, as are references to God being biologically male or Jesus being light, water, or bread. Truths are being pointed at, but a reader should not assume that facts are being presented.

The third and most tricky category is when history and allegory are mixed. Paul uses the Greek verb *allēgoroumena* translated *allegorized* in Galatians 4:24 when explaining that the historic story of Sarah and Hagar and the sons of each figuratively indicate the two covenants, old and new. Readers of the Bible need to be on the lookout for when facts have layers of allegory embedded in them. Jesus indicates it was history mixed with allegory when Moses stuck a pole in the ground with a serpent attached, upon which all who look are healed. Readers of the Bible should be taught to look for parallel situations such as Pentecost in the New Testament, when people of different languages understood each other, reversing the story of the tower of Babel in the Old Testament. Fact and allegory are often, not always, entangled.

Boethius teaches nothing eccentric in *De Fide Catholica*. Categorizing facts, allegories and mixtures of the two are a basic lesson in literature and film-studies classes. Much of life, maybe most of life, should be understood as a mixture of fact and allegory. God commands Hosea to live-out a role play, to mix fact with allegory. He is to marry a promiscuous and unfaithful woman. This marriage will be a fact and allegory. God's commitment to the people of Israel, all humanity, and all creation, is lived by Hosea.

Sailing extends the Boethian way of reading to a way of understanding reality. *Boethius* and I sail biblically thinking in terms of Boethian categories. As pilgrim-sailors in Alexandrian waters, *Boethius* and I are on the lookout for facts, allegories, and mixtures of the two. Often, maybe most of the time, we think we, like Hosea, are living out various mixtures.

DONE WITH LUNCH, having cleaned the galley and returned my book to it proper place, I climb back through the companionway, grab the tiller, and cinch the mainsheet. I feel *Boethius* speed up. Gallagher's Cove is up ahead where Santa Catalina affirmed that reading and snorkeling serve each other. We are on a close reach in bookish waters. Our goal is not to understand. Our goal is to experience and think about our experiences. Like Dante, we are on a boat headed further up and further in. The winds are God-breathed. In the beginning was the Word, and the Word was Life, and the Life was Light.

Close in, the island concentrates the wind along its edge. *Boethius* and I skate into Toyon Bay—only a generous cartographer would name this a bay. We tug the motor on and luff up into the wind. I climb up to the base of the mast to loose first the jib halyard then the main halyard. With the sails flogging hard, I gather them in and tie them off. We then motor further in. The wind calms and we anchor to the north of the camp's pier in an out-of-the way spot. As I stand at the bow watching to see if the anchor is holding, a group of kayakers from the InterVarsity camp pass by. As I start to gather the jib and tie it off, a skiff leaves the pier and motors toward us with a college-age kid, looking official, steering.

"I'm sorry, but you cannot anchor here," he says when he pulls up next to us and puts his motor on idle.

"I've anchored here before," I say.

"Our new lease restricts anchoring," he says.

I had heard leases are being re-negotiated up and down the island. Back at the beginning of the century, the Wrigleys had been very generous with leases and were dedicated to democratic access to the whole island. A hundred years later, leases are being re-negotiated. I suppose the growth of Southern California boating makes restrictions necessary.

"I'll move out," I say. We then start to chat as I start laying the jib out on the bow. The young man tells me he lives here full time, the camp is still owned by InterVarsity, but that may be changing. I tell him that I came to the camp back in 1975 with my church youth group and the reason I anchor here is that it reminds me of good times past. We continue to chat. He tells me about new buildings and new programs but assures me that the camp still is much as it was. As I go aft to start our outboard, he engages his and swings back toward the pier.

Anchor up, *Boethius* and I motor into the deep water further out from the tall cliffs of the island. A while later we motor past Avalon in the late afternoon light. Avalon has the look of a tight little Mediterranean village built into a hillside. High on its northwest side is the large Hopi-style house of Zane Grey, the extremely popular early-to-mid-century writer. In one of his fishing essays, he writes of returning to Avalon after a day at sea: "Avalon, the beautiful! . . . Avalon has a singular charm outside of its sport of fishing. It is the most delightful and comfortable place I have ever visited."[7]

Boethius and I pass Avalon thinking we will anchor further on off the quarry at the southeastern end of the island. The water is deep there, some sixty to eighty feet, but we have anchored there before. It will make for a quicker run to San Diego tomorrow. When we get down there, however, the southern winds are blustery and the near-shore waters rougher than expected. Anchoring looks sketchy, so we motor back to Avalon with the sun fully behind the island cliffs. Being cheap and planning to leave for San Diego before dawn, we do not waste money on a mooring. I drop the anchor off Descanso Bay in one hundred and twenty feet of water. This is where the harbor patrol sends the overflow on the big summer holidays. We have anchored here before. I put out one hundred and seventy-five feet of chain and near three hundred feet of rope. This is about a four to one scope which, given the long chain, should hold me fine even if the wind picks up during the night. As the chain clangs out at high speed over the bow roller, I worry that tomorrow my back will suffer from pulling it all up. Before making dinner I check the oil in the outboard. Tomorrow will be a long day. The weather report on the VHF predicts high winds and rain from the south, but nothing we can't handle with our sails reefed.

---

7. Grey, *Tales of Fishes*, 265–66.

After dinner, I stick my head out of the cabin and the wind appears not to be calming. Before I go to sleep, I check again, and the wind is building. I listen to the VHF radio and the weather report is more ominous. During the night, I wake up several times, and the wind is far beyond what I expected. I have been keeping an eye on our position relative to the hotel on shore and am confident our anchor is holding. At dawn, rain is slashing horizontal against the cabin windows. We are not in danger, but we cannot sail in this. The VHF radio is now recommending all boats stay in harbors. At a lull I take a picture of a rainbow over Descanso Beach. A boat and a rainbow, these are the first two signs in the Bible that the Fall is not permanent. We still live in the effects of the curse, but there is hope. After taking the picture I say a quick prayer of thanks and appreciation.

Rainbow over Descanso Beach, Santa Catalina Island. (Author's photo.)

During the lull in the storm, a harbor patrol boat motors over to talk. The boat driver is a thin friendly guy in his thirties. Over the years I have dealt with him several times, but I am sure he does not remember me. He deals with thousands of boaters every year. He calls out from his boat, rocking back and forth a few feet from mine. The Harbor Master, he says, is recommending that all anchored boats come shelter inside Avalon Bay. There is more storm coming. More gusts of gale-force winds are expected.

"Okay," I say, "I'll come in."

He clunks his two outboards into gear and motors off as I go forward to pull up the anchor. I wrestle up all the rope and about half of the chain. I tie off what I have brought in so far and, sitting on the front of the cabin top, I lean back on my hands. My back aches. I go at it some more, but, nothing more will come up. I tell myself that I will never drop a deep anchor again without a good windlass. Mechanical advantage is God's gift to sailors. I rest then try some more. I realize I can't do this alone. As I again rest with the chain tied off, I see the harbor patrol boat roaming around and flag him down. I tell him that I think the anchor is caught in kelp down below. He ties a line around my chain where it enters the water, fraps the other end to a tugboat-style bollard in the center of his pickup-truck-like stern. He guns his two outboard motors and for what seems a long time nothing budges. Soon, though, something below gives way, and the patrol boat drags us out into deep water. I begin wrestling with the chain again, but I am too tired and too old. A hundred feet of chain plus the anchor are hanging straight down. The patrolman, drifting close by to watch, smiles at me with the kind of smile the wise give to the stupid. He is thinking that I should not be sailing alone if I can't handle my gear. He is kind though. He re-ties his line to my chain and drags us across the entrance of the bay to the edge of a shallow cove used by the glass bottom boats. This makes it so I have to pull up only short lengths of chain until finally bringing up the anchor. With his motors idling, he continues to stay close keeping watch. He is a real guy, but he is also a guardian angel, a patron saint. He is a mixture of fact and allegory. When I get the anchor to the surface, it is wrapped in a thick clump of kelp. I wrap the anchor chain around our bow cleat, lean far over the side, and with a knife cut away the clump. After bringing the anchor the rest of the way up, the patrolman comes alongside *Boethius*. I pay for a tight fore-and-aft mooring, close to shore deep in the harbor, near the Tuna Club. I wave to the patrolman as he goes off to help someone else, then twist the throttle handle of our outboard. After tying up, I send a text to Sue saying we will be stuck in Avalon for at least two more nights. She replies she is happy. She doesn't want me sailing in a storm.

After cleaning up, I inflate the little raft in which my daughter learned to row, plop into it, and row to the dinghy dock. The sky is overcast and the wind is blowing hard, but the rain has subsided. I might as well take a long walk and have a good lunch. When I bring students here we always have a good time walking and talking about the political and spiritual ideas invested here by the Wrigleys during the early and middle parts of the twentieth century.

High above the south side of town, William and Ada Wrigley built an East Coast colonial-style house that is now a hotel. High on the north side, their son Philip and his wife Helen built a romantic Spanish-style house called Casa del Monte. The Wrigleys, as owners of most everything on the island, could have created here their own private Xanadu in the manner of William Randolph Hearst's gated castle/estate up the coast north of Morro Bay. But they didn't. The first two generations of Wrigleys were a chewing gum and baseball family. Good people. The Wrigleys cultivated on Santa Catalina Island a Progressive era, North Chicago/Pasadena, style of thinking. They believed in healthy living and leased their island coves to populist organizations such as YMCA, Boy Scouts, and InterVarsity. There is no good biography of William and Ada, but there is a good biography of their son by Paul Angle, *Philip K. Wrigley: A Memoir of a Modest Man*. Angle writes about how both William and Philip believed that capitalists should be moral and the excesses of capitalism should be curbed. After his father died, Philip would often give this account of his father:

> Once, food merchants on the island boosted prices until Dad felt that our Mexican laborers were getting gypped. He put in a commissary for them and sold at cost until the merchants came to reason. Once the barbers got their heads together and boosted prices too high. Dad felt that they were gypping visitors to the island. He told them to get in line, or he'd put in a barber shop and give away shaves and haircuts. He insisted on fair treatment for everyone. He didn't want the island to be a hold-up place.[8]

The first two generations of Wrigleys were not church-goers. Angle writes that Philip was never baptized and his father would bluntly ask new acquaintances, "What form of superstition do you practice?"[9] William and Ada's avowed superstition was homeopathy, a pleasant belief that asserts that within the cosmos there is a powerful force of balance. Similar to many people's belief in capitalism and ecology, homeopathy believes that imbalances do happen and a bit of management is required. In general, however, nature has balancing forces hard-wired into it. William and Ada Wrigley were not odd for being homeopaths. They fit nicely within the broader tradition of optimistic, Progressive-era, believers in metaphysical forces of goodness. As a duke and duchess of the California Bight, they wanted to help Santa Catalina Island be a model of nature's wisdom.

8. Angle, *Philip K. Wrigley*, 55.
9. Angle, *Philip K. Wrigley*, 11.

The Alexandrian Waters of San Pedro and Santa Catalina

Although not homeopaths, Philip and Helen Wrigley adopted in the 1960s the similar ideals of Southern California's most flamboyantly big-thinking architect, William Pereira. Irvine Ranch on the coast opposite the island was being developed according to an almost utopian plan orchestrated by Pereira. The second generation Wrigleys employed Pereira to design a high-minded development plan for the island, but it did not work out. After the Santa Barbara oil spill in the winter of 1969 and subsequent call for the creation of the California Coastal Commission, Philip and Helen, decided instead to create the Catalina Island Conservancy which today manages most of the island.

Even before the Wrigleys bought the island, what is now the village of Avalon attracted more than its share of people who believed the harsher Darwinian principles need not inform the ideals of their community. The Tuna Club remains a monument to the high-minded ecological principles of the island. Charles Frederick Holder, one of the California Bight's most prolific nature writers and the author of *The Channel Islands of California; A Book for the Angler, Sportsman, and Tourist*, helped found the Tuna Club on principals of balance and stewardship. Members are still supposed to "fish like gentlemen." Sport fishing, they declare, should be about giving the fish a fighting chance. Members purposely use traditional, weaker, gear and avoid modern equipment that offers technological advantage. Zane Grey, maybe the most popular author in America when he built his house overlooking Avalon, was as avid supporter of the values of Holder and a member of the Tuna Club.

For me, the most interesting of the wise naturalists of Avalon is Gene Stratton-Porter. She was already a major American novelist and naturalist when she moved to the Bight and built a vacation home in the flat, middle-ground, of Avalon. Her house is now the Singing Waters Christian Center. Sadly, she did not get to spend much time in the house before she died in 1924. She did, however, write her last novel here in Avalon, *The Keeper of the Bees*. Hollywood made the book into a movie. It is the story of a wounded war veteran who comes to the California Bight and finds spiritual and physical health as a beekeeper on the coast of Santa Monica Bay near Pacific Palisades. In the novel, commenting on books about bees, Stratton-Porter criticizes naturalists who tend to "dodge God and side-step Him and call Him 'the Spirit of the Hive.'"[10] These naturalists, she writes, wax eloquent about "Instinct" or "Nature" but refuse to recognize that they are

---

10. Porter, *Keeper of the Bees*, 145.

verging into the religious. She praises Charles Darwin as "a great scientist, one of the best," but notes that he almost went crazy trying to avoid God. She has one of her characters say Darwin "would have been a heap better off if he'd been willing to put God in where He belongs."[11] Her character points out that "a wise man," when confronted by the wonder and mystery of bees and beehives "will just take off his hat and lift his eyes to the sky and very politely he will say, 'Just God.'"[12]

Today, having come ashore, I go looking for Avalon's new history museum. Browsing the books, I pick up a new book just published: *The Life and Legacy of D. M. Renton: Pasadena and Santa Catalina Island, California, 1902-1936*. Angle had mentioned Renton in his biography of Philip Wrigley. With more storm coming, I buy the book, some groceries, and a block of ice then row back out to *Boethius*. After re-organizing the ice box and rain beginning to thrash about on deck, I lay down in my bunk with nothing to do for the rest of the day and night but read my new book.

David Renton and his wife, Elizabeth, were the Wrigley's Presbyterians. The Wrigleys, as is common with the super-rich, needed administrative assistance. They needed good managers who run things decently and keep things in good order. They needed either a Presbyterian or someone with Presbyterian ability to wrangle committees, steward resources, and keep deadlines. The Wrigleys lived mostly in Chicago. On Catalina Island, they needed an on-site general manager they could trust to develop the infrastructure, keep the books, and facilitate community-life. Renton was the man for the job. When he arrived as a young man in Pasadena looking to repair his health and find a career, the owner of a construction firm recognized him as "a good Presbyterian of high moral character" and hired him.[13] Later Wrigley hired him for the same qualities.

With Renton as the official general manager and his wife Elizabeth as the unofficial co-manager, the two set out to promote the happiness, grace, and beauty of Santa Catalina Island and its showpiece village of Avalon. Renton was a developer-designer who understood the pleasant qualities and idealistic politics of Spanish-style architecture and design. The biography has a picture of what Renton called "The Sunshine Terrace" where he developed Philip and Helen Wrigley's house along with a gathering of others, including his own. Renton envisioned, along with Philip, the

---

11. Porter, *Keeper of the Bees*, 145.
12. Porter, *Keeper of the Bees*, 145.
13. Renton, *Life and Legacy of D. M. Renton*, 7.

The Alexandrian Waters of San Pedro and Santa Catalina

pleasantly tiled waterfront with low undulating walls that are still the focal point of community life. Renton, himself, developed the wonderful Paseo el Encanto, the inside of which makes visitors feel like they are in the public square of a tiny Spanish village. The biography notes that Elizabeth Renton

> lent her considerable organizing skills to charitable and cultural organizations, drawing on her Pasadena contacts to provide speakers for social clubs and visiting musicians for community enjoyment. She quickly became a leading social figure in the town, heading committees and organizing community-wide events, as fitting complement to the dedicated General Manager. The family joined the Community Congregational Church with Elizabeth leading Sunday school classes and frequently entertaining the young participants in her home with one of [her sons] Malcolm and Arthur. She accepted an invitation to join the Mary Williams Club, the most prestigious local cultural organization for women, and soon became active as an officer, taking on major organizational responsibilities such as Chair of the Easter Sunrise Service Program and Chair of the Christmas festivities, both elaborate annual events in which most townspeople participated.[14]

I continue to read late into that stormy night and finish the book the next morning. I poke my head out of the companionway. The sky is blue, but the flags on the roof of the iconic casino building are flapping wildly. The VHF is still announcing small craft warnings. I row the dinghy ashore and begin a long, meandering walk. It is not a bad thing to be stuck in Avalon. I walk up to the combination elementary, middle, and high school. Long rows of electric golf carts and other electric vehicles are lined up. Hospitality workers are the dominant year-round population, and there are lots of kids living in Avalon. The doors of the town's one Protestant church building are unlocked. I wander in, look at the pictures on the wall, and check out the bulletin board. All seems to be going well. I say a quick prayer for the church. I then wander over a few blocks to the Roman Catholic church. Their doors are also unlocked. Inside in the foyer there are all the signs of busy church with lots of activities. I read some of the brochures in the free-literature rack. In the sanctuary I check out the artwork. I pull down the kneeler of a pew on the left side, about halfway back. I am a pilgrim. After praying for all the usual suspects in my life, I tell God that I don't want to be wrong about believing in the life and the life after death of Santa Catalina. I ask God to let me know if I am being a fool to think she

---

14. Renton, *Life and Legacy of D. M. Renton*, 280.

and San Pedro have a role here in California history. Am I a fool to think she watches over this little island church? I wait a bit in silence. I don't hear any words back, but I sense an affirmation. I willingly and spontaneously believe. As I am on my way out, I stop, and stand silently in front of a statue of Santa Catalina holding a Bible.

Santa Catalina in the foyer of St. Catherine of Alexandria Church, Avalon. (Author's photo.)

Philosophia stands next to me. I look up at her. She is at least three inches taller. She is dressed as she usually is in jeans and a red fleece. Next to her, much shorter, wearing matching untucked colorful Hawaiian shirts over baggy white shorts, are Beatrice and Dante Alighieri. They both have sun glasses pushed up into the hair above their foreheads. All three are looking at the statue.

"I should have added her to my poem," says Dante.

"Your poem's plenty long," says Beatrice.

Dante leans forward to look down the line of us at me. "I do have Boethius in it," he says. "Canto ten."

He pauses, leans his head back, then recites in a deep-timbered voice:

> The body whence 'twas hunted forth is lying
> Down in Cieldauro, and from martyrdom
> And banishment it came unto this peace.[15]

---

15. Dante, *Paradiso*, 127–29.

The Alexandrian Waters of San Pedro and Santa Catalina

Philosophia interrupts rather grumpily, "You could have named him. Readers today have to go to the footnotes to understand the reference to Cieldauro. You could have at least given the name of the church in the more recognizable form of San Pietro in Ciel d'Oro."

"It poetry!" Dante snaps back.

I break in to ask, "What are you two talking about?"

Beatrice speaks up. "Boethius is buried in Pavia in a church named St. Peter in the Golden Sky. St. Augustine is also buried there."

"Augustine, Santa Monica's son," I ask incredulously, "is buried in Pavia in the same church as Boethius?"

"Yes," says *Philosophia*. "Venerable Bede tells the story of how Augustine's bones were removed to Italy and buried there."

Dante then pipes in: "Bede is also in Canto ten." He then starts to quote himself,

> See farther onward flame the burning breath
> Of Isidore, of Beda, and of Richard . . . ."[16]

"Okay, okay," Beatrice interrupts. "We've got to get going. The ferry back to the mainland leaves soon." She tells *Philosophia* and me that Dante has promised her some American ice cream before they get in line for the boat.

"I'll go with you," says *Philosophia*. "I would like some ice cream."

As they walk out, I turn to look again at Santa Catalina. She has her book and wheel. She is the great matron of this island and the waters of between here and San Diego. I smile at her and walk out.

---

16. Dante, *Paradiso*, 130–31.

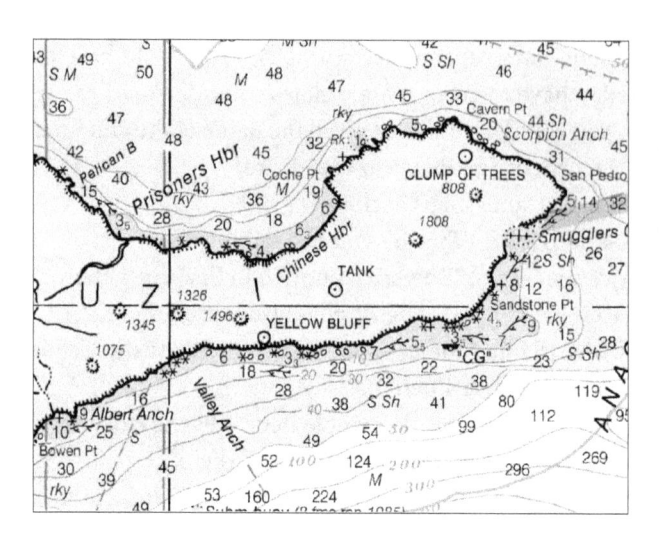

The east end of Santa Cruz Island, note Pelican Bay west of Prisoner's Harbor on the north side. (NOAA charts.)

Prisoners and Pelicans on Santa Cruz Island

Tomorrow, we will sail to Santa Cruz Island, the island of the Holy Cross, an island named for the central moment in history, the fullness and fulfillment of time, the event in which death trampled death. Tonight we are anchored in twenty-five feet of water near Bird Rock on the outer edge of Isthmus Cove, Santa Catalina Island. I sit in the cockpit looking up at our cross-shaped mast, highlighted against a dark starry sky by the battery-powered lamp I am using in the cockpit. Jesus said: "Whoever wants to be my disciple must deny themselves and take up their cross and follow me," and soon after his death, resurrection, and ascension into heaven the cross, an instrument of execution, became the most important, enduring, symbol of Christianity.[1] The Patron Saint of Ventura tells us that St. Francis of Assisi not only heard Jesus speak to him from a cross, Francis' prayers to be like Jesus were answered by being allowed to suffer like Christ. Nail wounds appeared in his feet and hands along with a sword cut in his side.

1. Matthew 16:24.

Christianity is not an easy religion. To be a Christian is first and foremost to be part of the fellowship of Christ's suffering. Christianity is about humanity screwing up everything, and the Creator fixing things by humbling the divine self as a God-man, submitting to death on a cross. Santa Cruz Island is a sign pointing to this reality. Even back to the earliest centuries, Christians have been advised to be on the lookout for cross-shapes. Justin Martyr, one of the earliest of Christian writers, put the mast of sailboats at the head of his list of cross-shapes to contemplate.[2] Tomorrow we sail as pilgrims into a sign of this reality to investigate with wonder and speculate with devotion.

The Golden Legend, the late medieval anthology of Christian stories that serves well as a cruising guide to the thicker aspects of the California Bight, tells stories even about the wood used to build the cross on which Jesus hung. First, the wood originally came from the *Tree of Mercy* in the Garden of Eden. After the banishment of Adam and Eve, the archangel San Miguel gave a shoot of this tree to one of Adam's sons who had come back to the gates of Paradise to get help for his sick father. This shoot was eventually replanted in Lebanon, became lost as part of a forest, and unknowingly was used in the construction of Jerusalem. In one story, the wood was unknowingly used in the construction of a bridge. The Queen of Ethiopia learned of this and saw the bridge in a vision that also told her the savior of the world would hang from this wood. She sent a letter about this to King Solomon, who then buried the wood. After a thousand more years, the wood surfaced at the time of Christ. When told to build a cross for Jesus' execution, Roman soldiers unknowingly used this wood. *The Golden Legend* goes on to say, three hundred years later, archaeologists working for Emperor Constantine's mother, St. Helena, rediscovered the cross. The holiness of the wood was unclear until a sick boy being carried nearby was miraculously healed. Santa Cruz is named for this relentless wood, born of *The Tree of Mercy*, a bit of the First Paradise hidden in this fallen world, destined to serve in the recreation of the Second Paradise.[3] St. Paul writes "the message of the cross is foolishness to those who are perishing, but to us who are being saved it is the power of God."[4]

Santa Cruz is the most meaningful of the signs and symbols of the California Bight that the patron saint of Ventura says we must investigate

---

2. Justin Martyr, *First Apology*, 55.
3. Jacobus de Voragine, "Finding of the Holy Cross," 277-284.
4. 1 Corinthians 1:18.

with wonder and speculate about with devotion. I remember in graduate school discussing the history of the cross in the fourth floor hallway of Phelps Hall at UC Santa Barbara. Professor Harold Drake had the office across the hall and was writing an article on the search for the cross during the Constantinian period of Roman history. Eventually, some of what he told us graduate students appeared in his excellent book: *A Century of Miracles: Christians, Pagans, Jews, and the Supernatural.* I fondly remember those conversations. I shared an office with Miriam, the wife of Tim Vivian, and we were both fascinated by the history of Christianity. From the large-windowed conference room down the hall from our office we could see Santa Cruz Island. We lived in the presence of Santa Cruz Island. Tomorrow, *Boethius* and I sail to the island, into the presence of the Holy Cross, into the center of time.

Tonight, in the lamplight, I study, not *The Golden Legend*, but a nautical chart of the northern California Bight. I have it spread in the cockpit on the seat across from me. The light of the lamp is not bright, and I have to lean close. The chart delineates an ecosystem of angels and saints coordinated by an island named for the Holy Cross. It is an anthology of names with stories behind each. Gathered as a whole, the chart is an index to the whole story from Paradise Lost to Paradise Regained. Place names on the chart have levels of meaning ranging from great significance to little, and I do not pretend to understand the whole. Some seem merely descriptive: "Yellow Bluff" and "Cavern Point." Some memorialize the history of the people on the island: "Chinese Harbor" and "Smugglers Cove." Some, such as "Scorpion Anchorage," seem random but are worthy of investigating whether they contribute to the larger whole. Tomorrow we will anchor at Scorpion on the east end of the island.

I lean back and look toward the glow of San Pedro across the channel. We are anchored in Alexandrian waters. I am encouraged to stretch my mind. I apply physiologic method: Is there anything in the Bible that connects a scorpion to the Holy Cross? Maybe. The Book of Hosea has a line about ransoming people from the power of Sheol: "O Sheol, where is your sting?"[5] Paul in the New Testament has it: "O Death, where is your sting?"[6] In the ecosystem of faith, death has no sting because of Santa Cruz. Death is merely an inevitable passage into another stage of life.

---

5. Hosea 13:14.
6. 1 Corinthians 15:55.

Prisoners and Pelicans on Santa Cruz Island

Physiologic method encourages me to keep reaching for meaning. I need to find a biblical allegory of death. Baptism! Baptism is a symbol of the passage from life to life through a short, temporary, death. *Physiologia* recommends now I create a parable, an analogy, to expand upon the subject. I like to scuba-dive along the edge of Scorpion Anchorage. Above water, I see dry land, muted colors, and scruffy vegetation. Then, suppressing instincts of self-preservation, I allow air from my vest to bubble free as weights around my waist pull me down below the surface of the water. Submerged, the island reveals itself teeming with life and color. Life then life after death, but only after I let go of one world in hope of another. I am not sure this is sermon worthy, but we pilgrims are supposed to push ourselves using such methods of thinking. I discover hope by studying a nautical chart published by the United States government.

I suppose many think such mental meanderings foolish. I should be checking my gear for weaknesses and looking at the chart merely for data. *Boethius* and I agree. We are fools by the standards of many. As pilgrims though, being foolish thickens our experience.

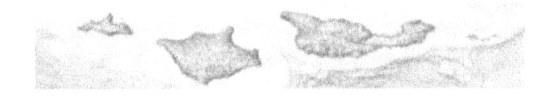

IN THE MORNING, after a cup of coffee, we motor to the fuel dock and wait for it to open. After the attendant arrives, we go through the process of stringing a big fuel hose onto *Boethius* from the dock. The attendant seems a little put-out that I only want a couple of gallons. I smile and try a little small talk, but he says little and turns his back on us. We loose ourselves from the dock, round northward after getting out into San Pedro Channel, and begin motoring under a thick marine layer through a flat glassy sea. We expect the wind to fill in later in the morning. After we are past the end of the island with no land visible ahead, I settle in to reading a book while the autopilot steers. The motor produces enough electricity to keep the autopilot pulling and pushing the tiller back and forth as we climb up and over swells that have travelled thousands of miles.

A few hours later, around noon, there is still no wind. After another hour, there are whispers of wind creating patches of surface turbulence, but for the most part, the bow continues to plow through gentle undulations of glassy water. The marine layer has not dissipated and visibility is only a mile or so. I put down the book and become more vigilant as we near the shipping lanes. Another hour later, I feel a bit of something on my cheek and the flag raises up with a flutter. I twist the throttle of the motor back to idle, stand up, and try to turn my body into a wind-gauge. The flag droops. We languish and roll side to side. "Situation Unitarian!" I declare loudly to the sky, then twist the throttle back to its former position. A couple hours later, heading into late afternoon, the surface of the water is still glassy and the marine layer persists. The island should be in sight, but I cannot see it. My handheld GPS shows twelve and a half nautical miles to Scorpion Anchorage. I am frustrated. I surmise that we are experiencing classic symptoms of a strong Catalina Eddy. There are probably high winds to the west of us blowing southward outside of San Miguel and San Nicholas Islands. To the north of us, a slice of that wind is blowing eastward through the Santa Barbara Channel. To the south of us, underneath Santa Catalina Island, another slice of those winds is swirling eastward into San Diego. To the east of us, there are light winds flowing northward that have swerved up the coast after heading into San Diego. *Boethius* and I are becalmed in the eye of a wind-eddy. Winds all around us blowing in three different directions, and we've got nothing right here, right now.

There is a long tradition among frustrated sailors who complain about lack of wind or too many things going wrong. To a sailor, the sign of Jonah is sign of being cursed. For Christians the sign of Jonah is a sign of Jesus being cursed, Jesus taking on human sin and descending into hell for three days. Jesus tells a group of Pharisees who are demanding a sign they will not get one, "except the sign of Jonah."[7] It is not clear in the Bible whether the story of Jonah is a mixture of fact and allegory or just allegory; however, Jonah is a savior willing to sacrifice himself for his fellow sailors. He is a type or figure foreshadowing the story of Jesus. Jonah's three days in the belly of "a great fish"—maybe Leviathan itself—points to Jesus spending Friday night, all day Saturday, and early Sunday, three days, in Hell. *Boethius* and I are sailing, or more accurately, puttering, toward the island of the sign of Jonah, an island about a curse, a place where three days does not mean seventy-two hours, a place where an instrument of execution means life.

About an hour later in the afternoon, in sight of the island, wind arrives. I turn off the motor, haul up the sails, and *Boethius* sinks her leeward hull as she surges toward the passage between Anacapa and Santa Cruz islands. A big blow is running eastward in Windy Lane dumping on us a

---

7. Matthew 12:38–41; 16:4. See also Luke 11:29–32.

Prisoners and Pelicans on Santa Cruz Island

sidetracked wind. The bow intermittently lifts spray up onto the cabin top. In the passage we tack back and forth between the islands. Around seven o'clock we get into the lee of Cavern Point and drop anchor in Scorpion Anchorage. The trip took twelve hours from the Isthmus to Scorpion. This is fast run for *Boethius*. Motoring most of the day on a flat sea makes us travel quicker, but not better.

Boethius in foreground at Scorpion Anchorage, Santa Cruz Island.
(Author's photo from cliffs near Cavern Point.)

THERE IS A STORY, learned from a descendent of the *Cruzeño* Indians named Fernando Librado, (also named *Kitsepawit*), about a queen named *Encarnación* who lived here on the east end of Santa Cruz Island. Librado is the source of many of the names of people and places prior to Spanish settlement of the Santa Barbara Channel. He learned the story of *Encarnación* from his grandparents who had learned it from theirs. The story of *Encarnación* begins with the islanders feuding with each other. A prophet tells the pregnant-wife of a village leader, probably at Scorpion, her baby will unite and rule over all the villages of all four islands. A girl is born, and when she is grown, the islanders don't want to be unified under her rule. Feuds continue until the prophet calls the village leaders together for a peace conference. Librado said the islanders "decided to make peace by declaring the woman captain, or princess, of all four islands. She was above all other captains, and her name and official title was *Luhui*, which means 'native.' Her Christian name was *Encarnación*."[8]

Without Librado we would know nothing of this, but it appears that for a short period, a princess of peace and unity ruled in some way over all four islands from her capitol near where *Boethius* and I are anchored. Coincidentally, she was named for the Christian doctrine of the God-man, the Incarnation, the history of the Prince of Peace who come to earth to die on Santa Cruz, eventually the name of this island.

Boethius and I collect and ponder stories contrary to academic expectation such as an empress of the four islands and coincidences such as her name coordinated to the later name of the island. This is an island that demands big thinking that sets aside the expectations of logic. We are anchored to an island named for the foolishness of the Holy Cross.

I am stretched athwart in the cockpit, leaning against a cushion, looking up at the stars, braced against the roll of the boat. Awkward swells that have turned the corner of the island, come at us broadside. Sometimes they pitch us violently side to side as they roll underneath us. Appropriately braced, I stare at the stars. I laugh. These stars destabilize my sense of time. There is no one "now" when I look at them. Each twinkle of light reports a different origination time in the distant past. My "now" is a gathering of millions of different "nows." Here at anchor, the night sky teaches a complicated, mysterious, biblical sense of time.

Boethius, in *De Fide Catholica*, refers to the three days of Jesus' death on Friday afternoon and resurrection on Sunday morning with the biblical language of *In ultimis temporibus*, "the last days of time."[9] These three last days are symbolized by the one day, the Friday on the cross. The End of Time, its fullness, its completeness, is declared by Jesus when he gasps, "It is finished." Chronology is not a line. It is a tide. We today live in the ebb. Salvation occurred when three days collapsed into one moment. The sum of the salvation equation is in the middle.

The Patron Saint of Ventura cites the son of Santa Monica and quotes Boethius when he says numbers are the language of the Creator.[10] But

---

8. Librado, *Eye of the Flute*, 15.
9. Boethius, *De Fide Catholica*, 66, 67.
10. Bonaventure, *Soul's Journey into God*, 75.

Prisoners and Pelicans on Santa Cruz Island

Bonaventure, Augustine, and Boethius were not referring to merely the numbering systems of modern clocks, calculators, and measuring sticks. All three wise men agree that we should keep an eye out for threes. The triune Creator embedded threeness into creation. Threeness is a oneness. Bonaventure, in his pilgrim manual, says there are seven different kinds of numbers. The one *Boethius* and I enjoy the most is *expressive numbers*. These numbers "proceed from the soul into the body, as seen in gestures and dance."[11] Sailing is a form of *expressive numbers*.

Star gazing while anchored to Santa Cruz Island encourages me to ponder the mysteries of numbers and time. I look up at the cross-shaped mast and spreaders of *Boethius* as they wave back and forth in front of the stars with every swell that circles round Cavern Point and rolls us from to side. *Boethius* and I are pilgrim-sailors. We are cosmologists between water and sky. At this thought, I laugh. I then get up and walk forward across the deck to check the anchor. I can't see it, but I bend down and can feel the tension on the rode. Yes, the anchor is holding.

IN THE MORNING, coffee mug in hand, I watch a line of California Brown Pelicans fly close in through our anchorage. When I was young this kind of pelican was headed toward extinction. The pesticide DDT made their egg shells weak. Today, with pesticide regulation, the California Browns flourish. Most days as *Boethius* and I leave or return to our mooring, we watch, and are watched back, by pelicans sitting on the top of piers, at the end of docks, and on the stern rails of tied-up fishing trawlers. Along the shore of the Bight, sometimes alone and sometimes in long lines, they glide, wings outstretched and unmoving, just a few inches above the water, disappearing and reappearing in the roll of ocean swells. *Boethius* and I keep watch for anything having to do with pelicans. Dante writes of Jesus as "Our pelican."[12] *Boethius* has what is called a pelican hook—it looks like a pelican—as part of its safety system. Part of the fun of being a Christian is the daily treasure-hunt for signs, symbols, and sacraments.

---

11. Bonaventure, *Soul's Journey into God*, 74.
12. Dante, *Paradiso*, 113.

Pelican hook on *Boethius*. (Author's photo.)

Santa Cruz Island has a Pelican Bay. It is best remembered historically for the hospitality of Margaret Eaton. She was an immigrant of deep Catholic piety whose story is told in *Diary of a Sea Captain's Life: Tales of Santa Cruz Island*. Born in 1876 and raised as an orphan in Canada, she immigrated to California to work in the tourist industry. The great beach hotels of the era needed lots of cheap labor and would recruit and pay for young women to immigrate. Margaret first worked at the Hotel del Coronado in San Diego then transferred to the Potter Hotel in Santa Barbara. After marriage and the death of her first baby, she followed her fisherman-husband into a squatters-life on various beaches around Santa Cruz Island. Vague laws and generous custom allowed poor people to live in the intertidal zone of the more isolated parts of the Bight. On Santa Cruz Island, Margaret lived homeless, all the while raising a daughter and dealing with an unfaithful and inattentive husband. In her "diary" assembled by her daughter, she appears as both a happy woman and a Woman of Sorrows. She thanks God often for her blessings. The happiest chapter of the book tells of an all-island Christmas dinner. Down and out fishermen, living along the edges of the islands, were invited to the Eaton's camp and each was to bring something from the bounty of the sea to contribute. "It was an ideal Christmas morning," she writes, "the weather was cold and clear, and the birds were singing in chorus. A very happy feeling came over me; I imagine it was the Christmas Spirit."[13]

Her most unhappy story is of drunken rowdies coming after her and her daughter at Scorpion Anchorage. Her husband is away. A visiting friend calls out to some Portuguese fisherman to come closer in to rescue the women. Margaret, her daughter, and the man push a skiff off the beach and point it into oncoming surf. After they jump in a steep wave stands the

---

13. Eaton, *Diary of a Captain's Wife*, 110.

skiff straight up on its stern, but a strong pull by the friend on the oars roll it forward over the top of the breaking wave. By then the rowdies on the beach are throwing rocks. Gunfire hits the pilothouse of the fishing boat. Margaret and Vera clamor over the side and lay down on bags of live crawfish. The next day, finding her husband in Santa Barbara, she tells him she wants to move to Pelican Bay. She writes, "While in Santa Barbara I took Vera to the beach every day. I looked across the channel to the islands and longed to be back there again. I knew that at Pelican Bay everything would be fine. I was tired of town already."[14]

Back on the island, Margaret's gift of hospitality brings her into contact with the movie industry using the island for films. By agreement with the island owners and the movie production companies, Margaret oversees a kitchen, dining hall, tent-dormitories on the cliff above Pelican Bay. But this happiness is not sustainable. A Woman of Sorrows, she is forced to divorce her alcoholic and unfaithful husband. The island owners also refuse to continue giving her permission to do this work. They hope to build their own hotel at Prisoner's Harbor. And the federal government, in the interests of environmental preservation, insists on eradicating squatters from the inter-tidal zones of the islands. Alone, getting old, late in the 1930s, Margaret moved to Hollywood to live with her daughter.

As I watch the pelicans and think of Margaret Eaton's love of life in the tidal zone of Santa Cruz Island, I think also of Rachel Carson's book *The Edge of the Sea*. She too lived on the seashore and loved life in the tidal zone. She described the shore as an "enchanted place on the threshold of the sea" where "the realities that possessed my mind were far from those of the land world."[15] Like me, she was raised Presbyterian with Presbyterian sensibilities about the Creator and creation. She loved the Christian-nature novels of Gene Stratton Porter whose house is in Avalon on Santa Catalina Island. In *The Edge of the Sea,* she ends her chapter on "The Marginal World" believing what I believe here in Scorpion Anchorage:

> Underlying the beauty of the spectacle there is meaning and significance. It is the elusiveness of that meaning that haunts us, that sends us again and again into the natural world where the key to the riddle is hidden. It sends us back to the edge of the sea, where the drama of life played its first scene on earth and perhaps even its prelude; where the forces of evolution are at work today, as they

14. Eaton, *Diary of a Captain's Wife*, 168. See 162–68.
15. Carson, *Edge of the Sea*, 423.

have been since the appearance of what we know as life; and where the spectacle of living creatures faced by the cosmic realities of their world is crystal clear."[16]

Between here and Pelican Bay is Prisoner's Harbor, which seems to me to be a blatant Boethian mixture of history and allegory. The story of its name is best told by an eyewitness: Angustias de la Guerra, the young woman whose little sister Anita was the bride at the wedding described by Richard Henry Dana. When Angustias was about fourteen or fifteen years old, a ship arrived in Santa Barbara carrying convicts sent up from Mexico to be relocated in California. Delivered on the beach, most of the convicts were naked, weak from the journey, and without provisions. Angustias remembers her father, José de la Guerra, the visionary head of the most powerful family in California, eventually the patron of California's first academy and supporter of Governor Figueroa's plans for stabilizing California's future, coming down to the beach, then demanding the prisoners be given baths. De la Guerra personally supplied them with clothes and blankets before gathering them in the courtyard in front of his house, the yard where a few years later Dana will see the wedding fiesta. Angustias remembers her father telling the gathered prisoners of California's bounty if they will take up an honest living:

> He assured them that he would be like a father to all who behaved well. If anybody found himself in need, that person was to come to my father for help. This may seem as if I am singing my father's praises, but besides being the truth, my reason for relating this episode is my desire to firmly impress upon people that those unfortunate Mexicans never gave any reason for complaints. They all behaved well after that.[17]

Here on the California Bight prisoners were offered redemption. De la Guerra wants to facilitate a type of atonement. Some of these prisoners went to work for the de la Guerra family and various other families in Santa Barbara. There were, however, some prisoners who appeared to be dangerous criminals. The commandant of the presidio insisted that they should be isolated on Santa Cruz Island. The island, the commandant decided, might serve as a self-governing prison colony. The colonists were given provisions, including cattle and horses, and were landed at what is now called

---

16. Carson, *Edge of the Sea*, 426–27.

17. Beebe and Senkewicz, *Testimonios*, 213. See also Pubols, *Father of All*, who interprets this quote differently.

Prisoner's Harbor. They did not, however, take to the island opportunity. Not long after, Angustias says, there was a fire on the island. She remembers seeing it from Santa Barbara. The prisoners by way of raft returned to the mainland, letting the channel current take them down toward Carpinteria where they were jailed and whipped. Eventually, Angustias says, they returned to Santa Barbara and were offered a new life. In the telling of this, she tells also of earlier prisoners from Mexico that were accepted into the population of the Bight. She says that children like her were not allowed to know who those former prisoners were. "Thus we could never, at any time, point out a family that had the misfortune of being related to a person who had been a criminal."[18] Criminals redeemed! Prisoner's Harbor on Santa Cruz Island and Casa de la Guerra in Santa Barbara tell happy stories of prisoner's set free.

But we must remember that the story of the Holy Cross is a violent story of the end of a curse. Anchored still at Scorpion, I make a second cup of coffee and return to the cockpit to ponder the violence, suffering, and death poured into this island over the last few decades in an attempt to return it to what it was like before humans started screwing it up. Over the fifteen years I regularly took California history students to this island, the rangers who talked to us became increasingly optimistic about their ability as good managers, stewards, and economists to re-create the islands' natural balances. In 2017, the National Parks Service produced the video "Restoring the Balance: Santa Cruz Island"[19] about saving an indigenous species of island fox by replacing fox-hunting Golden Eagles with non-fox-eating Bald Eagles. Sad to say, but necessary, for the work, thousands of invasive wild boar had to be sacrificed, shot from helicopters and left to die. What were experiments back in 2005 or 2006 when rangers first talked to my students have become triumphal stories of scientific eco-management.

T. C. Boyle, a popular novelist who lives on the Bight, in *When the Killing is Done*, turns the history of such killings on the island into a lesson on the moral complexities of ecology. The most interesting characters in the novel are Anise Reed and Alma Boyd Takesue. Anise is an animal activist who grew up on the old cattle ranch here at Scorpion where her mother Rita was the cook. Alma is a biologist from UC Berkeley working for the

---

18. Beebe and Senkewicz, *Testimonios*, 214.

19. "Restoring Balance: Santa Cruz Island," *National Park Service*, https://www.nps.gov/chis/learn/photosmultimedia/restoring-balance-santa-cruz-island-long-version.htm.

National Parks Service, helping manage the programmatic killing of invasive species. Anise and her mom are pure lovers of Santa Cruz Island. They lived here. The two are reminiscent of Vera and Margaret Eaton in *Diary of Sea Captain's Wife*. Alma, the outsider ranger-biologist, is also a lover of the island, but the love is more abstract and comes with an academic environmentalist's perspective. The novel ends with Alma, Rita, and the ashes of Anise at Scorpion Anchorage and Ranch. They arrive on the same boat. Alma has come to a triumphal meeting with others in the National Park Service to celebrate what they are acheiving. Anise is now dead, a casualty in the fight for animal rights. Rita takes her ashes high up to a bluff to pour out, sits under some oak trees, and sings folk songs. The book ends with a small island fox, one of the species that Alma has saved from invasive Golden Eagles, in the distance, listening to Rita sing, honoring the passage of Anise.

This island, named for the Holy Cross, has much to teach. Like a florist I arrange my ponderings. At anchor, *Boethius* and I enjoy the sound of small breakers on the pebbly shore. We listen to the wind begin to freshen in our rigging. We are anchored to an island mixture of facts and allegory. Above us is a cross-shaped mast.

ON OUR RETURN to home waters we sail first to Ventura Harbor, then along the coast southward. As we leave Ventura, following the shoreline down to Point Hueneme, my investigations and speculations turn from thoughts of Santa Cruz to the curse of sin. Jesus' death on Santa Cruz restores the balance and begins the new-creation, but we still live in the ebb tide of that fullness. We are still cursed, flawed in our nature. Adam and Eve sinned for us all, and there is nothing good that we cannot screw up. Miriam Pawel in her new biography of César Chávez says that somewhere along this coast Chavez and a Presbyterian minister named Chris Hartmire planned to create a communal farm that would serve as the mother-house for a new religious order. Chávez was a religious visionary much more than a union organizer. He believed he was called by God and helped by Our Lady of Guadalupe to uphold the cause of the poor, encourage Chicano pride, promote the equality of all peoples, and establish communities of peace and justice. He modeled his political strategy on the passivism of Mahatma Ghandi and St. Francis of Assisi. Like Junípero Serra, he optimistically believed he could bureaucratically create little cities-on-a-hill that God would bless and multiply. Like Junípero Serra, he drove himself and others hard. His first established community is now the César Chávez National Monument in the Tehachapi Mountains, named *La Paz*. It is dedicated to Our Lady of Peace. With his long-time friend and aid, Chris Hartmire, Chávez wanted to establish another Christian commune along this coast called *Los Menos*, "The Least," as in the Bible where Jesus, in parable form, says "Truly I tell you, whatever you did for one of the least of these brothers and sisters of mine, you did for me."[20] Here along this coast Chávez wanted Hartmire to help him build a utopian farm community centered in a trans-denominational church, a school, and a dining hall where all would eat together.

Sadly, in this sinful world, Satan is able to use power, fame, and high ideals for evil. The *Snake Path* is a truth. The serpent depicted in La Jolla does not rest. Chávez became too sure of himself. Already at *La Paz*, Chávez had become infected with the abusive doctrines and methods of Synanon, a cult-like encounter-group whose mother house was on the beach in Santa Monica. Chávez's vision of communal life became fused with encounter sessions that involved yelling at one another, undermining people's self-worth, and infecting relationships with doubt and distrust. Chávez, himself, destroyed many of his highest hopes and closest friendships. He turned against Hartmire, and all plans for a *Los Menos* on this coast were lost.[21]

As *Boethius* and I start to separate from the coast on our southward course we can dimly see the west side of Point Dume through a thin marine layer. Joan Didion lived over there when I was in college. I remember being assigned her relatively new collection of essays called *Slouching Toward Bethlehem*. She wrote of the flower children, supposedly happy and free. In the essay, Didion exposed the dysfunctional reality of the counter-culture, of family disintegration, male abuse of drug-addled women, abortions, and children being raised without love and wholeness. She saw the true heart of darkness in what others were portraying as stardust and golden. From her house just outside of Santa Monica Bay, she saw a blood dimmed tide rising and the beast slouching toward Bethlehem.

Many on this coast have warned that the center does not hold in this fallen world of sin. The reality of Satan, many affirm, must be confronted.

20. Matthew 25:40.
21. Pawel, *Cesar Chavez*, 361–62; 461–62.

This is the coast that inspired Thomas Mann's *Doctor Faustus* and Bob Dylan's "Gotta Serve Somebody." This coast is inhabited by many in the entertainment industry who know the most powerful stories portray the reality of personal evil. Jon Braun, one of the founders of St. Katherine University, while living in Isla Vista, wrote the book *Whatever Happened to Hell?* The book is about how Bible-based, traditional, Christianity cannot avoid the reality of Satan and hell. At the same time Braun was writing his book about hell, the history department at UC Santa Barbara hired Jeffrey Burton Russell who was writing the second of his five volume history of the devil and evil. Russell is now retired, but I took classes from him in my twenties. I suspect that it was Professor Russell who first recommended I read Boethius's *The Consolation of Philosophy*. Russell taught us that history points to truths. History is not merely, as cynics would have it, the tricks we play on the dead. Russell inspired his students to believe history is a tool that illuminates realities that are wider and deeper than what most university disciplines are able to illuminate. His books on the history of Satan teach that personified good and evil are realities and their existence can be traced in the ways people have reported their experiences of them over thousands of years. God and Satan, heaven and hell, have evidence for their existence in the accumulation of beliefs and experiences.

 I was teaching in Indiana when Russell sent me a copy of the last in this series of books. It came with good news and bad. The good news was that the book is dedicated to me and a group of my friends including Tim and Miriam Vivian. The bad news is that I have a book dedicated, in part, to me, titled *The Prince of Darkness: Radical Evil and the Power of Good in History*.

 Philosophia joins *Boethius* and me as we sail with Santa Monica Bay to port and Point Vicente lighthouse up ahead. It is late afternoon and we are sailing happily in Presbyterian conditions. The wind is from our starboard quarter. *Philosophia* sits athwart the cockpit next to me. Our feet pressed against the leeward cockpit to give each of us stability. I smile at her but don't have anything to say. She smiles back then turns to admire the transition from south Santa Monica Bay's gentle curve of beaches to the rugged cliffs of Palos Verdes. After a half hour of silence, I again look over at her. She smiles but does not face me. She is watching several nearby pelicans. I turn back and together we watch a pelican gracefully fly close in to us with wings spread wide. Abruptly, it flies sharply upwards to seventy-five, maybe a hundred feet, circles, stalls, partly folds in its wings, stretches out its neck, then shoots, arrow-like, a downward course toward the water. Splash! It hits the water, disappears for a second, then pops up to the surface in buoy form. With self-satisfaction it flings its head back to let a fish slide down its throat.

"This world!" she declares loudly after watching the pelican's liturgy. "So beautiful. So terrible."

Together, we continue sailing, watching more pelicans as we pass the lighthouse at Point Vicente and surge toward the lighthouse at Point Fermin. At dusk, in the brisk wind that concentrates at Point Fermin, we gybe and are driven hard toward the stubby light-station on the breakwater that marks the entry to Los Angeles Harbor. There is an industrial sadness in the air. Huge tankers hunker in the distance and tall cranes loom in the twilight. As we round Los Angeles Light and pass into flat water, I haul in the sheets and bring the bow up far into the wind. *Philosophia* sits silently, pensively, as we tack up into the free anchorage in the lee of Point Fermin.

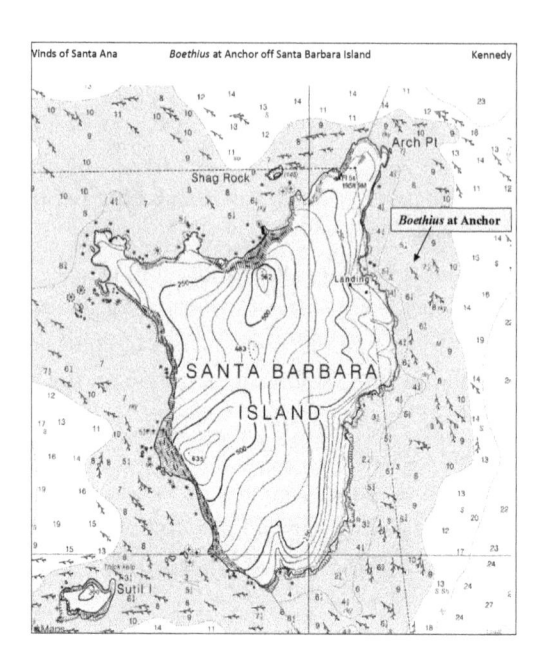

Santa Barbara Island. (NOAA charts.)

Santa Barbara Island

There is six thousand feet of water under *Boethius* and no land in sight. We are stretched out. The wind is perfect. The sheets eased. We are sailing large. The sky is blue and the sun shining. The water makes a whooshing sound as the bubbles of our wake spread out and conform to the low undulating swells behind us. We have been to Santa Barbara city and are on a four-day return pilgrimage to our home waters in San Diego Bay. Tonight we will anchor off tiny Santa Barbara Island. "Off" is the key word. The island is the top of a mountain that rises steep out of deep water. There is no protected anchorage. I have taken students to the island a couple times. In the waters on the east side of the island, we dropped kayaks at the outer edge of a kelp forest to explore the nearby majestic arch, venture into the surge beneath the high cliffs, and enjoy a sense of wild isolation. As the students paddled away from the yacht, two in each of three inflatable

Santa Barbara Island

kayaks, I warned them not to take risks. I stood watch on the cabin roof. Getting onto Santa Barbara Island from a small boat is not easy. There is a metal ladder that leads up to a platform at the bottom of a metal staircase that climbs, almost vertical, to the top of the island. Nautical charts mark it as a "Landing," but it is dangerous for small boats in anything but calm water. I watched as the students approached it, but the surge against the rocks was strong. They wisely paddled away.

On this day, I have no students with me. It is early afternoon, and *Boethius* and I are still miles from the island. I sit, back to the wind, feet wide and braced, left hand on tiller, facing forward, body leaned slightly aft. During the hours when no land is in sight, I steer solely by compass, relying on the mysteries of magnetism, relying on the ability of the compass to register the flow of things I cannot see. I am one of those who still believe magnetism has soul. Nautical charts teach the restlessness of magnetism and mark its local anomalies. Magnetic North is nature's north. Sailors are supposed to buy new charts every three years because nature's north wanders in unpredictable ways. The compass on *Boethius* registers the directional flow of rivers of unseen electromagnetism that run between a real north and a real south. So called "True North" is not real. True North is a geometer's abstraction, a useful fiction. Out here with no land in sight and deep water underneath, *Boethius* offers me her compass by which to steer.

Out here, crossing a deep sea, powered by winds, using a compass as guide, I distrust the academic fictions to which society is overly committed. Those who trust in True North are the same kind of people who say St. Barbara never existed. There is no good evidence to place her on a timeline. Chronological and geographical charts can't designate her precise longitude and latitude. Lots of people who live on land in Santa Barbara comfortably refer to her as a myth. Students and faculty at a university named for her smile at those who think the story true, as told in the *Golden Legend*, how she was abused by her father and executed by him because she clung to her faith.

I remember, back around 1990, skimming through a booklet on St. Barbara while standing in the mission gift shop in Santa Barbara. The author, a Franciscan, admits up front that her story seems more poetry than history. "Her spirit found expression in the lyrics of the bards where she lived in fact and in fancy."[1] At the booklet's end, however, was an account of endangered soldiers in the Vietnam War calling upon her for help (oddly,

---

1. Haas, *Santa Barbara*, 2.

she is the patron saint of artillery brigades). The soldiers who prayed told of receiving her help and sensing her presence. While I could have dismissed their testimony as thin evidence, I was instead affirmed. Like the magnetic flow registered by a compass, history records many accounts of Santa Barbara looking after those who have called upon her. Should I deny the truth of these testimonies because the True-Northers have doubts? As I took the booklet to the cashier, I said to myself "I believe." I still do. I recognize I might be wrong. I allow for my error and will never insist on the historical existence of St. Barbara. On the other hand, I was, at the time, standing in her mission. I have lived in her city, gone to her university, and sailed in her channel. Today I am sailing to her island. The California Bight encourages me to give her the benefit of the doubt. I am a child of this coast and these islands.

We are having a great day. *Boethius* is like a big dog straining ahead, pulling against its leash. Although my upper body swings back and forth with the rush of the boat through swells, I feel no need to reef sails. We laugh, *Boethius* and me. Out here under a clear sky, over a deep sea, it is easy to believe. We are evangelicals! We are believers in good news for all creation. We are pilgrims splashing in concert with the pilgrimage of the California Bight. I start to sing loudly and boisterously the old hymn with the bouncy Mozart tune:

> Joyful, joyful, we adore thee,
> God of glory, Lord of love;
> Hearts unfold like flow'rs before thee,
> Op'ning to the sun above.
> Melt the clouds of sin and sadness;
> Drive the dark of doubt away;
> Giver or immortal gladness,
> Fill us with the light of day!
>
> All your works with joy surround Thee,
> Earth and heav'n reflect your rays,
> Stars and angels sing around Thee,
> Centre of unbroken praise
> Field and forest, vale and mountain,
> Flow'ry meadow, flashing sea,
> Chanting bird and flowing fountain
> Praising Thee eternally![2]

---

2. Van Dyke, *Hymn to Joy*, verses 1–2.

Santa Barbara Island

The Bight is best experienced by sailing its waters. Out here, we sail large and full. Out here, we sail among a cloud of witnesses: Santa Catalina, San Buenaventura, San Diego, Santa Ana, San Pedro, Santa Monica, San Gabriel, Santa Clara, San Miguel, Santa Rosa, San Nicholas, Santa Clara, San Clemente, Santa Margarita, and San Luis Rey. Tonight we will anchor under the patronage of Santa Barbara. Today we sail inside of a hymn. We are loved, watched over, and encouraged to tell the world about the mystery of our faith: Christ has died. Christ is risen. Christ will come again.

By mid-afternoon the island is in sight. Late-afternoon we drop anchor in forty-five feet of water just outside of large swaths of floating kelp. I lay out one hundred and seventy-five feet of chain and another two hundred feet of rope. We anchor far enough from the island to have plenty of room to swing with the night winds. If the swells turn ominous, we have plenty of room to do what we need to do to get out quick. We are alone in the anchorage. I haven't seen another boat since morning.

Having cooked and eaten dinner, I go forward to stand on the bow. I stare intently at where the anchor chain comes out of the water. I am looking for any communications from below. I then take a long look at the silhouette of the island in the softening light. The island is about one square mile and owned by the National Parks. One ranger lives out here intermittently. A tourist boat ferries visitors the seventy-some miles out here from Ventura. The landing structure appears to have been remodeled since the last time I was here. On top of the island is a small campground and ranger quarters, but I see no sign of occupation.

Empty of people and barren, Santa Barbara Island feels haunted, even enchanted. In *The Encantatas or Enchanted Islands,* Herman Melville wrote of the Galapagos Islands as having an "air of spellbound desertness."[3] In the short story, he gathered together observations and stories of the various islands. He sensed deep mysteries, even the workings of good and evil in the sea life, birds, and human history. He wrote of the islands as charmed. Melville had been to the Galapagos on a whaler about seven years after Darwin. They were both great observers and deep thinkers. It is common

---

3. Melville, "Encantadas," 48.

today for people of the Bight to refer to the Channel Islands as California's Galapagos. Standing at the bow watching shadows lengthen as the light shines low from the west onto Santa Barbara Island, I think of both Darwin and Melville. *Boethius* and I appreciate Darwin, but we sail with Melville.

The classic academic study of what *Boethius* and I are doing is *Image and Pilgrimage in Christian Culture* by the anthropologists Victor and Edith Turner. "The pilgrim," they write, "embarks on an adventure, drawn by a kind of magic, the call of the saint."[4] The Turners think of pilgrimage as a "liminoid phenomenon."[5] The pilgrim has entered a middle-kind of existence, a liminality that "is not only *transition* but also *potentiality*, not only 'going to be' but also 'what may be.'"[6] As I stand at the bow, I listen to the surf, birds, and sea lions. To disenchant this world makes no sense.

WITH MORNING COFFEE and granola bar in hand, I sit in the cockpit of *Boethius*. There are no other boats to be seen. We are overwhelmed with the morning-joy of this place. With breakfast done and the galley clean, I walk forward to stand again on the bow. The ocean is flat. There is no wind. The sky is grey. There appears to be almost no surge rising and falling against the island rocks. I decide to raise the anchor, motor closer to shore, drop anchor, row ashore in the inflatable dinghy, and explore the island.

After re-anchoring, I flop the inflated dinghy over the side and lower myself in. Sitting low, I row with little plastic oars toward the Landing. I go close in to the pillars hoping to tie up to a ladder, but there is no place to safely get ashore. A seal starts barking at me to go away. Nearby I see a relatively flat boulder covered with tidal plants. I maneuver sideways to the boulder, tie the dinghy's painter to my pants, ride up with the surge, grab a handful of plants with both hands, roll myself out of the raft onto the rock, and scramble up to a secure spot. Safe, I pull the dinghy up behind me and tie the painter to a small boulder. Proud of myself, I edge along the rocks over toward the metal stairway. While in the dinghy, I had noticed a sign at the base of the stairway saying, I thought, "Watch Your Step." When I got

---

4. Turner and Turner, *Image and Pilgrimage in Christian Culture*, xv.
5. Turner and Turner, *Image and Pilgrimage in Christian Culture*, 1–39.
6. Turner and Turner, *Image and Pilgrimage in Christian Culture*, 3.

Santa Barbara Island

close, it said the island was closed to visitors. Dang it! I carefully go back to the dinghy, push it back into the water, and roll back into it at the top of a surge. Balancing myself within it by skootching around, I row half way back to *Boethius* and stop. A sea lion is watching me. I survey the barren island rising steep in front of me. I sit silently in the little inflatable boat for a while. Enchanted.

Boethius and I then leave Santa Barbara Island. There is no wind, and the sea is glassy. I hook the autopilot to the tiller after pointing us toward the southeastern tip of Santa Catalina Island. Up forward on the bow I feed the anchor chain down into the chain locker. I have an ABS pipe rigged under the deck to guide chain down low below the V-berth back toward the center of the boat. This helps balance of the boat. With the chain stowed, I sit with my back against the sloped front of the cabin roof.

I say a quick prayer of thanks for the opportunity to pilgrim out here. *Boethius* and I are blessed. Great is the Lord, and greatly to be praised. *Boethius* and I sail inside a Pacific coastal version of Psalm 48. The California Bight is beautiful, one of the joys of the whole earth. It is a holy place. These waters, this coast, these islands deserve to be investigated like Mt. Zion in the psalm:

> Walk about Zion, go around her,
> count her towers, consider well her ramparts, view her citadels,
> that you may tell of them to the next generation.[7]

---

7. Psalm 48:12–13.

The author in *Alert*, a Dana 24 built by Pacific Seacraft. (Author's collection.)

The Santa Ana Condition

I SOLD *Boethius* in the fall of 2019. The boom broke again, this time while sailing with two friends in Santa Monica Bay. We fixed it on the dock in Marina del Rey by riveting a whisker pole inside of it. When I got home, Sue asked about the boom, and what it is like to fit three old men for several nights inside of *Boethius*. She laughed at my answer, and said I should buy a bigger boat. She even said that she and any future grandkids might sail with me if we had a boat with a bathroom in it. I started looking at used boats. It made sense. I had learned to sail in small dinghies. My teen years were spent mostly on a Hobie Cat. In my twenties and thirties, I trailered daysailers. *Boethius* was the keelboat of my forties and fifties, a coastal weekender. Now that I am into my sixties, it is time for an ocean-going boat in which I can stand up straight while cooking dinner. The bucket can return to the service for which it was designed. A private toilet with a holding tank will allow me to stay longer in a nice harbor or anchorage.

When I bought *Boethius* in early 2001, the ocean-going boat I actually wanted was a Pacific Seacraft Dana 24. An internet search found a 2002

The Santa Ana Condition

Dana 24 for sale up the coast in Morro Bay. The price was reasonable. I read all the reviews and checked prices of all available Danas in North America. Dana 24s, built in the late 1970s and early 1980s, were listed on the Atlantic coast for more money than the 2002 boat in Morro Bay. Out of love for *Boethius*, I offered only two thirds of the asking price. I knew the offer would be rejected. I promised *Boethius* that I would not negotiate. For a couple more months, I heard nothing while *Boethius* and I sailed together happily. My offer had apparently been insulting to the owner.

But then the broker called. My low-ball offer was accepted. Everybody I asked affirmed it was a great deal. Boat owning is a form of stewardship. Good boats get passed from one generation to the next. I was the third or fourth owner *Boethius* had mentored in these waters. I passed *Boethius* on to a young surfer from Oceanside. *Boethius* and I took him sailing, and we all were happy with each other. The buyer was new to sailing but is a water-guy. He and his dad planned to fix her up, love her, and sail her back-and-forth to Catalina Island. I sold the boat cheap, fifty years old but still seaworthy.

I now took on a new mentor, a twenty four foot Dana, twenty seven feet long if you count the bow sprit that holds the anchor and supports the forestay. Pacific Seacraft named this design after Richard Henry Dana Jr. The boat was built in Santa Ana, thirty-two years after *Boethius*. For several decades Pacific Seacraft thrived on the California Bight as a high-end, high-quality, deep water boat builder. It sold expensive boats to people willing to pay for the sense of security that comes from knowing a boat has been designed and built for crossing oceans safely with comfortable motion in rough seas. She is not a racer. She is heavy, slow, and so small that a woman sailing quickly past us in San Diego Bay laughed, pointed, and yelled to me my boat is cute.

I called on my retired friend Jeff to help me sail the four hundred miles from the boat's mooring in Morro Bay down to San Diego. He and I met at the train station in San Luis Obispo, him coming from the north and me from the south. An Uber took us over to Morro Bay where I had paid a boat yard to check over the boat, paint the bottom of the hull, and get her ready for a sail to San Diego. I gave the boatyard a list that included, of course, making sure the diesel engine was in good shape and ready for such a trip. Jeff and I loaded the boat in the late afternoon and motored up the channel to Morro Rock where we turned southwest. We were just leaving the channel when the engine gave out! It had not been properly serviced. With no wind, the harbor patrol helped us back to a dock. During the night we got her going with some parts left over from the old owner.

Eventide was the name written on a board attached to the boat's stern ladder. The board was rotting, and the name was barely readable. My first day cleaning her up in Morro Bay, I removed the board. I sensed no commitment from her or me to the name. We would have to get to know each other, then choose a new name. Jeff and I discussed names on the way south and, on the second day of the trip, we agreed that a Dana 24 on the California Bight should have a name that honors the book *Two Years Before the Mast*. We mulled over possible names for another day. We were northwest of San Nicholas Island when the three of us settled on *Alert*. Dana sailed two boats on the Bight: the *Pilgrim* and the *Alert*. He wrote fondly of the *Alert* and sailed in it back to Boston. A short name seemed right for a short boat. Also, it also allowed the boat to admonish the pilgrims she carries: Be alert! Jesus often told his disciples to Be alert!

AT DAWN THE morning after our engine debacle, *Alert*, Jeff, and I leave Morro Bay. The incoming tide comes fast at us, but the boat's diesel chug takes us past the waterfront shops and close up past Morro Rock glowing in the October morning sun. Being off the coast north of Point Conception, we enter waters known for high winds and rough seas. I am somewhat familiar with this coast. Back in the 1970s I sailed here in both a Hobie Cat and a thirty-five foot Ericson sloop. Today, we are headed toward Point Conception for which every coastal guidebook offers extra warnings. When we planned the trip, we expected in the afternoon to be reefed and riding big swells. Instead, we pass San Luis Obispo Bay in a flat calm. South of us, within the Bight, the VHF weather report warns of extreme Santa Ana Conditions. Up here, to the north of the Bight, we've got nothing. We continue motoring southward hoping for wind. In the late afternoon, still in flat water, we steer outside of Irene, a huge oil rig.

Having used the engine all day and begun to take it for granted, the dang thing conks out at sunset when we are about five miles off the coast between Point Arguello and Point Conception. Darkness is coming fast. The wind is still Unitarian. The engine is dead. We appear to be drifting toward

The Santa Ana Condition

what we know to be a rocky shore. Jeff goes to work on the engine, while I put up the sails and try to nurse some movement out of the boat. Jeff gets queasy reading a manual with a flashlight while his head is in the engine compartment. He comes up on deck for some air. Happily, Unitarian conditions are turning Presbyterian. There is soft wind being dispersed westward out of the Santa Barbara Channel. We no longer drift and begin to create a consistent wave at our bow. We are safe, headed south, on a port tack.

Jeff and I discuss the gale being announced on the VHF radio. This is a Big Santa Ana, the kind that Dana wrote about when all boats in Santa Barbara slip anchors and sail out to where they have plenty of space to ride out a storm. The radio tells us tonight the Santa Barbara Channel will blow Pentecostal. Jeff, me, and the boat agree not to try to anchor anywhere. We had planned to anchor tonight at Cojo in the lee of Point Conception. But Cojo in a Santa Ana will be a lee shore. We look at the chart and talk about other anchorages, but we have another problem. We have never used the anchor and rode that came with the boat. When buying the boat, I looked at the anchor and found attached twenty-five feet of thick chain and another two hundred feet of strong rope: A little short for deeper anchorages but good enough for normal conditions in a moderately shallow anchorage. Trouble is: Good enough and trusting it in a heavy blow are two different things. The radio says gale-force winds are expected in the channel out to San Miguel Island. Jeff and I agree we are safest at sea, sailing south, keeping well outside of San Miguel Island, well outside of the California Bight. We suit up in foul weather gear and tether ourselves to the boat with heavy-duty carabiner clips and web-strapping. In the morning, we will figure out what to do about the engine. At present we have a Presbyterian wind. If Pentecostals hit us during the night, we are prepared to reef sails and ride out whatever comes at us. We will trade off sleeping. Each of us will have long night hours alone at the tiller. We are not worried. The *Alert* is designed for heavy seas.

As I take first watch at the tiller, I look back to the Point Conception lighthouse. She is flashing her name: Fl 30s 133ft 26M Horn. I don't hear the horn but count the seconds between the flashes. I see the outline of the low headland disappearing in the growing darkness. *Boethius* and I, as part of our pilgrim-investigations, had tried to come out here at the upper edge of the Bight. Now here I am, without *Boethius,* fleeing this corner of the Bight. At home I have written a rough draft of some of this book. Here, off Point Conception, I question what I have written. Can a region such as the California

Bight be on a distinct pilgrimage? Of all places, can this coast, islands, and waters be purpose-driven to declare the good news of hope for all creation?

In this state of mind, I think of Santa Ana. She is the patron saint of all who don't know what is happening—which, I suppose, is everybody. This is the Santa Ana Condition: Be alert! Something's happening here. What it is, is not exactly clear.

Key to the story of Santa Ana is the fact that she does not know who Mary actually is. In the Church of the Immaculata overlooking Mission Bay there is a beautiful statue of Santa Ana teaching her young daughter who is holding the Bible. We who look at the statue can see the poignancy of the moment. Santa Ana's face is in shadow as she looks down to Mary. The light from above, to which Santa Ana points, shines on Mary's face. Santa Ana is teaching about God to the mother of God and doesn't know it. San Gabriel will later come to Mary to reveal that she is blessed above all women. It will be Mary who later tells her mother about the angel visit and who her grandson will be. At the time depicted in the statue, Ana is simply doing what a good Jewish mother should do: teach the scriptures and direct her child to the Light. The Santa Ana Condition depicted by the statue is a poignant mix of ignorance, belief, trust, and hope. They see through a glass darkly. Someday they will see face to face. Theologians will later debate the miracle of conception and the nature of the baby, but at the time depicted in the statue, the Santa Ana Condition is merely a sense that something special is in the works. Here, as we sail in the dark away from the lighthouse, I ponder the possibility that Point Conception, as a jutting lowland infused with a meaningful name, is a divine geoglyph, a message from the Creator to creation.

Santa Ana and Mary, Chapel of St. Anne, Church of the Immaculata, San Diego (author's photo with the permission of the church).

The Santa Ana Condition

STILL NO BLAST of wind from the east. It is long past midnight and visibility is good. Where is this predicted gale? Jeff has taken a turn below, and I am steering. Above us are stars, crisp and clear. Off to the starboard, oil rigs are brightly lit. I don't often wear a full-suit of foul weather gear, but I have it on now. I am ready. But nothing yet, nothing but pleasant winds and a clear night. I hear water gurgling along the hull. I start thinking about California historians who have gone before me. If I am an academic fool, I am not alone in my foolishness. Kevin Starr, as California's state librarian and a professor at the University of Southern California, wrote what is called the *California Dream Series,* a series of volumes published by Oxford University Press that attempt to identify a teleology specific to California.

While in graduate school at UC Santa Barbara I was told to read Starr's books by Harold Kirker. He was my mentor-professor and a friend of Starr. Back in the 1980s, Starr was the most vigorous proponent of a California angle in the project to identify a distinctive "American Character." Other historians had identified a New England Mind and a Southern Culture. Starr proposed a California Dream distinct within the larger American Dream. While most of the historians of regional cultures were comfortable with the vague rhetoric often called exceptionalism, Starr was more serious and precise. His was a Roman Catholic project rooted in classical and Christian tradition. Starr was in graduate school at Harvard when Erich Auerbach's *Memesis: The Representation of Reality in Western Literature* became widely studied among historians of culture. Auerbach, by then a professor at Yale, wrote that medieval Christianity offered methods of "figural interpretation" that linked seemingly unrelated lives, events, literature, artworks, and architecture together in an earthly "horizontal" realm by interpreting them as "vertically linked to Divine Providence." Auerbach noted this medieval Catholic way of understanding cultural history is "impossible to establish by reason," but it offers a "conception of history magnificent in its homogeneity."[8] To see the homogeneity, Auerbach taught, one has to

---

8. Auerbach, *Memesis,* 64–65. Gerald R. McDermott notes Auerbach's influence on the modern study of biblical typology in his own promotion of a typological understanding of creation in *Everyday Glory,* 35–36.

think in the manner of St. Augustine in *City of God*: all creation, earth and heaven, is entangled while on a pilgrimage from disunity to ultimate unity.

Kevin Starr, who died near the end of the pilgrimages I record here, was a ready believer. He had been raised in a Roman Catholic orphanage in Northern California and was educated in Catholic schools and universities in San Francisco before he went to graduate school at Harvard. Throughout his life, he was a product, patron, and promoter of Roman Catholic intellectual life. For Starr the California Dream is a Christian pilgrimage, a regional Augustinian pilgrimage, an entangled culture, purpose-driven through history. Starr, in his autobiographical novel *Land's End,* declared "I have always been too obsessively, baroquely if you will, Roman Catholic for my own good."[9] A few pages later he describes his teleological understanding of the cosmos: "the universe streams toward the Risen Christ as a river to the sea."[10] All creation, he believes, evolves "in some mystical yet truly historical process towards its own ultimate resurrection and glorification, its unification with the Risen Christ, the Lord of History, in some future mystical and physical implosion of Christ, creation, and mankind that will make us one with God himself and end all History."[11]

Looking up at the night sky, I take comfort in the work of Kevin Starr. I am merely one of a long tradition of pilgrims in a pilgrim land. Jeff comes up through the companionway to trade duties. I go below to get some sleep.

AFTER SUNRISE THE little wind we had died. Jeff and I are both in the cockpit dressed and harnessed for a storm. The VHF weather channel continues to speak of gales and Santa Ana Conditions, but we have entered into the stillness at the center of a wind swirl. We are a hundred miles off the coast, ten or so miles below San Miguel Island, trying to enter the Bight. We have turned southeastward in hope of sailing above San Nicholas and San Clemente Islands into the Gulf of Santa Catalina. We continue to listen to the computerized drone of the VHF weather channel. It tells us, eventually, we will not have winds out here near San Nicholas Island for at least two days.

9. Starr, *Land's End,* 56.
10. Starr, *Land's End,* 69.
11. Starr, *Land's End,* 69.

The Santa Ana Condition

We both laugh at ourselves for being overdressed. Jeff takes a picture of us, then we remove our foul weather gear. I make coffee, a pleasure now that I can stand at a gimbaled stove in this new boat. No more crouching below. I hand a mug up to Jeff, and we both sit for a while in the cockpit, enjoying an early morning at sea. The boat is just sitting in glassy water, mainsail flogging back and forth with the swells. Eventually, with our mugs empty, we decide to get to go back below. I wash dishes while Jeff reads the engine manual. I go up to the cockpit when Jeff starts to work on the engine. We desperately need an engine if we are going to get back to San Diego before my Monday classes.

Author and Jeff Cann on the morning after no gale (author's collection).

Jeff figures the impeller on the water pump is the problem. The bigger problem is that a bolt is stripped, and we have few tools. There appears to be a back way to get at the impeller, but we both struggle to make it work. Eventually I resort to prayer. Kneeling in front of the small Yanmar diesel engine, tools in my right hand, I look up and tell God that I am sorry to be a bother. There are more important things for God to fix in the world, but we need help with this engine. We have plenty of food. We are not in danger. We might actually enjoy spending a few extra days floating out here. But both of us need to get back to San Diego. Jeff has plane reservations, and I have students to teach. Please help us. After the prayer, I feel better. No miracle occurs, but within the next thirty minutes the problem is somewhat fixed. We start the engine. It does not overheat. I say a prayer of thanks. Jeff and I then discuss at what speed we should run the engine. We agree not to put any strain on the pump. Until we get some wind, we will chug slow.

In the middle of the following night, I am steering while Jeff sleeps, I can see San Nicholas Island lit up in the distance with the lights of the US Navy. As I keep an eye on the compass, the cross-shaped mast is in the foreground of millions of stars. We are in an outer region of the California Bight where I have never been. No sails are up. The small diesel engine continues to do its duty. Answers to prayer are a mystery. We Christians are supposed to think that the Creator of the whole cosmos wants to talk with us and hear about our mundane concerns. There is a prayer that seems to have been answered in amazing ways recorded at the beginning of *The Charismatic Century: The Enduring Impact of the Azusa Street Revival* by two Southern California Protestant pastors, Jack W. Hayford and S. David Moore. They note that on January 1, 1901 Pope Leo XIII dedicated the twentieth century to the global work of the Holy Spirit. Given that the Holy Spirit soon after hit Los Angeles hard and Southern California became a global leader in the Pentecostal and Charismatic movements, not to mention the Jesus Movement, worship music movement, and the intellectual branch of fundamentalism and evangelicalism, Hayford and Moore are justifiably amazed at God's answer to the pope's prayer of dedication.

As I watch the mast wave back and forth in front of the stars, I too am amazed. Why did the Holy Spirit pick Protestants on the California Bight to be the most evident answer the pope's prayer? Who knows? Maybe we here had been prepared for it after being founded as a Spanish mission field. I smile. I can image priests in the Vatican, after hearing the news of a new Pentecost in Los Angeles, asking each other: "Can anything good come from Los Angeles?"

That the Southern California coast seems to have an outsized role in the global history of the twentieth-century Christianity fascinates me. The subject is worthy of pilgrimages and ponderings. I sold *Boethius* but still read and teach *The Consolation of Philosophy*. It is one of the books I have assigned to my honors class, a class I need to be back home to teach. Tonight under a clear sky in the calm waters north of San Nicholas Island I am reminded of one of *Philosophia's* prayers:

> What brings all things to order,
> Governing earth and sea and sky,
> Is love . . . .
> O happy race of men,

The Santa Ana Condition

If the love that rules the stars
May also rule your hearts.[12]

WE TURN THE engine off and raise sail when we pass San Clemente Island and enter the Gulf of Santa Catalina. With the wind growing strong from the southwest, the *Alert* dips her portside and shoulders her way past La Jolla Point into her new home waters. Nearing the San Diego Bay channel, we gybe the sails to starboard and sail north into the bay. During the final approach before motoring to our mooring, I can see in the distance the tower of the Church of the Immaculata.

Jeff flew home the next day. During the following two years, years of the pandemic, I wrote much of this book and often sailed with *Alert*. We have been on several more long pilgrimages together. She does not handle as well as *Boethius*, but she takes better care of me. She is slower than *Boethius*, but slow is good.

---

12. Boethius, *Consolation of Philosophy*, 2.poem 8, 227.

Acknowledgements

Tim Vivian, Jim Meals, Elizabeth [Kennedy] McKay, and Steven Kennedy offered much editorial support as the book grew then shrank. Jeff Cann, Matt Bell, Doug Sweeney, Karen Lee, Barry Hankins, Don Yerxa, Ron Morgan, Gerald McDermott, Ben Cater, Josh Reyes, Victor Labenske, Sue Martin, Gerard Reed, Ron Wells, Jason Sexton, Robin Lang, Harold Drake, Paul Willis, Jerry Jackman and Tim Wood read drafts and offered encouragement.

Bibliography

Altschul, Jeffrey H. and Donn R. Grenda, eds. *Islanders and Mainlanders: Prehistoric Context for the Southern California Bight*. Tucson, AZ: SRI, 2002.

Angle, Paul M. *Philip K. Wrigley: A Memoir of a Modest Man*. Chicago: Rand McNally and Co., 1975.

Arviso, George. "Consecration Speech." St. Bartholomew's Chapel, Reservation of the Rincon Band of Luiseño Indians, California. February 14, 2010.

Ashley, Kathleen and Pamela Sheingorn, eds. *Interpreting Cultural Symbols: Saint Anne in Late Medieval Society*. Athens, Georgia: University of Georgia Press, 1990.

Auerbach, Erich. *Memesis: The Representation of Reality in Western Literature*. Translated by Willard Trask. New York: Doubleday Anchor, 1957.

Babcock, Maltbie, D. "My Father's World." In *Thoughts for Every-day Living from the Spoken and Written Words of Maltbie D. Babcock*. Edited by Katherine T. Babcock and Mary R. Sanford, 180–82. New York: C. Scribner's Sons, 1901.

Barber, W. T. A. *Raymond Llull: The Illuminated Doctor: A Study in Medieval Missions*. London: C.H. Kelly, 1903.

Beebe, Rose Marie and Robert M. Senkewicz. *Junípero Serra: California, Indians, and the Transformation of a Missionary*. Norman, OK: University of Oklahoma Press, 2015.

Beebe, Rose Marie and Robert M. Senkewicz, eds. *Testimonios: Early California through the Eyes of Women, 1815-1848*. Norman, OK: University of Oklahoma Press, 2015.

Benston, Henry. *Outermost House: A Year of Life on the Great Beach of Cape Cod*. New York: Holt, 2003.

Blackburn, Thomas, ed. *December's Child: A Book of Chumash Oral Narratives*. Berkeley: University of California Press, 1975.

Boethius. *Boethius: The Theological Tractates and The Consolation of Philosophy*. Translated by H. F. Stewart, E. K. Rand, and S. J. Tester. Loeb Classical Library. Cambridge, MA: Harvard, 1973.

Bonaventure. *Bonaventure: The Soul's Journey into God, The Tree of Life, The Life of St. Francis*. Translated by Ewart Cousins. New York: Paulist, 1978.

Boscana, Gironimo. *Chinigchinich: A Historical Account of the Origin, Customs, and Traditions of the Indians at the Missionary Establishment of St. Juan Capistrano, Alta California Called the Acagchemem Nation*. Translated by Alfred Robinson. New York: Wiley and Putnam, 1846.

Bowens, Lisa M. *African American Readings of St. Paul: Reception, Resistance, and Transformation*. Grand Rapids, MI: Eerdmans, 2020.

Boyle, T. Coraghessan. *When the Killing's Done*. New York: Viking, 2011.

Bibliography

Braun, Jon. *Whatever Happened to Hell.* Nashville: Thomas Nelson, 1979.

Brown, Peter. *The Rise of Western Christendom: Triumph and Diversity, AD 200-1000.* London: Blackwell, 1996.

Chiles, Frederic Caire. *California's Channel Islands: A History.* Norman, OK: Oklahoma, 2015.

Carson, Rachel. *The Sea Trilogy: Under the Sea-Wind, The Sea Around Us, The Edge of the Sea.* Edited by Santra Steingraber. New York: Library of America, 2021.

Castor, James G. "The Last Days of Don Juan Perez, The Mallorcan Mariner," *Journal of the West* 2 (1963): 15-21.

Cronon, William, ed. *Rethinking the Human Place in Nature*, New York: W. W. Norton, 1996.

Curley, Michael J., trans. *Physiologus.* Austin: University of Texas Press, 1979.

Dana, Richard Henry, Jr. *The Journal of Richard Henry Dana, Jr.* Edited by Robert F. Lucid. Cambridge, MA: Harvard, 1968.

———. "Leonard Woods." *Scribner's Monthly Magazine* (1880): 138–144.

———. *Two Years Before the Mast: A Personal Narrative of Life at Sea.* New York: Modern Library Classics, 2001.

Richard Henry Dana Sr. *Poems and Prose Writings.* 2 vols. New York: Baker and Scribner, 1850.

Dakin, Susan Bryant. *The Lives of William Hartnell.* Palo Alto: Stanford University Press, 1949.

Dante Alighieri. *Paradiso.* Translated by Henry Wadsworth Longfellow. Boston: Ticknor and Fields, 1867.

Deverell, William. *Whitewashed Adobe: The Rise of Los Angeles and Remaking of its Mexican Past.* Berkeley: University of California Press, 2004.

Dillard, Annie. *Pilgrim at Tinker Creek.* New York: Harper Perennial Modern Classics 2013.

Dochuk, Darren. *From Bible Belt to Sunbelt: Plain Folk Religion, Grass Roots Politics, and the Rise of Evangelical Conservatism.* New York: W. W. Norton, 2012.

Drake, Harold. *A Century of Miracles: Christians, Pagans, Jews, and the Supernatural.* New York: Oxford, 2017.

Duns Scotus. *Philosophical Writings*, Translated by Allan Wolter. Indianapolis: Hackett, 1987.

Eaton, Margaret Holden. *Diary of a Sea Captain's Wife: Tales of Santa Cruz Island.* Santa Barbara: McNally and Loftin, 1980.

Eguiluz, Antonio. "Father Gonzalo Tenorio, O.F.M. and His Providentialist Eschatological Theories on the Spanish Indies." *The Americas* 16 (1960): 329–56.

Eire, Carlos. "The Good, the Bad, and the Airborne: Levitation and the History of the Impossible in Early Modern Europe." In *Ideas and Cultural Margins in Early Modern Germany*, edited by Robin Barnes et al., 307–24. Burlington, VT: Ashgate, 2009.

Englehardt, Zephrin. *San Luis Rey Mission.* San Francisco: James H. Barry, 1921.

Eskridge, Larry. "And the Most Influential American Evangelical of the Last 25 Years Is…." *Evangelical Studies Bulletin* 17.14 (2001): 1–4.

———. *God's Forever Family: The Jesus People Movement in America.* New York: Oxford, 2014.

Evans, C. Stephen. *Natural Signs and Knowledge of God.* New York: Oxford, 2010.

Fagan, Brian. *Before California: An Archaeologist Looks at our Earliest Inhabitants.* Lanham, MD: AltaMira, 2004.

Bibliography

———. *The Cruising Guide to Central and Southern California: Golden Gate to Ensenada, Mexico, Including the Offshore Islands.* New York: International Marine, 2001.

Farris, Glenn. "Jose Panto: Capitan of the Indian Pueblo of San Pascual, San Diego County." *Journal of California and Great Basin Anthropology* 16.2 (1994): 149–61.

Filler, Martin. "A Mystic Monumentality." *New York Review of Books* 64.11 (2017).

Geiger, John. *The Third Man Factor: Surviving the Impossible.* New York: Hachette, 2009.

Gillquist, Peter. *Becoming Orthodox: A Journey to the Ancient Christian Faith.* Ben Lomond, CA: Conciliar, 2010.

Gray, Paul Bryan. *The Struggle for the Rancho Santa Margarita.* Spokane: Arthur Clark, 2002.

Grey, Zane. *Tales of Fishes.* United States: Derrydale Press, 2001.

Gumprecht, Blake. *The Los Angeles River: Its Life, Death, and Possible Rebirth.* Baltimore: Johns Hopkins, 1999.

Haas, Capistran. *Santa Barbara: Her Story.* Santa Barbara: Old Mission, 1988.

Hayford, Jack W. and S. David Moore. *The Charismatic Century: The Enduring Impact of the Azusa Street Revival.* New York: Warner Faith, 2006.

Holder, Charles Frederick. *The Channel Islands of California: A Book for the Angler, Sportsman, and Tourist.* Chicago: A.C. McGlurg, 1910.

Hunter, Doreen M. "America's First Romantics: Richard Henry Dana, Sr. and Washington Allston." *The New England Quarterly* 45 (1972): 3–30.

———. *Richard Henry Dana Sr.* Boston: Twayne, 1987.

Irwin, Robert. *Robert Irwin: Primaries and Secondaries: With Essays by Hugh M. Davies and Robert Irwin.* San Diego: Museum of Contemporary Art, 2008.

Jacobus de Voragini. *Golden Legend: Reading on the Saints.* Translated by William Granger Ryan. Princeton, NJ: Princeton University Press, 2012.

Justin Martyr. "The First Apology." *New Advent.* https://www.newadvent.org/fathers/0126.htm.

Kennedy, Rick. *A History of Reasonableness: Testimony and Authority in the Art of Thinking.* Rochester, NY: University of Rochester, 2004.

———. "Educating Bees: The Craft of Humility in Classical and Christian Liberal Arts." *Christian Scholar's Review* 42 (2012): 29–42.

Lewis, C. S. *The Allegory of Love: A Study in Medieval Tradition.* New York: Oxford, 1958.

Librado, Fernando (*Kitsepawit*). *The Eye of the Flute: Chumash Traditional History and Ritual.* Edited by Travis Hall et al. Santa Barbara: Santa Barbara Museum of Natural History, 1977.

Lindsell, Harold. *Battle for the Bible.* Grand Rapids: Zondervan, 1976.

Llull, Ramon. *Ramon Llull: A Contemporary Life.* Translated by Anthony Bonner. Rochester, NY: Tamesis, 2010.

Marsden, George. *Reforming Fundamentalism: Fuller Seminary and the New Evangelicalism.* Grand Rapids: Eerdmans, 1987.

Matovina, Timothy. "A Response to Stafford Poole." *The Catholic Historical Review,* 100:2 (2014): 284–91.

———. *Theologies of Guadalupe: From the Era of Conquest to Pope Francis.* New York: Oxford, 2018.

McClain, Molly. *Ellen Browning Scripps: New Money and American Philanthropy.* Lincoln: University of Nebraska Press, 2017.

McDermott, Gerald R. *Everyday Glory: The Revelation of God in All of Reality.* Grand Rapids: Baker Academic, 2018.

Bibliography

Melville, Herman. "The Encantadas, or Enchanted Isles." In *Herman Melville: Four Short Novels*, edited by G. Thomas Tanselle. New York: Bantam, 1959.

———. *Moby Dick or, The Whale*. New York: Library of America, 1983.

Migliazzo, Arlin C. *Mother of Modern Evangelicalism: The Life and Legacy of Henrietta Mears*. Grand Rapids: Eerdmans, 2020.

Milton, John. *Compete Poems and Major Prose*, edited by Merritt Y. Hughes. Indianapolis: Odyssey, 1957.

Mourelle, Noel Blanco. *Every Knowable Thing: The Art of Ramon Llull and the Construction of Knowledge*. PhD diss., Columbia University, 2017.

Noreen, Kristin. "The Virgin of Guadalupe, Juan Diego, and the Revival of the *Tilma* Relic in Los Angeles." *Church History* 87:2 (June 2018), 514.

Norris, Kathleen *The Cloister Walk*. New York: Riverhead, 1996.

O'Dell, Scott. *Island of the Blue Dolphin: Complete Reader's Edition*. Edited by Sara L. Schwebel. Berkeley: University of California Press, 2016.

Palóu, Francisco. *Historical Memoirs of New California*. Translated by Herbert Eugene Bolton. New York: Russell & Russell, 1966.

Pawel, Miriam. *The Crusades of Cesar Chavez*. New York: Bloomsbury, 2014.

Pelikan, Jaroslav. *The Christian Tradition: A History of the Development of Doctrine*, vol. 3, *The Growth of Medieval Theology 600–1300*. Chicago: University of Chicago Press, 1978.

———. *Mary Through the Centuries: Her Place in the History of Culture*. New Haven: Yale University Press, 1996.

Phelan, John Leddy. *The Millennial Kingdom of the Franciscans in the New World*. Revised Second Edition. Berkeley: University of California Press, 1970.

Pointer, Richard. *Encounters of the Spirit: Native Americans and European Colonial Religions*. Bloomington: Indiana University Press, 2007.

Poole, Stafford. *Our Lady of Guadalupe: The Origins and Sources of a Mexican National Symbol, 1531–1797*. Tucson: University of Arizona Press, 1995.

Porter, Gene Stratton. *The Keeper of the Bees*. United States: Eirenikos, 2015.

Pubols, Louise. *The Father of All: The de la Guerra Family, Power, and Patriarchy in Mexican California*. Berkeley: University of California Press, 2010.

Renton, David M. and Kathryn E. Renton. *The Life and Legacy of D. M. Renton: Pasadena and Santa Catalina Island, California, 1902-1936*. Riverside, CA: Renton Investments, 2018.

Ritter, Mary Bennett. *More Than Gold in California: The Life and Work of Dr. Mary Bennett Ritter*. Edited by Gesa Kirsch. New York: TwoDot, 2017.

Ritter, William. *The Unity of the Organism: Or the Organismal Conception of Life*. 2 vols. Boston: Gorham, 1919.

Russell, Jeffrey Burton. *The Prince of Darkness: Radical Evil and the Power of Good in History*. Ithaca, NY: Cornell University Press, 1988.

Sanders, Fred and Jason S. Sexton, eds. *Theology and California: Theological Refractions on California Culture*. Burlingon, VT: Ashgate, 2014.

Sandos, James. *Converting California: Indians and Franciscans in the Missions*. New Haven: Yale University Press, 2004.

Schroeder, Susan and Stafford Poole. "Seminaries and Writing the History of New Spain: An Interview with Stafford Poole C.M." *The Americas* 69 (2012): 237–54.

Bibliography

Serra, Junípero. *A Marian Novena Attributed to Fray Junípero Serra.* Translated by Francis J. Weber. Los Angeles: Archives of the Archdiocese of Los Angeles, 1988. https://udayton.edu/imri/mary/j/junipero-serras-marian-novena.php.

Smith, Chuck. *A Memoir of Grace.* USA: The Word for Today, 2009.

Sorrell, Roger D. *St. Francis of Assisi and Nature: Traditions and Innovations in Western Christian Attitudes toward the Environment.* New York: Oxford University Press, 1988.

Kevin Starr. *Americans and the California Dream.* New York: Oxford University Press, 1973.

———. *Land's End.* New York: McGraw Hill, 1979.

Teal, Edwin Way. *A Naturalist Buys and Old Farm.* New York: Dodd Mead, 1974.

Thurman, Michael E. *The Naval Department of San Blas: New Spain's Bastion for Alta California and Nootka, 1767–1798.* Glendale, CA: Arthur H. Clark, 1967.

Turner, Victor and Edith Turner. *Image and Pilgrimage in Christian Culture.* New York: Columbia University Press, 1978.

Van Dyke, Henry. *The Poems of Henry Van Dyke.* Project Gutenberg Ebook. https://www.gutenberg.org/files/16229/16229-h/16229-h.htm.

Veléz, Karen. *The Miraculous Flying House of Loreto: Spreading Catholicism in the Early Modern World.* Princeton: Princeton University Press, 2018.

Vivian, Tim. *St. Peter of Alexandria: Bishop and Martyr.* Minneapolis, MN: Fortress, 1988.

Waldie, D. J. *Holy Land: A Suburban Memoir.* New York, W. W. Norton, 2005.

Walsh, Christine. *The Cult of St. Katherine of Alexandria in Early Medieval Europe.* Philadelphia: Routledge, 2007.

Warren, Rick. *The Purpose Driven Life: What on Earth am I Here For?* Grand Rapids: Zondervan, 2002.

Weber, Francis J. *Memories of an Old Country Priest.* Mission Hills, CA: Saint Francis Historical Society, 2000.

———. "The Pious Fund of the Californias." *The Hispanic American Historical Review* 43.1 (1963): 78–94.

Wells, Ronald A., ed. *California Dreaming: Society and Culture in the Golden State.* Eugene, OR: Pickwick, 2017.

William Whiting, "Eternal Father, Strong to Save." *Songs and Hymns.org.* https://songsandhymns.org/hymns/detail/eternal-father-strong-to-save.

Wimber, John with Kevin Springer. *Power Evangelism.* San Francisco: Harper and Row, 1986.

Wright, N. T. *Surprised by Hope: Rethinking Heaven, the Resurrection, and the Mission of the Church.* New York: Harper One, 2008.

Wulf, Andrea. *The Invention of Nature: Alexander von Humboldt's New World.* New York: Knopf, 2015.

Index

Acajachemen, 54
Alighieri, Dante, 130, 131, 140, 148, 149
Allston, Washington, 49, 50
Alvarado, Juan Bautista, 107
Anaheim Vineyard Christian Fellowship, 74
Anacapa Island, 15, 16, 115, 116, 154
anthology, 3, 151, 152
Arnel, Guillermo, William Hartnell, 107, 125
Arviso, George, 108–10
Asberry, Richard, 61
Asuza Pacific University, 75
Asuza Street Church, 61, 62
Augustine, 2, 34, 52, 131, 138, 149, 157, 178
Auerbach, Erich, 177

Balaam, 43, 44
Barbareños, 121
Beatrice, 131, 148, 149
Benedict XIV, 90
Bennett, Denis, 66
Berry, Wendell, 15
Beston, Henry, 15
BIOLA, Bible Institute of Los Angeles, 64
Boethius, 12, 84, 149
 Consolation of Philosophy, 12, 13, 36, 37, 39, 138, 164, 180, 181
 De Fide Catholica, 138, 139, 156
Bonaventure, Patron Saint of Ventura, 3–5, 7, 29, 31, 39, 59, 68, 83–85, 91, 100, 111, 124, 151, 156, 157

Boyle, T. C., 161
Braun, Jon, 136, 137, 164
Breyer, Paul, 132
Brown, Peter, 68
Bucareli, Antonio Maria de, 60

Calvary Chapel, 23, 73, 74
Camp Pendleton, 7, 99–103
Campbell, Donald, 32
Cann, Jeff, 174, 175, 177, 178–81
Carson, Rachel, 159
Center for Christian Thought, 64
Chan, Francis, 25
Charismatic Christianity, 25, 58, 66, 180
Chavez, César, 162, 163
Chumash, 121, 122
Chumash Heritage National Marine Sanctuary, 122
Church of the Open Door, 64
Coast Survey, United States, 113, 116
Colegio de San Jose, El, 125
Corona del Mar, 76
Crespí, Juan, 6,
Cronon, William, 29, 30
Cruzeño, 155

Dana Point, 12, 40, 41, 45–49, 51, 53, 54, 92, 93
Dana, Richard Henry Jr., 21, 40, 41, 46, 47, 49, 50, 52–54, 114, 125–29, 160, 173, 174
Dana, Richard Henry Sr., 49–51
deFreitas, Kevin, 12, 108
de la Guerra, Ana María (Anita), 125

191

Index

de la Guerra, Angustias, 127, 128, 160
de la Guerra, José, 125, 127, 160
de la Guerra (Arnel/Hartnell), Teresa, 107, 125
Deverell, William, 59–61
Didion, Joan, 136, 163
Dillard, Annie, 15, 28, 29
Dochuk, Darren, 54
Drake, Harold, 152
Dylan, Bob, 63, 135, 164

Eaton, Margaret, 158, 159, 162
Eder, Tamara, 45
Eire, Carlos, 77
Eskridge, Larry, 79
Ethiopia, 13, 68, 69, 151
Queen of, 151
evangelical, evangelicalism, 3, 23, 25, 48–54, 58, 64, 65, 75, 78, 79, 96, 136, 168, 180
Evangelical Orthodox Church, 136
Evans, C. Stephen, 28

Figueroa, José, 94, 106–8, 160
First Presbyterian Church, San Diego, 74
florilegia 2, 3
Forest Home, 66
Francis of Assis, 3, 4, 6, 7, 17, 25, 39, 43, 54, 58, 72, 79, 80, 83, 84, 86, 90, 100, 150, 163
Frisbee, Lonnie, 74
Fundamentalism, 64, 180
Fundamentals: A Testimony to Truth, The, 64

Gabrieleño, 121
Gálvez, José de, 6, 7
Gideons, 62
Gill, Irving, 36, 38
Gillquist, Peter, 136
Gospel Swamp, 57
Graham, Billy, 62, 65, 66, 79
Graham, Robin Lee, 24, 25
Grey, Zane, 141, 145

Hartmire, Chris, 162, 163

Hartnell, William, (see Guillermo Arnel)
Hayford, Jack, 75, 180
Herodotus, 13, 59
Hollywood Presbyterian Church, 65, 136, 145
Humboldt, Alexander von, 38

Immaculata, Church of the, 78, 79, 81, 181
InterVarsity Christian Fellowship, 132, 141
Irwin, Robert, 34
Isla Vista, 44, 114, 133, 136, 137, 164

Jacoway, Robin, 12
Jeffers, Robinson, 135
Joan B. Kroc School of Peace Studies, 79
John Paul II, 91
Justin Martyr, 151

Kahn, Louis, 35, 36
Kinner, Ann (Captain Ann), 115, 116
Kirker, Harold, 177

LaHaye, Timothy, 78, 79
La Jolla, 31–36, 38, 39, 43, 76, 92, 94, 163, 181
Las Flores (Indian pueblo), 94, 107, 108
Lewis, C. S., 138
Librado, Fernando (*Kitsepawit*), 121, 122, 155, 156
Llull, Ramon, 96, 97, 111
Lorenzana, Apolinaria, 5
Los Angeles, city, 5, 8, 59–62, 72, 74, 76, 115, 180
basin, 7, 54, 56–76
port, 58, 132, 165
river, 56, 57, 59, 60, 63, 65
Luiseño, 106, 108

Mallorca, 96, 97, 111, 151
Mann, Thomas, 135
Matovina, Timothy, 91
Mary 2, 6, 20, 79, 112, 176
as Our Lady of Guadalupe, 87–89

Index

as Our Lady of Immaculate
   Conception, 7, 58, 59, 76
as Our Lady of Peace, 163
as Our Lady of Refuge, 7, 112
as Our Lady of the Angels of
   Portiuncula, 7, 58, 59, 76
Maritime Museum of San Diego, 20,
   46, 113
Californian (schooner), 46, 113, 115,
   121
Mason, Charles, 61
McClain, Molly, 38
McPherson, Amee Semple, 61
McPherson, Miles, 25
Mears, Henrietta, 65, 66
Melville, Herman, 25, 26, 169, 170
micro-christendom, 68, 69
Milton, John, 33, 34
Mission Bay, 77–82, 86, 90, 91, 176
Mission La Purisima, 112
Mission Santa Ynez, 121
Missions, disease at, 97–99
Moore, S. David, 75, 180
Mount Soledad, 32, 33, 35, 78, 94

National Parks Service, 122, 161
Nauman, Bruce, 32
Newport Beach and Harbor, 44, 45, 46,
   56, 60, 71, 73–76
Neve, Filipe de, 60
nishmath chajim, 45
Norris, Kathleen, 15

Ockenga, Harold, 64, 65, 75

Palóu, Francisco, 7, 119, 120
Pawel, Miriam, 162
Pentecostalism, 16, 58, 61, 62, 66
Pereira, William, 31, 32, 145
Perez, Juan, 120, 123
Peyri, Antonio, 106
Phillip II of Spain, 97
Philosophia, 12, 13, 36–39, 53–61,
   66–69, 71–73, 75, 76, 98–101, 103,
   131, 148, 149, 164, 165, 180
Physiologus, physiologic method,
   27–29, 153
Pico, Pio, 107, 108

Pious Fund for the Californias, 119,
   120
Point Conception (Humquq), 1, 15, 69,
   93, 111–25, 174–76
Point Fermin, 47, 116, 132, 165
Point Loma, 11, 12. 17, 19–21, 28, 46,
   77, 81, 115, 116, 119
Point Vicente, 116, 130, 135, 164, 165
portiuncula, 58, 59
Portolá, Gaspar, 113
Poole, Stafford, 88–91

Renton, David, 146, 147
Renton, Elizabeth, 147
Rincon Band of *Luiseño* Indians, 108,
   109
Rincon Reservation, 109
Ritter, Mary, 37, 38
Ritter, William, 37–39
Robinson, Alfred, 125
Russell, Jeffery Burton, 164

San Blas, 120
San Diego, 78, 91
   bay, 6, 11, 19, 31, 34, 39, 78, 79, 105,
      111, 113, 115, 166, 173, 181
   city, 5, 11, 20, 26, 32, 46, 77–80, 93,
      107, 112, 141, 158, 179
   mission, 5, 7, 78
   river, 78
San Fernando Rey, Ferdinand III, 96
   mission, 72
   valley, 66, 85
San Gabriel, 58, 76, 169, 176
   mission, 60, 116
   river, 12, 56, 57, 65, 74
   mountains, 58
   valley, 75
San Juan Capistrano, 7, 47, 48, 54, 94
San Joaquín, 15, 16, 115, 116, 154
   hills, 7, 76
San Luis Rey, Louis IX, 95, 105, 169
   mission, 94, 96, 106, 107, 116
   river, 92–94, 104–6
San Marcos, Mark, 66, 132, 136
San Miguel, Michael, 33, 151, 169
   island, 95, 112–17, 135, 154, 169,
      175, 179

193

Index

(San Miguel, Michael continued)
   church (St. Michael's and All
      Angels), 133, 137
San Pedro, Peter of Alexandria,
      132,133.
   channel, 1, 7, 40, 45, 69, 76, 115,
      118, 120, 131, 115, 118, 120, 131,
      136, 153
   city, 132
Santa Ana, 7, 72, 111, 176
   city, 5, 7, 10, 23, 25, 72, 73, 77, 169,
      173
   condition, 7, 8, 174, 176, 178
   mountain range, 58, 92, 103
   river, 7, 10, 44, 56, 65, 66, 71, 73,
      76, 80
   wind, 7, 24, 108, 175
Santa Barbara, 169
   city, 5, 13, 18, 45–47, 70, 91, 110–26,
      133, 158–61, 166, 167, 175
   channel, 1, 3, 6, 15, 42, 44, 84, 93,
      112, 114, 115, 116, 118, 119, 121,
      122, 124, 154, 155, 175
   island, 166–71
   mission, 112, 125–27, 167, 168
   oil spill, 70, 145
Santa Catalina, Katherine of Alexan-
      dria, 132–34, 136–37
   eddy, 154
   gulf, 1, 92, 99, 115, 178, 181
   island, 7, 10, 41, 53, 57, 63, 69, 73,
      121, 130–32, 144–46, 150, 154,
      159, 171, 173
   university, 164
Santa Cruz Island, 16, 44, 72, 93, 112,
      114, 116, 117, 119, 121, 124,
      150–62
Santa Isabel of Portugal, 19, 20
Santa Margarita, 91, 94, 95, 107, 169
   rancho, 107, 108
   river, 92–94, 106
Santa Monica Bay 1, 25, 53, 76, 115,
      116, 118, 131, 135, 145, 163, 164,
      172
Santa Monica's Son (see Augustine)
Santa Rosa, 112, 169
   island, 113–17, 120, 122, 124
Santa Ynez Mission, 121

Schock, W. D., 7
Scottus, John Duns, 97, 111
Scripps, Edward, 38
Scripps, Ellen, 38
Scripps Institution of Oceanography,
      37, 38
Serra, Junípero, 97–100, 105, 111, 112,
      120, 163
Seymour, William J., 61
Shaw, Bill, 10
Shumaker, John L. Jr., 72
Sheldon, Ian, 45
Signs and Wonders Movement, 73–75
Smith, Alexis, 31–34
Smith, Chuck, 23–26, 29, 73, 74
Solares, María, 121
Spontaneous and Willing Belief, 84, 85
Starr, Kevin, 54, 150, 177, 178
St. Michael and All Angels Episcopal
      Church, 133, 137
Stewart, Lyman, 64
Stonehill, Randy, 85
Stratton-Porter, Gene, 145, 146, 159
Syriac Orthodox Church, 137

Tac, Pablo, 106, 107
Teal, Edwin Way, 15
Tijuana River, 1
Tomol, Fellowship of the, 122, 123
Turner, Victor and Edith Turner, 170

University of California, Irvine, 29, 34
University of California, San Diego, 34
University of California, Santa Barbara
   3, 4, 44, 85, 86, 95, 114, 124, 152,
   164, 177
University of Southern California, 59,
   132, 177

Vanguard University, 74
Veléz, Karen, 87
Ventura, 3, 5, 7, 70, 73, 85, 88, 113, 121,
   162, 169
Ventureños, 121
Vivian, Miriam, 152, 164
Vivian, Tim, 133, 137, 152, 164

Waldie, D. J., 67, 68

Index

Walsh, Christine, 133
Warren, Rick, 54
Weber, Francis J., 72
William of Ockham, 39
Wimber, John, 74, 75
Woods Family, 52, 53
   Leonard Jr., 52
   Leonard Sr., 52
   Sarah, 51, 52
Wrigley Family, 140, 143–46
   Philip K. and Helen, 145, 146
   William and Ada, 144, 146
Wulf, Andrea, 38

Younger, Bill and Nancy, 74